synthesis
REMEMBERED

Awakening Original Innocence

Charles L. Moore, JD, STB

ΣΥΝΘΕΣΙΣ

Charles L. Moore, JD, STB

Jacket and Book Design: Suzanne Wright
Back cover photo: Charles D. Robinson

Printed in the United States of America.

ISBN-10 1-60145-070-2
ISBN-13 978-1-60145-070-8

Mooredune Publications, LLC
PO Box 476
Soquel, CA 95073

NOTE TO READERS

Each Canto in this book taps into a mingled or shared dream held by visionaries throughout time, people who have guided us to self-evident truth. Each of the designated speakers in the dialogues or poetic writings speaks of their observations and concerns, while historical facts are intertwined in service of activating essential questions.

Some spelling and use of words and phrases may seem unfamiliar, or inconsistent with our current custom and practice. This is intended as a means to enrich our experience. All language is representative of and filtered through the multifaceted lenses of culture and context, as well as numerous editors and publishers. To have a sense of the origins and early spellings and meanings of our words expands our understanding of how we arrived here in our current world.

The Glossary and Chronology are merely a beginning. You are enthusiastically encouraged to continue your own lines of inquiry and discovery.

Acknowledgments and Bibliographic References

Though many seem to work alone, no one ever does. We are all connected to the same source and come to original realizations in the company of many others. I first wish to acknowledge in alphabetical order people who have taken the trouble to write their vision of the imminent unanimity that we perceive in common.

Thomas Aquinas
Sir Francis Bacon
Michael Baigent
Dorothy Bryant
Tony Bushby
E. A. Wallis Budge
John P. Dourley
Albert Einstein
Riane Eisler
Father Newman Eberhardt
Dion Fortune
Benjamin Franklin
Laurence Gardner
Manley P. Hall
William Henry
Graham Hancock
Thomas Jefferson
Carl G. Jung
Olga Kharitidi
Richard Leigh

Henry Lincoln
David Loy
Malachi Martin
Thomas Merton
John Michelle
Sir Isaac Newton
Plato
Pope John XXIII
Pythagoras
Eleanor Roosevelt
Franklin D. Roosevelt
Carl A.B. Ruck
Acharya S
William Shakespeare
Zecharia Sitchin
John Steinbeck
Michael Talbot
Mark Twain
Eleanor Wasson
Paramahansa Yogananda

In addition, I wish to acknowledge those who have provided symbolic inspiration and living participation in the dream, in forms other than writing:

Acevia A. Bennett	David and Anne Jevons
Geoffery Ash	Katherine Maltwood
Gerald Askevold	Marsha Morgan
Shelley Ipimi Brown	Andrew Mount
Pim Chavasant	Daniel O'Conner
George S.J. Crain	Al Olsen
Mary & Larry Delaney	Rudy Proctor
Eleanor of Acquitane	Mona Schoenwisner
David Cushing Feuss	Siddartha
Robert Graham	Socrates
Daniel S.J. Harkin	Thomas Nason (LittleBear)
Steve Hildebrand	Jaques Verduin
Hildegard de Bingham	Jack West
Homouk	Bishop Aloysius Willinger
Peter Hueber	Mary Yavner
Michael Taylor Jackson	Eleana Young
Jesus, the Nazarite	

I wish to acknowledge with gratitude those whose names I may unintentionally have omitted. Also, I wish to remember with compassion all those who have risen in outrage to defend the truth.

Many people have worked to bring forth this book and must be specifically acknowledged for their talents and passion for this material. I wish to extend hearty thanks to: Marcos Warshaw for the ongoing dialogues, for bringing the initial manuscript into a unified form and reviewing my references to math and science; Gary Don Blevens for his concept for the cover; Dawn Griffin for her concepts for structuring the material presented here; Joyce Diamond for her thoughtful editing of the whole manuscript as well as thorough research for the glossary; Denise Renee O'Connor for her meticulous wordsmithing and copyediting; and Shams Kairys for his insightful reflections and final editing. Susan Kinsey Smith provided invaluable ongoing support and guidance for the project. Special thanks to Patricia Carney for her loving and skillful attention to myriad aspects of producing this book, holding the overall vision for it while marshalling all the parts that needed to be refined and joined to bring it into your hands.

Contents

Introduction

In the spring of 1957, after 30 years as a Presbyterian, I was baptized as a Roman Catholic at Old St. Mary's Church in San Francisco's Chinatown. I received my first communion at St. Francis Church in North Beach, and went shortly thereafter to Santa Cruz, where I had been District Attorney, and visited Monsignor Phelan at St. Joseph's Church in Capitola. After mass he motioned me back to the sacristy. His greeting was, "Well, Charles, so you're a Catholic now! Why don't you become a priest?" "But Monsignor," I replied, "I've only been a Catholic a week!" "Oh," he said, "that's nonsense. I'll write the bishop today."

It wasn't long before I was on my way to see the bishop in Fresno. I took back roads, enjoying the hillsides of poppies that were like sunlight emanating from the California earth. When I arrived and entered the office of the first bishop I had ever met, he greeted me with a gruffness covering a genuine gentleness, and said, "So you want to be a priest, huh?" I replied, "I don't know whether I want to be a priest or not, I just want in, that's all, and I'll scrub floors the rest of my life if necessary!" The bishop said, "That's good enough for me; I'll put you in the seminary tomorrow! It's a Jesuit seminary, and I would like you to go see the Jesuit provincial in San Francisco, if you don't mind."

I knew little of the Jesuits, except that they were controversial. I would later learn they are also scholars in dedicated pursuit of knowledge. Upon my arrival the provincial received me with elegant decorum, yet without formalities. He asked, "Are you familiar with Thomas Aquinas?" I replied, "A little bit." He said, "You will become more familiar. As you study, remember that we have followed the synthesis of his *Summa Theologica* for eight hundred years. It's out of date." I took that to be a commission from John XXIII's Vatican to write this book, although it is likely the present Vatican administration would be horrified.

Since that time my studies have made it clear to me that any "synthesis" must extend into our origins, and that the entire Christian religion was out of date long before Thomas Aquinas, starting with the Council of Nicea in 325 CE. This is when the Church of Constantine presented us with a Jesus as God who gave us commandments to be obeyed under threat of hell at the last judgment. But Jesus never claimed to be God; nor did he speak of hell, or issue commandments, or require beliefs. Jesus only gave us himself as a master of truth. Like any true master, his purpose was to stimulate a memory of what is already known in our heart-minds.

My hope is that this book will be a catalyst of such memory, the memory of the self-evident truth. To those who may find that suggestions in this book seem contradictory to their convictions, remember that Jesus is not made less real by what I have stated. For the Bible, like all books, has a bibliography of some kind, whether referenced or not. And no human instrument is infallible, including you and me!

✳

This book is by nature oxymoronic. It attempts to express in language what may only be comprehended by spontaneous individual memory. That said, I make this offering in the hope that the words will elicit your own memory—not of the mind alone, but something much larger that is common to us all.

My inherent curious nature came to full bloom as a student at Grant High School in Portland, Oregon when I first read the words inscribed on the marble plaque at the entrance: "All ye who enter here, never abandon persistent curiosity." This maxim has guided me throughout my life. I have never allowed any doctrine or teaching to supplant the curiosity which always urged me to go deeper.

Although my curiosity is broad, I focused my pursuit of knowledge on the twin pillars of the archeology of Earth and the archeology of language. My guide in the archeology of the Earth is Zecharia Sitchin, who led me to remember who the gods of Israel, Greece, Rome and India really are. My initial exposure to the archeology of language began in Latin class at Grant High School when our stern instructor shocked my pubescent mind by declaring, "There are three genders of Latin nouns: feminine, masculine and hermaphroditic neuter. If you don't know what that word means, look it up!" A rabid Protestant fundamentalist at the time, my religious convictions were shaken and my curiosity awakened.

Religion and Bonding

This book examines organized religion to discover its relationship to our personal spirituality, and our quest for a sense of the meaning of life.

I am an ordained Roman Catholic priest as well as an attorney admitted to practice in California. In my quest for my spiritual life I find that the principle obstacle in my way has been my own conformity to received doctrine. Beyond confessing that this conformity is my own responsibility, lie these questions: 1) From whom did I receive the doctrine? 2) What doctrine did I receive? 3) How is it that this doctrine becomes an impediment to the understanding it is intended to facilitate?

I'll return to these questions in a moment, but first it seems important to also ask: What is religion? The archeology of language helps us to understand. The word comes from the Latin verb *ligo*, meaning to form a bond. *Religo*, therefore, means to re-form a bond.

As a law student at Stanford my principle course was contracts. A contract is defined as "A promise or set of promises that the law recognizes as legally binding." Therefore, a contract is also about bonding.

We can talk about bonding from the perspective of chemistry as well, which teaches us that salt occurs when sodium bonds with chlorine. Actually all of life is made possible through the bonding of elements.

Patriotism is also about bonding, as described by the word allegiance, derived from *ad* + *ligo*, to bond to.

In Catholic seminary I was told that Moses made a covenant with the burning bush, from which sprang Judaism, Christianity and Islam.

A covenant is a bond between heart-minds. A contract is a bond between minds. Religion in its purest expression is about covenants; however, in its role to enforce doctrine it is about contracts.

Of all bondings, of course, the most important is a recognition of the bond that can never be broken—a bond with the living universe—the mysterious, nameless essence of all that is. It is through the celebration of this bond that the heart is filled with ecstasy and awe. Love is after all the ecstasy of a deeper bonding between spirits. Shall we then, like Homer, be bards in praise of the odyssey of bonding?

3

Received Doctrine and Schizophrenia

As to the question raised earlier, "From whom did I receive the doctrine?" the answer is both simple and complex. The simple answer is the Church, which in my case included both the Presbyterian and Catholic Churches. I remember sitting in the pews of the Mt. Tabor Presbyterian Church in Portland, Oregon, at the age of eleven, reading along as the "Creed" was recited. The part that struck me was, "I believe in the Holy Catholic Church." I was shocked and said to myself, "I believe in the Holy Catholic Church?! Then what am I doing here in the Presbyterian Church?" I've really never recovered from that shock of realizing that all Christian churches are based on the same doctrine.

My religious education, however, began at a much earlier age. I had read the Bible by the time I was five under the influence of Ailla, our housekeeper. She was a "holy roller" who took me to Sunday school at a small Wesleyan Methodist Church. Sometimes she took me to Wednesday prayer meetings. I remember going to such a meeting when I was five with Ailla and her boyfriend, Kermit, who was frequently "possessed by the spirit" and "rolled" very convincingly. At the end of his sermon the minister cried out, "Which of you will come forward now and confess Jesus as your personal savior?" Expecting a great rush of confessions, I was puzzled when no one made a move. Being the precocious child that I was, I confidently walked to the front to confess. The minister looked down at me from what seemed a treetop height and said, "Little boy, who brought you here? Did your mother bring you?" "No," I said. "Did your father bring you?" "No," I said. "Well, who sent you up here?" "God did," I replied, at which the minister became appallingly confused and could not speak. I glanced up at him with what I am sure was ill-concealed contempt, and went back to sit with Ailla and Kermit.

I suppose that was the beginning of my life-long inquiry into the lack of intelligence, compassion and connection in the teachings of Christianity. As scholar and psychologist Carl Jung said, "The collective unconscious has a thousand ways of killing those who lack the sense of the meaning of life." My quest has led me to conclude, in agreement with another reflection from Jung, that "Christianity is the illness that we are" (and I don't think Judaism and Islam are far behind). When I read this statement, I was moved deeply that Jung included himself in "the illness that we are," and I became convinced that I should look for that illness in myself. So I asked, "Does that illness have a name?" An analogous name appeared at once: schizophrenia—the most terrible mental-emotional illness. What is schizophrenia? It is a disassociation of sensory input, feelings and emotions on one hand and thoughts on the other. In other words, it stems from the conflict that occurs when one denies what is sensed, felt, or remembered in his or her own heart-mind in order to conform to a conflicting set of beliefs.

I co-authored a book titled *A Schizophrenic's Spiritual Search* with the late Margaret Ingram, in which she tells the story of having adopted a young man from Philadelphia who was a diagnosed schizophrenic. When she was consulting with one of the psychiatrists on the case, he warned her, "A schizophrenic can kill you." History holds multiple examples of this, a prime one being the perpetrators of the Inquisition.

Why would Christianity be likely to induce such daemonic consequences? The real answer is subtle and frightening. It goes back to the Apostle's Creed, the summary of required beliefs I was taught in the Presbyterian Church, which relates back to the Holy Catholic Church, the source of so many problems and sorrows:

"I believe in God the Father Almighty,
Creator of heaven and Earth,
And in Jesus Christ his only son, Our Lord,
Who was conceived by the Holy Spirit,
Born of the Virgin Mary,
Suffered under Pontius Pilate,
Was crucified, died and was buried.
He descended into hell.
On the third day he rose again from the dead.
He ascended into heaven
Where he sits at the right hand of God the Father Almighty.
He will come again to judge the living and the dead.

I believe in the Holy Ghost,
The Holy Catholic Church,
The Communion of Saints,
The Forgiveness of Sins,
The Resurrection of the Body,
And the Life Everlasting."

The trouble with the beliefs stated above, or similar ones, is that they are totally unbelievable. Individuals are threatened with hell not only if they don't believe them, but even if they question them. Yet, most of the required beliefs, if not all of them, go directly contrary to the self-evident truth in one's own heart. These beliefs induce conflict that disempowers people, causing them to either tergiversate (turn their backs and walk away), or worse yet, to surrender their freedom, slowly sinking into schizophrenic denial, despair and aggression. The only real survivors are those who don't take them seriously in the first place.

One day in France, years ago, I was talking to a French matron about my concerns with Christianity. She said, "Oh, you Americans. You take it all so seriously! We stopped listening long ago!"

One might argue that there is much truth in the Christian religion and that Christianity has done a great deal of good, especially in its care of the poor. These things are true. But has the damage Christianity has done been dwarfed by its good deeds, or is it the other way around?

Founding of Christianity

A key question is, who founded Christianity? Without thinking, one would answer, "Why Jesus, of course!" The Catholics will add, "Upon the Apostle Peter at Caesarea Philippi."

Research clearly indicates that Jesus never founded the Christian church at all, and certainly not upon Peter. The New Testament leads one to believe that Paul of Tarsus fashioned the Christianity we know, inventing several important doctrines including the Divinity of Christ, Original Sin and the Eucharist (the "body and blood" of Christ consumed at Communion), but most particularly the idea that Jesus Christ died on the cross for our sins. No quotes attributed to Jesus in the New Testament support any of the above. Further research shows that it was neither Peter nor Paul who founded Christianity. The Christianity we know was founded by the Roman Emperor Constantine for the purpose of ruling the Roman Empire. He was assisted by Eusebius, Bishop of Caesarea, who formulated the accepted Creed of the Church at the Council of Nicea in 325 CE based upon the work of Irenaeus of Lyon, France 189 CE.

Constantine and those who followed him had their own religion based on the Solar Hero named Mithra by the Persians. Those who had been influenced by Christ and continued to spread his teachings were considered a radical element that threatened to undermine Constantine's power. So Constantine founded Christianity as a religion for his army by selectively adopting Jesus' teachings and turning him into a Solar Hero, like Mithra. Ultimately, Theodosius (379-395 CE) proclaimed Christianity the religion of the Roman Empire.

All of the above was known but not hotly disputed until 1945, when a group of local farmers found the *Gospel According to Thomas,* together with a group of "Gnostic" writings, at Nag Hammadi, a small desert town in Egypt. Carl Jung was there at the time. Thomas' gospel gives us a Jesus who sounds a great deal more like Siddhartha the Buddha than like the founder of Caesaro-Papist Christianity.

The history of western civilization is really the history of Empire, continued in the form of the Holy Roman Church. The Pope historically shared the role of Emperor, as the Church representative in the Church-State partnership, beginning with the Holy Roman Emperor Charlemagne in 800 CE, and continuing until the end of World War I. Although the Holy Roman Empire vanished from the map at the Treaty of Versailles in 1919, at least in its "state" function, that influence still exists today, in spite of the seeming separation of church and state.

From the Roman Catholic Church sprang Protestantism headed by Martin Luther who had been a Catholic priest who suffered the full rigors of the Augustinian Order. The final event that prompted his leaving was witnessing the paedophilic behavior of Pope Leo X at a birthday party in Rome. Luther declared, "There is nothing spiritual about the spiritual practices of the Christian Church." Unfortunately Luther's protests strained out the gnat and swallowed the camel, as the saying goes. He accepted too much and denied too little. But to his credit, he opened the door to finding a Jesus closer to the portrayal in the Gnostic *Gospel According to Thomas.*

The Gnostic teachings imply that Jesus grafted a Buddhist shoot on a Jewish root. Gnosticism is still considered by adherents to orthodoxy to be the greatest heresy. Gnosticism leads one to finding the self-evident truth in his or her own heart-mind rather than memorizing the opinions of others as orthodoxy requires. Gnosticism is the true basis of democracy and freedom, whereas orthodoxy is the support of hierarchy, obedience and slavery. That is why for centuries the Roman Catholic Church worked to eliminate all Gnostic writings.

Prehistory and History

Prehistory is based on archeology—the excavated ruins of cultures and cities, along with skeletal remains from thousands of years ago.

The word *history* means a story, any story. As an event, history is whatever happened, but as a fact it is a written account of what witnesses say they remember. Intentionally or not, all stories are fictional to a degree, no matter how "objective" the historian tries to be. It is like quantum physics—the subjective state of the physicist alters the process of observation making the experiment unrepeatable, at least in part.

The earliest written records we have are Sumerian clay tablets that contain accounts of the history of our species, including the creation of our Earth from a planet then in the orbit of our present asteroid belt called Tiamat (Tohu in the Book of Genesis). The *Meh*, the *Tablets of Destiny*, describe their sciences of both the mind and heart-mind and contain an amazing amount of advanced mathematical and astronomical detail. These tablets describe events in literal detail with no supernatural overlay, portraying a pragmatic, hard-working people. Therefore, their accounts do not seem to have any ideological agenda, and I accept them on their own terms. Parts of the Old Testament are clearly derived from the Sumerian tablets, though the material has been manipulated and the tone altered.

The dividing event between prehistory and history described by the Sumerians is the coronation of the first human emperor, En-me-dur-an-ki in Sumerian, or Enoch in the Old Testament. This date marks the beginning of the Jewish calendar, and the beginning of time for Christian fundamentalists (5766 years ago as of 2006).

Remembered Truth

This book has much historical data woven into the fictional form. Its metaphorical nature is intended to elicit deeper truth. This brings up the question, what is fiction? Fiction comes from the Latin verb *facere* that means to make. A fiction novel is said to be a story constructed by the author, but in many cases such stories are based on actual experiences combined with the interior processes of the author. Stories are also about dreams—whether waking or sleeping—one's unconscious or alternate experience of "reality." It is often in a dream-vision state that deeper meanings are revealed. To paraphrase Shakespeare, "The dream, the dream, the dream's the thing, in which I'll catch the conscience of the king." How is reality a dream? Well, if we are together, you think you see me, and I think I see you. But actually I don't see "you," I see the light reflected off of you. But is that what I see? No, it's the effect that that light has upon the retina of my eye. But is that what I see? No. It is the code that the retina sends to my brain via my optic nerve. But is that what I see? No, it is what my brain makes of the code. The analogy of a television set decoding a TV signal is very close indeed.

So you, as a reality, actually come to me from a four-step visionary experience, even though my perception appears to come from the direct experience of standing in front of one another. Reality really is a dream or illusion! As I write my dream, you interpret it based on your dream. So, you may be asking, how can the truth ever be known? The answer is always only through what Buddhists call your own heart-mind. When you find that self-evident truth, there will be no need to confirm it, nor to convince others that what is true for you is also true for them. So I offer this book to assist you in breaking free from any doctrine that keeps you from knowing what was always yours to know.

By the way, I do believe this process, as challenging as it may be, should be lighthearted. As Lao-Tsu might put it: Lightness of heart is the fountain of youth and the doorway of eternal life. Nothing is more serious than lightness of heart and nothing is more frivolous than unrelieved sorrow.

It is time to remember a deeper synthesis. I begin with stories and verse to spark your memory of your origins and your ancestors as we begin a journey of discovery. I invite you to relax into what follows and see where it takes you.

Canto I

The Dragon

Time: 4 billion years ago
Place: The orbit of the asteroid belt
Proto-Personae: Nibiru – A planet visiting this solar system
                Tiamat – The Proto Earth
                The witnessing voice – Oracular Discernment

The dragon dreams of other stones
That fly the ways of night
And work their magic darkly
To become the wombs of light.

In the singing silence of the dreamless dream
A wandering planet came
A galactic voyager
An orphaned child.

He crossed over
Like the *Abiru* beyond the birth of time
Over the Living Void
He came.

Over the singing silent void he came
A listener to the music
That is everywhere
In the apparent emptiness.

He came
Carrying with him a seed he came
From beyond the universe of the lesser gods
A seed planted by holographic dreaming.

A seed of life he brought,
The double-spiraled seed of life
Wandering, masterless, sunless
Wrapped in self-contained adequacy.

10

Yet lonely as the windless memory of space
He came on
Deep in the viscera of his volcanic soul
He felt the old familiar pull.

The old, almost forgotten yearning
Of allegiance to a parent star
His vanished parent of long ago
Sirius of the three faces.

He burst with eager suddenness
Upon the scene of spawning planets
Intent to be an Adopted Child
To find his home among them.

To feel again the solar wind
To revel in the balance of relationship
Forgetful was he of the danger
The danger of mutual doom.

Forgetful was he of the subtle order
That decreed where a planet might fly
Around his terrible beloved parent
Straight on he came.

Bringing his circling satellites
Like David with his sling
The order of subtle gravity seized him
Pressed on inexorably to a certain orbit.

An orbit already occupied by the Watery One
Spinning peacefully in slumbering comfort
The Watery One groaned in terror
Her sea veil lifted high to hide her.

In waves mountain high
Her inner volcanic nature awoke in rage
Her sides were warped with agony
Satellites of liquid granite poured out of her like a horde.

Stone missiles to do battle
With this assailer of her peace
But too late
A stone dragon, planet-sized
Struck her full
And terrible was her demise
Her seas were cast into space
Ice castles in the sky.

Her mantle was shattered
Her liquid granite mantle bled into the void
More than half of her granite crust
Dispersed into fragments.

There was no sound
For there was no hearer,
But the pulses of her screaming
Were shrill and thunderous.

Thunderous
Beyond the imagination of dragons
She reeled in vortiginal spin
And fell away bleeding across the void.

Leaving in her wake her remnants
To circle forlornly in stone and ice
A world of asteroids
Keeping vigil for her in the orbit she had known.

And the sea followed her
Ice castles in the sky it came,
Ice crystals veiling her like a bride it came
In frozen mountain chains of ice the seas followed her.

Tiny flakes of mist they followed her
Yes the sea came
But not all the sea.
Some lay locked in asteroids beyond the orbit of Mars.

Canto I

Some followed the Orphan of the Crossing
Back into deep space
But the Orphan himself did not escape
Captured was he by the great net of the sun.

In a great ecliptic arc he returns
Bringing comets in his wake
Shaping the patterns of those left behind
In a certain measured cycle he comes again.

True to his ecliptic course
Wandering but steady he comes again
To the station where he slew the Watery One
Bristling for the encounter.

And, as he comes
His adopted brothers and sisters
Groan in the gravity of his presence
Trembling in the attraction of his grace.

Upon the Way Station, the red planet
The Child of Wars, great fissures open
The surface trembles, volcanoes roar
Ancient sea beds writhe.

Far, but not too far
From the station of the Orphaned Child
Among the asteroids
Upon the surface of what was once the Watery One,
Seas surge upon their beds
Ice shatters, great shelves collapsing in the sea
Rift valleys open
Islands, continents are born and die.

Thus comes the instrument of creation
The Omphalos of origin
Bearing in its ecstasy
Wild catastrophe and new beginning.

The Stranger too lost his balance
Catapulted by diagonal force
He was unable to claim the orbit he had sought
On a comet's path he flew.

An Adopted Child of the sun was he
But a Comet Child
In long periods
Three thousand six hundred year periods.

He returned as comets do
To the neighborhood of his parent star
And his captured ice mountains
Became comets.

But she, the Wounded One,
Careened into the pathway of her little sister
And great slabs of her fell into her sister's face
Shattering her and leaving her disfigured.

Then she, the Wounded One, settled into the vacant orbit
And the little sister
Unable to persist
Fell into orbit around her healing sibling.

There upon the yawning surface of the once Watery One
The waters began their fall
Millions were the years of their falling
Slowly the seabeds filled.

Tortuous were the fissure cracks
Of continents aborning
Slowly the fiery furnaces
Fell beneath her crust.

And as the waters gathered
Around the nurturing vents
Down in the gathering darkness
A habitat arose.

But something more was left
Planted by the Visitor in the circling water
Something small, very small
Something containing within itself the birth of significance.

It was the seed of life.

For the dragon dreams of other stones
That fly the ways of night
And work their magic darkly
To become the wombs of light.

Interlude

To what shall we liken the Golden Age?
The Golden Age is like the true original condition of mankind:
Original Innocence.

In eternity no beginning and no end can be found,
only flow
in and out of manifestation,
into and out of what we call the material world.

For it is love and love alone that rules for aeternity.

Canto II

Bonding

Time: 66 Million BCE

Place: A river that one day would be the
Paluxy River in Texas

Personae: A diplodocus
A man
A pterodactyl

There were redwood trees along the river, and low hills. A ptero-dactyl soared in search of prey. The weather was warm with rain showering softly.

The Earth shook in a spasm and a great fissure opened. Hot ash spiraled upward. The pterodactyl shrieked with alarm and wheeled away to the south. Another spasm and the river boiled, scattering ash, lava and dust. The Earth heaved up, and a great mixed pyroclas-tic flow filled the little valley, moving south in the river's course, coming to a slow halt fifty miles away. Another eruption, more groaning from the Earth, as the bodies of small dinosaurs were swept away with the volcanic flow. The wave passed and left a foot of hot residue across the valley. Burning trees fell and were rolled in the steaming river. Another tremor. Then twelve days passed.

From the north came a dinosaur, a diplodocus moving slowly toward the soft flow. Just behind her was a human figure following in her tracks. They were not hunter and prey. The man was black, well-muscled and nude. He carried nothing. The diplodocus stepped into the flow which was still warm and soft, and almost pleasant. She looked beyond the river and saw a low pass through the hills beyond and suspected a nurturing marsh past the trees.

The man was silent, and his expression spoke of a passionate calm as his feet left the print of round heel and five toes in the flow alongside the dinosaur tracks. Then he crossed over and stepped into a track of the great beast as a perfect frame around the perfect track of his own foot.

There was some connection between the man and the animal, some invisible telepathic bond.

As the dinosaur came up out of the pyroclastic flow and moved toward the small pass in the hills where good pasture beckoned from the marsh beyond, she turned her serpentine head to see how he fared, still in the flow. He was close to the border she had crossed.

Suddenly there was a wrenching shriek as the pterodactyl returned to its old haunts to find it obliterated. But it paid no attention to the devastation as there was a tidy bit of two-footed prey for the taking! Shrieking, it came down for the kill. The man looked up, turned suddenly, and fell helpless.

The great diplodocus, seeing the danger to her friend, turned, bellowing with threat, swinging her head at the pterodactyl. It veered off, just missing the fallen man. She moved toward him, extending her serpent-like head to comfort him with motherly concern. He stretched out his arms around her stout neck, locked his hands around her head. She raised him up, and he righted himself, sitting on her neck as she moved toward the nurturing marsh beyond the hills where she hoped to find others of her kind.

Interlude

Merkabah

If time and space are illusions,
as we grow more aware that they are,
and if the power of telepathic immediacy is present in us all,
is there any limit to where we may go in space or time?

Free of the cumbersomeness of wings
and without the bonds of external technology,
who is to say that we cannot do it together?

Canto III

Stranger in the Sky

Time: 65 Million BCE

Place: Paluxy River Valley in Texas
                 Bird's-eye view, 100,000 feet

The red and purple sunset cast great rays among the gathering clouds that rose above the forested plain. To the west and south there was a swelling elevation where some day the Sierra Madre would rise.

As the sky darkened, the great swamp destined to be the Gulf of Mexico was alive with monstrous crocodiles forty feet long, small rat-like creatures, velociraptors, pterodactyls, brontosaurus, triceratops, diplodocus, all the hundreds of dinosaur species from monstrous to tiny, some predator, some prey. From this altitude a great vista of stars seemed to slowly turn as the Earth moved at a thousand miles an hour away from the receding sun and toward the rising darkness, making the stars seem to move westward as the Earth turned eastward to where the heavens would seem to heave up the sun again.

The north-south compass path of the sun where the sun seemed to follow a north-south motion very slowly through the year held the puzzle of an Earth moving around the sun at a thousand miles a minute, about 60,000 miles an hour of orbital speed, a more or less normative speed for a celestial body.

Suddenly there was a stranger, an unknown object in the sky, moving at such a normative speed. Night by night it became more visible. As it approached there was a great commotion of bellowing and chirping in the millions of square miles of the great swamp as its inhabitants felt the danger. They sensed a message that moved them to fear, as did the tidal power of the full moon, yet it was an alien fear that had not been known before in the lifetime of the living.

There were humans in that world too; no one had ever known whence they came, or why. These were humans of highly developed telepathic power who could travel the night sky in telepathic unanimity. They too felt the dread, the primal fear of species extinction from the collective unconscious. They had traveled together the wormholes of space-time; they had visited the cataclysmic fires. They knew close-up the burning apparent chaos in which a star is born. They knew what happens when a great stone comes from outer space, as big as a dinosaur, as big as a small mountain, as big as an island, a continent, a planet. In time travel they had seen *Nibiru* throwing lightning bolts at *Tiamat*, Proto-Earth, out where the asteroid belt now circled in granite and ice. They had seen the two planets raging at each other, ripping great chunks out of their very stone flesh and sloshing seas and hurling them at each other like a horde of angry weapons. They had seen the great stone hurled from *Nibiru* strike the Proto-Earth and split her in two, smashing one half of her into asteroids of granite and water to spin forlornly in their orbit while what was left of her careened on a dizzying course to seek her present orbit, dragging the shattered moon and the sea behind her, ice castles in the sky.

These humans knew up close how many great and deadly stones were within striking distance of the Earth, the Earth they still called *Tiamat*, her ancient name that she breathed out in the celestial battle of the infant solar system four billion years ago.

These humans then knew to seek refuge from this immanent cataclysm of celestial destruction. But where?

Closer every night, larger loomed the Great Dragon in the Sky. The whole Earth trembled like a fair maiden scorched by the deadly dragon come to devour her, and all of her beloved dinosaurs cried out, feeling the coming doom.

Then, one night when the moon was down, the great stone made its rising at midnight, brighter than the moon had ever been. And as the despairing Earth creatures cried in dread, the moonlike stone split in two before their very eyes.

It was as if there had been an inner explosion in the monster stone that sent one part away from Earth as the other was accelerated toward it. No, it was not coming from the east, but from the west.

It came on toward the Earth, vanishing into the sunrise, then closer, greater. Earthquakes were everywhere; the seas followed the monster in great walls of water that marched across whole continents. The swamp was submerged in a wild sea and all her children perished.

Then she struck, just east of the narrow isthmus that would someday be called Central America. She scoured out a sea someday to be called the Caribbean, burying herself beneath the Windward Archipelago, making a line of islands bow out beyond her grave into the wild Atlantic Sea.

The cataclysm of the death of dinosaurs had only begun. The other half of the great stone that had shot straight up and arched away now came crashing down in a perpendicular path, unlike the skimming bounce of his sister half. He shrieked downward on the flooded swamp of the now dead dinosaurs to excavate that great elliptical crater to be called the Gulf of Mexico and buried himself off Yucatan. Another maelstrom of tsunamis swept the Earth and great saltwater rains fell full of sea creatures as shattered seawater returned from outer space. Afterwards, a long winter descended when the sun lay hidden behind a vast dust cloud. The forests died and all green things languished.

Postscript

Today a record still remains. The great asteroid has been found off Yucatan. In Texas along the Paluxy River the pyroclastic flow was uncovered by a flood which had the tracks of a dinosaur and human tracks beside them, round heel, five toes and all. One dinosaur track was like a frame with a perfect human print inside it, a fetching possibility that they knew and loved each other.

Interlude

Do Christians believe in telepathy?
If not, what are they doing when they pray?

Telepathy:
: The transfer of thought-feeling between heart-minds without the use of the five senses.

Clairvoyance:
: Ability to be present as a witness or participant in an event distant in space, or time, or both.

Precognition:
: Ability to be present as a witness or participant in a future event.

Telekinesis:
: Ability to move an object perceived as external with telepathic power alone.

Prayer:
: From the root, pry; as in pry open. An ability to open the heart-mind to the hearing of the still small voice.

Merkabah:
: A spiritual vehicle composed of several spirits.

Ekankar:
: Spiritual tourism in a Merkabah, a spiritual coven.

Golden Age:
: A time when internal technology of telepathic power obviated the need for external technology.

Golden Section:
: The Fibonacci series, the mathematics of life, the Flower of Life.

Canto IV

Primal Parenting

*We have paid so much attention to Original Sin that we
have forgotten Original Innocence.*
~ Innocent III, Pope of Francis of Assisi
in Thirteenth Century

Time: Unknown
Place: South Africa
Personae: Our first parents
             Ahuradeva–Androhermaphrogenous
             Earth Spirit

So speaks Ahuradeva, the tone, the logos, the deep-throated Earth
As she-he spins upon the axis of the pole star.
Her-his grace is gravity
Drawing her-him to the sun
As she-he spiral spins her-his magic.
Her-his gravity is grace.
His-her grace is gravity.
The attractive power of the living spirit.
And it is the power of spirit to remember.

Before the coming of the gods
Blood creature walked barefoot upon the warm earth
Endowed with swiftness of foot
Unenclosed by the encumbrance of the knowledge of time
When the knowledge of death yet slumbered.

He felt the tone of Earth's deep-throated turning
Flowing in profound nurture in his blood
And he heard her tone
Beneath the power of ears to hear
Singing a song of Love and Bonding
In the telepathic receptivity of his unblemished mind.

How sweet, how strong
How bathed in the ecstasy of Union
Like two coiling serpents
Tail to tail and head to head
In the bliss of bonding
Freely binding
In the purposiveness of Love
The ecstasy, the joy, of bonding between spirits.

Today the Earth was singing
Her memory of that timeless time
When time began for her
And for all the life that called her home.

She sang of the Dragon Stones
In whose number she counted herself
Flying effortlessly through the rich substance
Of spirit space
That is nowhere silent or empty.

Time began for her then
Because it was as far as her memory yet reached
Outward from the eternal moment
That is the seed of time.

Dragons!
Colliding in the womb of light
Glowing into suns
Whose relationship and bonds with one another
Would give birth to measure
And refractive relationship
That would sometimes be called space
Sometimes time.

Dragons!
Dreaming of the richness of ecstasy
And the boundaries of primal fear
Interactive
As the guardians of those forms
That consciousness would take

As it perceived itself
First as spirit
Breathing
Then as energy
Spinning
Then as Consciousness
Reflecting.
Spinning beginnings and ends
In the timeless spaceless fabric of Earth's dreams.

For dragons dream of other stones
That fly the ways of night
And work their magic darkly
To become the wombs of light.

Blood creature stood and remembered these things
His heart-mind pulsing with deep excitement
As Earth's memory became his memory
Flowing up through his feet upon Earth's face
And flowing up into his consciousness
Like a shooting star
In the night womb of the heavens
He remembered the immortal spirit that he is
Not was or would be
And yet was and would be.
Remembering the protective illusion of darkness and light
That made possible the mystery of his uniqueness
Veiled like a bride in her oneness
With all that is.

Blood creature stood
Remembering the others
Who were like himself
Particularly in their power to remember.

He stood feeling their presence in telepathic immediacy
And being glad
That they too were unique and different
In the joy of separation
That could not break
Even for a second

The joy of communion
That united them, always.

And not only his kind
But all kinds
Who had ever been or would be
Blood creatures!
He said wordlessly to himself
In ideas that no sound had ever clothed
How wonderful they are!
All those others
How marvelous to be one with them
In the spirit covenant of bonding
And yet how wonderful
To respect them as other than myself.

So the Earth sang her telepathic song
So strong was her grace
Flowing through his feet and legs
Coiling through his groin
In affectionate embrace
Flowing through the fragrant coil of his intestines
Entering into his heart from beneath
Distending his veins and arteries in bliss
Passing into his dragon brain stem
Pouring through the sending and receiving
Neurons of his brain
Encountering like two sea waves
The emanating power of his right brain
And delicately tripping lightly
Across the fragile bridge of sighs
That connected right to left
Where all the predatory instincts lay, still sleeping.

And so all of him was well
And self-healing
Before injury could take root
And he became again what he remained
And had always been
A blessing in his land.

To walk the building blocks of matter
To stride the distances between the stars
To be one with the spirit of manifestation
That grace that rises to the energy-spirit consciousness
That was in every being
In all its fullness
No matter how great or how small
To stride effortlessly and timelessly
The distances between the stars.

To fly the heavens
Without the cumbersome necessity of wings
To hear the sweet sound of the song of being
Quiet and without stint
In every being subject to perception.

How easy it is
To know
Without the encumbering baggage of logic
The oneness with the eternal un-manifested dark
From which flows that darkness
That is the womb of light!

She did not move
But the flow of her grace
Was so intense
That she was vibrant with motion
Motion toward him.
She was black but beautiful
And so was he
His beauty pulsing with his spirit
In the ecstasy of innocence
Innocence that drew her to him
As hers drew him.
There was no confusion
But a great sword of Primal Fear
Pierced them both
But sheathed itself in their primal ecstasy.

Their bodies did not yet yearn to touch
Their fear restrained them

But their spirits mingled freely
In an embrace so intimate
So complete, so nascent
That physical touch would ground it.
In disappointment
They stood face to face across the distance
Feeling the bonds of union unite them
To each other
And to the sentient universe
That seemed itself just born
Feeling the Earth's grace-gravity coil around them
As two halves of one being.
It was the covenant
The bond of union with life itself.
They were not eager
But at rest in the fullness of their union
At the peak of an awesome activity
So balanced as to be motionless
Yet surprisingly abundant in its activity.
So they stood
Answers to each other's unuttered prayer
And their own
Knowing they had come together
To share one another's burden
Of the fullness of joy
Compelled by time
And the eagerness of the spirit
That their kind should multiply upon the Earth.

What others would one day call loneliness
Not even what it means to be alone and unheard
Had ever occurred to them
And yet they now remembered
What it might have been
That loneliness
Though it was only empty
In regard to that fullness
They now experienced together
So they are suspended

In the memory of Earth
And so they remain forever
With all that followed for them
And all that had gone before
Perfect in their immortality.

They are our ancestors
And we are their descendants.
Their spirits still live.
They visit the Earth in their kindness
And come to us in our dreams
Sometimes as a voice
A voice that reminds us to remember
That we have the power to remember,
Sometimes as a sudden presentiment
A clearly perceived knowledge of truth
Which when recalled we had always known
But only dimly perceived,
Sometimes as a warning
To make good use of time
Even though time is an illusion and will pass away.

Many are the urgings of our beloved forebears
For whom the oracle urges us to have Kabode
That is to hold in perfect harmony
The Primal Ecstasy
And the Primal Fear within our hearts
Holding in awe that balance
Where ecstasy is forever strong
For it is not the matter that matters,
For it is the spirit that remains
In the flux of time.

Interlude

Nameless
Un-manifest
Spiral Lightning of Manifestation
Aum
Kether
Golden Age

Tiphareth   Tiphareth

Primal Fear   Primal Ecstasy

Golden Section
Ladder of Lights

Je me souvions   Malkuth   I remember

Deva

(Kether is the Malkuth of the Un-manifest)

31

Canto V

The Observer

Time: Circa 500,000 BCE, The Golden Age

Place: South Africa, Rift Valley,
             Savannah that boundries the jungle

Personae: 12 Ancestors
             The Human Observer
             The meercats and other jungle animals

There were predators out there by night and day. The meercat observer, was sitting on her haunches, watching while the young ones played, fragile ones, delightful, agile, unafraid but vigilant; never too far from their refuge.

The sun had not yet risen, but the rose dawn was creeping through the morning twilight. As the darkness retreated westward, there were still stars over the tree line where the jungle began and the rules of survival changed. Now and then an okapi, fitted for plains life but adapted to the jungle, would slip back under the jungle cover where it felt safer in the rising day. The dawn chorus of the birds was just breaking out along the arboreal line. Prehensile primates were chattering, hand-like feet busy from branch to branch. Out on the plains there was a locust tree here and there that the giraffes favored, and that the elephants, for some reason, had left standing. The year's last rains had just passed and the tall grass rippled sinuously in a passing breeze, still cool from the shadow of night.

Just beyond the shadow of a fig tree, ripe with fruit, lay a group of blood-kind humans, twelve in number, still sleeping, heads together in a circle, arms and legs akimbo, backs to the Earth, faces toward the lightening sky; men and women, all of black skin, all without clothing of any kind. As they began to stir their hands, palms up, moved to just touch each other, and as they touched, eyes still closed, a blissful smile moved across each face as if all faces were one. Their eyes, still closed, looked inward to find their unanimity of all as one. They held a common vision of the suns, moons and stars as one dream, unanimous in the one-spirited communion of their accustomed oneness.

This night they had visited together the star system that one day would be called Al Pharatz, the Pharaoh's star, out in the celestial vault, where the prime meridian of the Nile crossed the 30th degree of north latitude. They had spent a thousand years of apparent lapsed time as one spirit-being, visiting the planets and moons of that star. They had experienced the abundance of life in its multitudes on every heavenly body that circled that star, and had seen close up the fiery furnace of the star itself. They had learned telepathically the language of creatures the Earth would never know, feeling their joys and their sorrows, their ecstasies and their fears, and reached the understanding that *all*, including themselves, on no-matter-how-distant a star, were relatives and co-participators in a manifesting and de-manifesting universe pulsing in and out like a primal breath of life. They felt themselves pulsing in and out upon that primal breath of life, proceeding from and returning to a great oneness in which all are forever one while they are still forever many.

The human Observer was wakeful as the long vigil of the night came to an end. She was just on the outer edge of childhood, perhaps thirteen, but she knew well the ways of the nightly vigil. The Observer should not sleep, so the others could dream their one dream, safe from all the many perils of the predatory realm of the plains.

On this night there had been no moon, but the lions did not sleep. With the long vision of her inner eye she watched two marauding males sniff the wind and move off at a trot toward her sleeping voyagers. She tracked them until her two eyes could see their shapes in the starry light, their tails and ears up, dropping to a slink as they stalked their still invisible prey.

The Observer reached inward for her daunting weapon, the telepathic signal that would blind the lions' senses to the presence of their intended prey, those she loved. She felt the power flow out of her, a bolt of telepathic energy. She watched the lions stop, as the invisible force struck them, and they began to circle aimlessly having lost the scent. One lion even stumbled over a sleeper's leg and almost fell without suspecting what obstacle had caused his fall.

There were other instances, one a meander of buffalos whose deadly hooves were called away by a similar vital signal, though they never knew they had been herded.

Now, scanning the vicinity for unwelcome visitors she found none and turned her attention to the dawn sky. She sensed the exact place where the sun would rise, or seem to rise, as the Earth "heaved it up" into the "heavens." Just before the first dot of brilliance emerged, she began the tone of waking, a tone that would one day be called *Tiphareth*, or beauty. It rang out from her like a belltone, a tone that could shatter crystal, and the sleepers wakened in one gesture as each rose to spin slowly in his or her own place.

They smiled as they rose, remembering the joy, the common experiencing of their dream. And as they rose, the sun also rose and sent the searchlight of its first beam among them, a beam that was perceived as penetrating into the deep heart-mind of each. They joined in the exacting tone, slowly spinning, their arms floating out so hands occasionally brushed, as if orchestrated by the conducting precision of the Golden Section, the measure of the rotating force that is the manifesting essence of every manifested being.

Far out on the plains all the animals raised their heads and looked toward the source of this astounding tone and they bounded toward it. The dawn chorus of birds from the jungle's edge a mile away came flying in their multitude to form a winged vortex above them as they spun toning before the tree that had sheltered them and hung ripe with the fruit of their nurture.

Then the animals began to arrive, both predator and prey and began their own leaping circle around the dancers, leaping, running with the innocent joy of the meercats who also joined in the celebration.

For an hour the dance continued. The communion, the ecstasy of delight, the oneness with all that is, the vortiginal divinity of the Deva of the Dance.

The young Observer was dissolved in tears of delight in the humility of true power. She stopped her tone. The silence was sudden as only a singing wilderness can sing. Noiseless, all melted away into the pattern of their daily pursuits.

It was not just today that such celebration occurred. It was every day, for who grows tired of the warming fires of an experienced ecstasy of union with all that is?

At certain times there was more awareness than others: particularly on the night of equal day when the night equals the day over all the Earth, a moving dawn that spreads the ecstasy of oneness to all the Earth from pole to pole, from the prime meridian to itself again, and also particularly on the solsticial days when the sun-stand heralds the resurrection of the sun first at one pole and then the other as the day becomes one minute longer.

On such days, there was awareness that the tides of light moved around the Earth as it spun, first toward then away from the life-giving light. This awareness would grow in ages to come when humanity was more dispersed, and more deeply involved in the magic of the stones that sing.

Now the day having begun, it was time to play, time to join in the quest of the outer senses. Time for touching and seeing, time for feeling and hearing, time to taste the odors of sanctity. It was the time of the innocence of the children of immortality in the intimacy of the flesh, and so they began to play, the play of physical communion.

No one ever put food in their own mouth. Each found a delicate morsel to put in the mouth of another. As gratitude awakened in the heart of the receiver it was felt in the heart of the giver, ten times multiplied.

And the giver shone with grace and sent back the sacred response, wordlessly, "I am you, adopt me!"

The ceremony of communion continued as the trees provided their abundance and the people celebrated their hunger and their satisfaction, as if each were a cell and all were one body.

Then there were the wells, the springing wells of the deva where water flowing underground crossed water flowing underground, each having its own cylindrical standing wave of spin. As the waves mixed, a new spin was born, spinning upward from their crossing. Here beneath the equator, countersunwise-spin was healing; sunwise-spin brought the spirit down. Far to the north, beyond the latitude of the changing vortex, the equator, it worked the other way around. In their flights of the night stars they had found it so on all the whirling worlds among the stars.

They sought the devas, the devas of delight, and knew not to tarry where the devas of sadness spun. They would seek stones to place on the crossing places where the wholeness flows in the one or the many that gathered round. They would spin around the stone, four times in the direction of the light and once sunwise dark and then all move round the circle in the direction of the counter-sunwise light.

After the first full circle they would stop, hands clasped, arms and legs akimbo at the angle of the gentle spin and feel the low-toned power of the Earth drawing them down to her in the sense of foundation, feeling the pounding pulse of their hearts in one another's hands and how they were one with each other, with the trees, with the stones and with the flowers and the stars and all things without exception—alive!

Then they would spin again, coming to a standstill, joining hands and leaning toward the center. Two would stand in the deva place and raise their arms and join their hands as an arch. All would see the pair as two swans and themselves as swans. One by one in succession they would pass through the arch and leap upward as a swan would fly up. They would feel themselves as the substance of air, tangible to the senses and real in the telepathic power. They could see where there was no light other than the auric light from which substantial things arise.

Back to the circle dance and another standstill, the clasping of hands, the leaning to the center until all could see a dream pool of water, blue as the sky, clear as the air in all of its crystalline magic, motionless and full of the soundless sound of essential flow. Cool water, cool, clear water.

A fourth time, the circle. Again, the spin. Again, the stop. Joining hands; right hand over left, they held each other leaning back in the grip of trust, looking up to where the noon sun had stood. To see what eyes could not bear to see, to feel the warming, life-sustaining heat as it followed the blue path of imperceptible motion so seemingly slow but yet so fast. A thousand miles an hour! The red path of sunrise and sunset with its violet flame, even slower, even faster. A thousand miles a minute!

Closing their eyes they saw the violet flame, the rainbow serpent where the sun paths crossed, whirling on the wings of the deva to a single point, then emerging in a sunwise spiral to vanish over the rainbow among the stars.

Postscript

The imagery in this Canto is inspired Dorothy Bryant's allegorical fantasy novel, The Kin of Ata Are Waiting for You.

Mythical Interlude

The Hundredth Monkey Internet

Ken Keyes in his *The Hundredth Monkey* told of an incident that took place in some islands in the Pacific off Japan. When the fishermen found them each had its colony of monkeys. No one knew how they got there, as the islands are separated by hundreds of miles. The fishermen liked the monkeys and began feeding them. Every day they counted the monkeys who gathered to be fed and counted out the exact number of sweet potatoes, one for each monkey, and threw them in the beach sand.

One morning a potato fell into a tide pool. One female monkey sat and looked at it floating. It was her potato for that day. She pondered and looked and pondered some more. Then she put her hand in the water and pulled the water toward her. The potato followed. She picked it up, bit into it and, surprised, held it out and inspected it. She repeated this performance, and then gobbled up the potato. No sand! Sweet potatoes are much better without sand, so next morning, and every morning thereafter she threw her potato in a tide pool. Another female monkey watched her for about a week and then tried it herself. She too was hooked.

Then another monkey and another adopted this behavior. The number of monkeys reached about 30 percent, when, one morning, all monkeys on the island also washed their sweet potato. That same morning all the monkeys on all the islands separated by hundreds of miles washed their sweet potatoes.

Is this something like a large number of scientists all over the world coming up with the same new hypothesis at almost the same time? And if it happens to monkeys and men, how about dolphins and whales? And maybe, just maybe, it happens to every living thing, including you and me, and even the trees.

Internet indeed!

And how about stars?

And how about gods?

Interlude

Ex uno plures: Out of one many
E pluribus unum: Out of many one
Per aspera ad astra: Through the rough to the stars

Canto VI

First Contact

Time: 450,000 BCE

Place: Persian Gulf, a fresh water lake at this time

Personae: Lord Enki
            Gula, one of the 50 "rowers" of the ship Argo

Enki: Do you still see our vessel where it splashed down?

Gula: Yes, my Lord. It appears the others are safe.

Enki: We are compelled to return to the shelter of our craft before the sun-star rises. The whiteness of our skin is not safe cover, accustomed as we are only to the stars of night.

Gula: Perhaps we should only appear in protective cover if we must go forth by day.

Enki: No doubt. But I am eager to place foot on solid ground in this alien and yet welcoming world.

Gula: I am perhaps too young to remember when our home planet came close enough to the sun to provide a "day" in our world.

Enki: Understandable, Gula, that was more than three thousand five hundred sun cycles ago by the reckoning of this world. As our world has but lately arrived at its perihelion, it will be 3600 sun cycles before we come again to a comparable time.

Gula: Have you yet seen any of the expected life forms on this planet?

Enki: Not yet. That is really my purpose in this expedition, to make contact. No doubt the fresh water beneath us now contains many forms similar to those in our world, as these depths provide a shield from our adopted sun. But it is the life forms on solid ground that fascinate me in their probable variety. Our surveys showed the likelihood that vast areas are covered with rooted species that generally appear as green. Additionally, roving creatures of all sizes have been spotted in exposed areas.

Gula: Now that we have landed on this world, may I be permitted to ask why have we come?

Enki: For the gold, Gula.

Gula: Where on this planet do we expect to find it?

Enki: The survey showed that most of the gold of this planet is dissolved in its seawater.

Gula: How do we extract it?

Enki: The method which I most prefer extracts the dissolved metal by a process of percolation of seawater through quartz crystal. It is the least arduous, but is slow and may prove too expensive of time. We have the option to also mine it, but that would be very taxing work for us indeed. We shall see how things proceed. I am sure that if our gold production lags the need, we will be ordered to take the necessary steps to increase production.

Gula: But why do we want the gold?

Enki: It is a problem with the life-sustaining property of our atmosphere. The volcanism on our planet sustains the atmosphere and the decline of volcanism has reached a point that we are all in danger or soon will be. When gold is altered into a white powder and diffused it slows the decay of the atmosphere, but we have run through our own stock of gold and that is why we are here.

Gula: Are there any beings on this planet who might object?

Enki: That is another matter we are investigating. We see no sign of visible technology that would seem to be a threat, but we have found signs of agricultural development in the southern hemisphere, that we call the Abzu. Those signs indicate beings that are well advanced. We wonder why there is little external technology and need to investigate that.

Gula: Are there any cities?

Enki: No, none at all, and no sign that there have ever been any. It is my suspicion that these beings may be possessed with a degree of intuitive development that is greater than our own and that could present a problem.

Gula: Intuitive development? Do you mean telepathy?

Enki: Yes, exactly. We have some competence in that, as you know, and some of us are able to send and receive information over great distances of space and time. We who are intuitively knowledgeable are few in numbers as yet, but we will be very useful as our planet moves into the apohelion of its orbit. We suspect the presence of beings with such developed powers on this planet. We suspect that they are also able to access past and future times, and some of them are likely able to operate collectively. The area of "internal technology" whereby you can manipulate external objects with this power is almost unknown to us. We would not be surprised if there are beings on this planet that are more advanced in these areas than we are.

Gula: Look, my lord Enki! The moon has risen and you can just make out a shoreline!

Enki: Yes, and it seems that there are living creatures that appear rooted and reaching upward.

Gula: Over to the right there appears to be a break in the line and a sort of estuary. Shall we go there?

Enki: That may be one of the many rivers we saw from above. This appears to be a very fertile land. Yes, let's go in there to land and set first foot upon planet number seven.

Interlude

The Nameless Tao, hiding in plain sight,
does not ration the fullness of its presence to any being,
no matter how fragile or how strong,
for grace is gravity and gravity is grace,
beauty is truth and truth beauty.
This is all we know and all we need to know
if we could but remember in every moment of timeless time.

Canto VII

Sir Leonard Speaks of Ur

Time:	1927 CE
Place:	British Museum, London
Personae:	Sir Leonard Wooley A *London Times* correspondent

Corr: Good afternoon, sir! Sir Leonard, I presume?

Sir L: And I presume you are the *Times*?

Corr: Thank you for receiving me and being so prompt!

Sir L: My mother told me that to be early is noble, to be late is common, and to be prompt is royal. Though I have only attained nobility, I like royalty!

Corr: I understand that Oxford has published your findings at Ur?

Sir L: Yesterday. Glad you noticed!

Corr   Do I detect, Sir Leonard, that you are very fond of the ancient city of Ur?

Sir L: Yes I am.

Corr: Could you tell me why?

Sir L: Because it is there, and because its ruins tell a story that clears up the history of civilization, not to mention our religion.

Corr: I understand you financed the expedition yourself?

Sir L: At this stage, at least. I had my predecessors, other diggers at the site, as you know. And the University of Pennsylvania helped.

Corr: This emergent science of archaeology, how long have we had it?

Sir L: As to method, the first to keep meticulous notes was Schliemann. He died in 1890.

Corr: German, I presume?

Sir L: Yes, but also, by happenstance, an American. He was in California on July 4, 1850 when California became a state. His methods emerged as he excavated at Troy, the scene of Homer's *Iliad*.

Corr: In public school I learned a quote about Troy when memorizing Virgil: "...from the flaming walls of Ileum."

Sir L: Yes. "Pious Aneas who from the flaming walls of Ileum did the old Anchises bear." Before Schliemann it was all sort of hit or miss. Interest in ancient ruins is rather recent, you know. The dark ages pretty well squelched interest in antiquities for a thousand years.

Corr: I suspect the Church and its fondness for burning all records except their own.

Sir L: That has always troubled me. Since when do people who tell the truth try to conceal the evidence?

Corr: My sentiments exactly. But wasn't it Schliemann's discovery that got those Form Criticism theologians interested in Nineveh?

Sir L: I think so. Form Criticism started in Germany when Queen Victoria was young, 1830 or so. Theologians began to question whether the Bible was a true account of real facts or just mythological, but nobody was courageous enough to find out. It wasn't Iraq yet, you know. Winston Churchill made Iraq.

Corr: But why did the early archeologists go to Mesopotamia first instead of Palestine?

Sir L: Because the story of Abraham starts in Mesopotamia and that is the beginning of the story of Israel.

Corr: But why Troy?

Sir L: Most are not aware that Troy and Moses are probably contemporary. The work of Homer was effectively "lost" until the end of the low Middle Ages and his "rediscovery" had a lot to do with the coming of the Renaissance in Italy, the rebirth of learning. Many call it the "Greek Revival."

Corr: I never really noticed that before!

Sir L: You see the Form Criticism people made comparisons. They said: "It is clear that the *Iliad* is metaphor and so it is probable that the Bible is too."

44

Corr: And Schliemann disagreed?

Sir L: In a very scholarly way. He learned Greek well enough to read the *Iliad* in the original and it sounded like real history to him. So he went to the Dardanelles, the *Hellaspont* whose southern entrance Troy guarded, checked his reference points, found a tel, a mound that forms over an old city, and started digging. He made a vertical trench across the tel and kept precise notes at every step.

Corr: Was the discovery of Troy widely accepted as the true home of Homer?

Sir L: Of course not. Schopenhauer says: "When an ancient truth is rediscovered it is at first greeted with ridicule, then with violent opposition, and finally it is held to be self-evident. Archaeologists of that time were no exception.

Corr: So, where did they go next?

Sir L: Greece, of course, is where the other heroes of the *Iliad* came from. The Trojan War was really a struggle for control of the Dardanelles. Helen was just an excuse.

Corr: Where did our proto-archaeologists go after Greece?

Sir L: Nineveh.

Corr: Why Nineveh?

Sir L: Because it was the Assyrians who started the second captivity of Israel by taking away the northern tribes, according to the Bible. Babylon did the third captivity by taking away the southern tribes. The Israelites became the Jews while captive at Babylon, where they learned banking. They had been landowners prior to the Babylonian captivity. The first "captivity" was in Egypt, but it wasn't really captivity as they went there on their own.

Corr: So where is Nineveh?

Sir L: At modern Mosul on the Tigris river, Kurdish country now. In those days there wasn't much there. There were several tels near where Mosul now stands. So they asked the natives: "Which one is Nineveh?" They replied, pointing, "That one." They dug it up and the natives were right.

Corr: What kind of evidence did they find?

Sir L: Temples, statues, libraries, inscribed clay tablets, king lists, cylinder seals. In the king lists they found Jehu, King of Israel. He is listed by name as one of the captive kings, confirming the Biblical record.

Corr: So where did they go from Nineveh?

Sir L: A word of explanation: The records were in Assyrian mostly, in a lost language, not known, like Aramaic. They found a stone similar to the Rosetta stone in Egypt, but in parallel columns of Assyrian and Aramaic. So far so good, but there was a problem. The Assyrian proper names did not mean anything in Assyrian. They guessed that their proper names were from an older language to the south.

Corr: So they looked farther south?

Sir L: Exactly, and they found Akkad and records in Akkadian that told them what Assyrian proper names meant. But the Akkadian proper names meant nothing in Akkadian. So, south again.

Corr: One more time?

Sir L: Yes. This time they found Sumer, the Biblical Shinaar, which means land between the rivers, and in Sumerian both Akkadian and Sumerian names meant something.

Corr: So they knew that they were home and had finally resolved the puzzle?

Sir L: Not only that, they later found tablets in Sumerian cuneiform, not only in Akkad but in Assyria and Babylon. These turned out to be the ceremonial tablets used especially for the New Year festival proving that all of them, including the Akkadians and Sumerians, had conducted their ceremonies in Sumerian down until Babylon II, the period when the Jews were in their third captivity.

Corr: That brings you to Ur, doesn't it, and to your work published by Oxford University this year?

Sir L: Yes. 1927, a most amazing year this has been, with Lindberg flying the Atlantic from New York to Paris. Remember, Ur was the first commercial center of the world just as New York is now the commercial center of America.

Corr: Is that why you spent a fortune excavating Ur, because it was the commercial center of the world?

Sir L: No. I didn't know that when I first started excavating, but I know it now.

Corr: What was the religion of Ur?

Sir L: Ur was a city of at least 500,000 people. Its temple in the southwest corner of the city is a ziggurat, a spiral step pyramid. The name of its god was *Nannar Sin*. Nannar Sin has his markers on our modern map today. Sinai is named for him and so is India which was once known as Sind.

Corr: You mean that Nannar Sin is the god of Abraham?

Sir L: That would startle a few people. No, Nannar Sin is the god of Abraham's father, Terah. If you read Genesis carefully you will see that Abraham's god who spoke to him in Phadan Uram is not the same god as the god of his father. The one who spoke to Abraham is Nannar Sin's brother *El Hadad*, the god of Is-Ra-El.

Corr: So we shouldn't be capitalizing the word for god in the Bible?

Sir L: Exactly. You see we know the name of the father of Nannar Sin and El Hadad, who are brothers. Their father is Enlil, Lord of the Command. He, in turn, has a brother, Enki or Ea, Lord Earth or Lord of Water. Their father is Anu, who bore the title of Father in Heaven. None of these beings are the makers of the universe.

Corr: That would seem to be very damaging information for Judaism, Christianity, and Islam.

Sir L: Yes, and *very* dangerous, too. You need to be very careful when you offend somebody's prejudices, perhaps especially if they are afraid to be wrong.

Corr: So you think our newfound knowledge from Ur will ultimately revise all of our western religions?

Sir L: I am not sure. But if it doesn't cause them to revise themselves, it will surely contribute to their demise. It is paradoxical that the discovery of Ur makes Abraham's story move toward the factual, and, at the same time, it undermines the theologians who have constructed religions around his story.

Corr: For instance?

Sir L: The story of Abraham's journey to Chanaan follows a sort of tale of three cities, Ur, Phadan Uram, and Urgarit. Ur was on the Persian Gulf in its time, Phadan Uram was the transfer point of commerce from the Euphrates River to the camels, and Urgarit is the place on the Mediterranean where the camels were taken. All have been found and all contain the name Ur. The foundation of all three faiths is a conversation at Phadan Uram between Abraham and the god of that place. All the monotheistic religions assume that that god was God, the one and only.

Corr: I see what you mean by a problem.

Sir L: One might say that the fullness of the Divinity is in all beings, so it may speak through any one of them. No problem there, but that is a very different idea than having God show up without a mask. The gods may be seen as masks of God, as all beings are masks of God. The gods are no more or less God than you are!

Corr: You mean god with a small "g?"

Sir L: Yes. We have made God with a big G in the image of god with a little "g," not the other way around! It turns out that the temple at Phadan Uram was a temple of the god of Abraham's father at Ur, Nannar Sin. Nannar Sin had left Ur at the time and gone back to his planet. Phadan Uram is in the territory of his brother, El Hadad. It is plain that El Hadad, El, the god of Is-ra-el, is the one who spoke to Abraham. The question is, why? The answer is that El Hadad had a big problem: being only a god with a small "g," he had a wayward son called Baal who was trying to take Chanaan away from him.

Corr: Baal? Isn't that a big name in the Old Testament?

Sir L: Very big. The entire Biblical struggle in the region of that time, the war, is between Baal and his father, El. El Hadad was trying to set up an army in the desert to take Chanaan back if Baal should win. The story of David and Absalom in the Bible is a look-alike, and you don't have to read much Old Testament to find out that almost the whole thing is a war between Baal and the god of Israel.

Corr: Why do you suppose the monotheistic religions do things like that?

Sir L: You mean like promoting some god to be God? This occurs because they are all trying to inherit the Empire, and to inherit the Empire, God has to be on your side.

Corr: And that is the reason for that conundrum—a religious war?

Sir L: I'm afraid so. Those warriors will surely be displeased to find out that their god is no better than the other guy's!

Corr: Be not the bearer of bad tidings. Thank you, Sir Leonard. You are surely a man of courage. And if I may be so bold, a man of God, the true God that is!

Interlude

First City of Earth

Eridu

Translation: City in far-away-built,
far away from the home planet of the gods.

Who art thou, o Eridu?
A buried city on a buried sea?
Waterborne
Thy dust has lain
Dreaming in the mists of time.

But who hath waked thee Eridu, with memory of gods
As familiar to us
As ourselves
As comfortable
And as mysterious?

Canto VIII

Ziggurat of Ur

Time: 1919 CE

Place: Ziggurat of Ur, Southern Iraq

Personae: Sir Leonard Wooley
            A Jesuit
            Arab workmen

Sir L: Careful now, just one bucket at a time! And be sure to sift each one carefully. Keep a sharp look out for cylinder seals. They aren't very big. Look especially for the one showing Ninti holding her hands in the air with wide-eyed Adapa, the Adam, in the lower left-hand corner.

Jesuit: Ninti, who is that?

Sir L: One of the "Holy Trinity" of ancient Sumer: Enlil, Enki, and Ninti or Ninharsag.

Jesuit: What was the function of that trinity?

Sir L: Those three formed the High Council of the gods of Sumer. Each was a child of Anu, the Father in Heaven, but each child had a different mother. Only Enlil was a "legitimate" heir because his mother was Antu, known to us as Anna, Anu's half sister and wife.

Jesuit: A bit scandalous for gods, wouldn't you say?

Sir L: Not at all. Just too troubling for us, I'm afraid. The Sumerians were not ashamed of sex and never thought it was a bad thing. I think those moral ideas came from the Stoics, the philosophers of the Greeks, prudish as they were.

Jesuit: Are there genealogical lists in the Sumerian material?

Sir L: Yes, many of them. Those lists are clearly where the lists in the Bible came from.

Jesuit: We have long been puzzled about the so-called "begots."

Sir L: So have you been puzzled about begotten gods?

Jesuit: Treading on dangerous ground there.

Sir L: Would you be surprised to find that many favorite Christian beliefs could be put in severe peril by what secrets may lie here at Ur?

Jesuit: As a matter of fact, no, I wouldn't be surprised. I think I was sent here to find out about that. Would you like to elaborate?

Sir L: Well, the first thing you might notice is the name of the god of Ur, Nannar-Sin. Sinai and India appear to be named after him. That ziggurat there in the southwest corner of the tel was Nannar's temple. It appears that Terah, the listed father of Abraham, was a priest in that temple 4,000 years ago, give or take a couple of generations.

Jesuit: We have noted that Abraham's god and the god of his father appear in Genesis to be different, but we have no names to distinguish them.

Sir L: Perhaps a clue can be found in another city six hundred miles northwest of here. I believe you call it Phadan Aram. It appears it was originally Phadan Uram, a colony of Ur halfway to the west coast at Urgarit. There was also a temple of Nannar-Sin in Phadan Uram. Sin seems to have abandoned that one around Abraham's time and it reverted to El Hadad, Sin's brother. The voice that spoke to Abraham was likely that of El Hadad. Hadad is the Aramaic name for David, the beloved one. El seems clearly to be the name of the god of Is-ra-el.

Jesuit: Perilous ideas, certainly. You mean our god of Israel is El, and El is just one of the gods of Sumer?

Sir L: It looks that way and explains how El graduated to be creator of the Cosmos in the story of the Chosen People who incubated the idea during their stay in Egypt.

Jesuit: Is there some way we can induce you not to reveal these findings on the origin of our God? I fear that Christianity, as we see it, is severely threatened and its credibility would be severely undermined, not to speak of Judaism and Islam.

Sir L: I regret that, Father. For such an implosion of Christianity might dim the hopes and the faith of half the world. Perhaps the truth buried in this mound will have that effect. On the other hand, perhaps it will also stimulate a quest for further truth that will reveal the true nature of Jesus and his God. I fear it has been hidden too long.

Jesuit: Sir Leonard, I must confess that I share your feelings, as do many members of our order, yet we have a fourth vow: obedience to the Pope. The Vatican cannot bear the thought of such revisions. I think we should all pray to the real Jesus to help them as it is said he helped Thomas Aquinas.

Postscript

In the forest primaeval near a great eastern bend of the Congo River a forest wilderness exists where no human beings had entered for four hundred thousand years, as onsite evidence was about to suggest. An expedition was formed to enter this ancient land in the 1990s. As they moved away from the last human settlement, the animals became more numerous. After a long journey they came to open glades. Groups of primates, elephants, antelope, and some okapis were gathered enjoying the sunlight and the mineral springs. The people stopped, not wishing to frighten the animals. Then the wind changed and took their scent out onto the green. Some of the animals raised their heads and looked toward them, then, instead of running away, they walked right up to the people and sniffed as if wondering what they were. Shortly they went back to their former pursuits.

The party stayed in the vicinity several days and found evidence of prior human occupation, remnants of meticulously organized agricultural plots with signs of irrigation. There were useful plants not native to the area. The clear streams contained traces of human artifacts. When this evidence was later evaluated it was found to be 400,000 years old with no other proof of human presence for the intervening 400,000 years.

Since the ancient cuneiform records of the Sumerians place the first coming of the gods of Sumer at 450,000 years ago, could there be a connection? Especially since these Sumerian records place the breeding experiments to create the first modern humans in South Africa in order to provide workers for the gold mines there. Even today most of the gold mines in southern Africa are over 100,000 years old.

✳

Interlude

Ziggurat of Ur
Four-Step Pyramid

Is lack of trust the consequence of betrayal?   Black

And is betrayal a trait of the
Masters of Deceit do?   Red

And should we believe anyone who
asks us to believe in them?   Blue

And do we have the courage to seek
the truth in our own hearts?   Gold

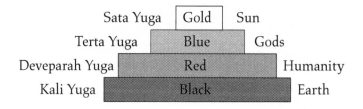

Canto IX

From Avalon to Eridu

Time: Circa 500 CE
Place: Isle of Avalon, Severn Estuary, Somerset

Personae: Merlin, (Emrys Merlinus Moordune)
             Arthur, age fourteen
             Vivian, Lady of the Lake

Arthur: Is it true, grandmother, that your spells can part the mists of Avalon?
Vivian: On occasion.
Arthur: Can I part them?
Vivian: Anyone can part the mists, young man, if they awaken the power.
Arthur: You mean the faery power?
Vivian: Yes, Arthur, the power that works outside of time.
Arthur: You mean you can go to any time you please?
Merlin: And any place as well. We all have the keys to the star gate that opens all times and all places to us.
Arthur: Will we still be here, while we are there?
Vivian: Yes, Arthur, though our attention may seem to be elsewhere.
Merlin: And to where, Bear Cub, do you wish to go, and to when?
Arthur: To the first city on Earth that ever was and to whenever it was.
Vivian: That would be Eridu.
Merlin: So it would. Eridu is older than *our* gods.
Arthur: How old, Merlin?
Merlin: Nearly half a million years, Bear Cub.
Arthur: Where did you learn of it, grandfather?
Merlin: At the lake village near the Tor, in the house of the Phoenician trader.
Vivian: Yes, I remember. We asked him who sculpted our Tor, our spiral mountain into its maze, and he replied, "Why the Sumerians, of course. They left their name on this land, Somerset."

Merlin: When we asked him, "Are you a Sumerian?" He answered, "Yes, after a manner of speaking. You see, I am from Phoenicia. As for Phoenicia, the name comes from the Phoenix bird that rises from its own ashes. Sumer is the original bird and Phoenicia is its reincarnation. Though some say we are named for the shellfish called *porphyro* that gives us the royal purple dye. Phoenicia was the west coast of Sumer, you know. Sumer was destroyed in the war between the gods on Sinai. We inherited its rich trade routes through the Black Sea to Scandinavia and through the Pillars of Hercules to this land where we now stand, and far across the Atlantic Sea to a world which few here know."

Arthur: Will we be able to sail there some day?

Merlin: Yes, Bear Cub, but not for a thousand summers.

Vivian: We then asked the trader, "How did Sumer come to be?" He replied, "In the beginning was Eridu, whose name means City-in-Faraway-Built. She was first built by Enki, first son of Anu, at the place of first landing on the Lake of the Well in the Sea, Bahrain, 400,000 years ago. The sea was lower then, and the present Sea of Ur, the Eurythrean or Arabian Sea, lay beyond the land of Makan. The sea rose and Eridu was re-built near the River Euphrates. Many cities arose after her, but the greatest was Ur whence trade routes went to the entire world, to Ur's great port on the Middle Sea that we call the Mediterranean, and to Urgarit in the land of my fathers. When Sumer was sadly swept away, my fathers arose to carry on the western commerce of Ur. Thus, we truly are that Phoenix bird, called Phoenicia, the winged one who rises from its own ashes."

Arthur: In Far-Away-Built? Built far away from what?

Vivian: From Nibiru, the planet of the gods, my boy.

Arthur: And who are these gods of Eridu?

Merlin: They are the ones the seers call the "olden gods."

Arthur: Which "olden gods" built Eridu?

Vivian: The Phoenician said to us that it was *Enki*, the powerful, son of Anu; he who is called Ptah by the children of the Nile in Egypt.

Arthur: Did Enki have a family?

Vivian: Oh yes! He had a brother named Enlil, Lord of the Command, a sister named Ninti, Lady Life, a father named Anu, The Father in Heaven, and many children. He had a nephew called Nannar Sin, the God of Ur, and another nephew named El Hadad, the God of Is-Ra–El, and a great nephew called Baal. Enki had a niece called Inanna who kept the sanctuary of his father at Erech.

Arthur: He came to Earth 400,000 years ago?

Merlin: Yes, so we have been told, Bear Cub, and our word Earth comes from Eridu, as does Arabic, *Ard*, and the Hebrew, *Eretz* and the German, *Erd*.

Arthur: Why did Enki come here?

Vivian: Because his father Anu sent him.

Arthur: Why would a father send his son so far, on such a dangerous journey?

Merlin: To get the gold.

Arthur: Was he out of money?

Merlin: No, Bear Cub. They needed the gold to save their world. Their atmosphere was decaying and only gold in the form of a white powder could save it.

Arthur: Doesn't that have to do with alchemy?

Merlin: Yes, Arthur. The Philosopher's Stone, the final quest of alchemy, is the white powder of gold, the fruit of the tree of life. The Philosopher's Stone is not sought to change base metal into gold, but to change gold into the white powder and to change material consciousness into spiritual consciousness.

Arthur: If I go to Eridu, will I find some white powder of gold?

Merlin: Perhaps, Bear Cub, but know that it is a dangerous journey, as Gilgamesh found out!

Interlude

Should we try to remember how that
Original Innocence was lost?
Or was it lost?
Is it not perhaps still within us all
Waiting for the call?
And can we not remember
Innocence is power,
The power that the Divinity has given us from the beginning
And was never taken away,
A power that is given not only to some, but to all?
For innocence means uninjured.
And what is uninjured?
Our power to know the truth.

Canto X

Granting of the *Meh*

Time: 3760 BCE, fall equinox, an hour after sunset

Place: Erech, Land between the Rivers

Personae: Duran, En-me-dur-an-ki, Enoch
              Inanna, Queen of Heaven
              A servant
              Anu, Father in Heaven
              Antu, wife and half-sister of Anu
              Lord Enki, Ea

Setting: The Ziggurat of Erech, High Holy place of Anu;
Euphrates River running northwest to southeast. Cool
river breeze taking the edge off a 120-degree day. The
city is coming alive again. On this day of great honor,
gracious Inanna is to welcome her grandfather Anu,
Lord of the Heavens, with his wife and half sister
Antu, mother of Enlil, Lord of the Command and his
half brother Enki, Lord Earth also known as Ea or
Lord of Waters. The "Eagle" would land in the E-kur,
as the ziggurat was called. Duran, the human
custodian of the Heaven-Earth Bond is in attendance.
Erech will be the realm of Gilgamesh someday.

Inanna: Good evening, Duran. My grandfather has a great opinion of you. You are the chosen one.

Duran: My Lady, what urgency of fortune compels such promise
from your lips?

Inanna: This I am bound by promise not to speak, but you shall
have your answer from Father Anu himself. See the moving star. His eagle will soon land. There! It stands upon its
fire even now above the sacred precinct. Be assured. He
comes not as usual for my sake, but for yours.

Servant: *(Naked to the waist, bowing obsequiously.)* My Lady,
Lord Enlil and Lord Enki beg your permission to converse
on this momentous occasion.

Exit Inanna and servant. Enter Anu and Antu.

Anu: I am told that I would find Duran, Keeper of the Bond, in this place. Are you he?

Duran: I am, and I am your unworthy servant, Lord Anu.

Anu: Servant you may be, but it is precisely because I find you worthy that I have come. Do you know that Lady Inanna is keeper of the *Meh*, the *Tablets of Destiny*?

Duran: She has not confided in me, but I have heard it is so.

Anu: Do you know what these tablets contain?

Duran: I have learned they are the double tablets of knowledge—one for the left hand, the other for the right. And as to the stars, one tablet records how we measure stars, and the other how they measure us.

Anu: The same is true with mathematics and numerology. All the sciences are dual in their nature.

Duran: Does the Bond I will protect depend upon them?

Anu: Even as you depend upon the Lady Inanna. But there are to be changes. It is time that a human, native to this orb, should rule the Empire and not an Anunnaki, one who from heaven to Earth came. It is you, Duran, whom I have chosen for this task.

Duran: I can only tremble at such an honor. I know not if it be from terror or joy, or from the awesomeness of their intercourse.

Anu: First Duran, I have set you a monumental task, a monumental labor as great as any that a human who bears like you, the blood of Heaven and Earth, has ever been asked to undertake.

Duran: Again I tremble, Great Heavenly Father. Let your will be my will that I may do as you desire.

Anu: Then go out from here and discover the brightest and the boldest and the most perseverant of the children of Sumer that they may learn at your hand the contents of the Meh, that they may assist you in the administration of your charge.

Duran: Great Anu, I am your servant.

Anu: If you succeed, I shall return after ten cycles of the sun and raise you to govern your people. When you have governed well for the season of a life, the eagle will come for you and you shall dwell with me on the Planet of the Crossing for the lifetime of a god. Farewell.

Canto IX

Exit Anu and Antu.

Duran: Then surely I shall be called En-me-dur-an-ki, Lord of the
          Encoded Information for the Maintenance of the Bond
          between the Heavens and the Earth! How shall I quell the
          restless tides of my self-doubt? Shall I now remember
          Adapa, the first human born of Earthwoman's egg and the
          seed of my Lord Enki through the labors of Lady Ninti?
          May I call upon the power of the Black Earth Woman
          native to this Earth, she who is mother to half my blood,
          to revive in me the powers lost so long ago? Or, shall I
          depend on White Father Enki's seed to teach me the skills
          of my hands? Is it too much to ask that instead of striv-
          ing against each other these two powers may flow togeth-
          er in harmony to bring an empowerment never yet
          known on Earth? Does this in me seem ambitious? Or, do
          I hold this memory in hope that my descendants on
          Earth, in the fullness of time, may share such a heritage,
          the worthy gifts of the Manifestor of all things, who is
          father even to Anu?

Enter Enki.

Enki: My son, you are valorous that you do not crumble
          beneath the ponderous weight and glory of such dreams.
Duran: My Lord Enki, do you attend me now with your love in
          the hour of my trial? How shall my heart so filled with
          self-doubt make room for the gratitude I feel for your
          love?
Enki: A heart that finds room for such thanksgiving has already
          been moved by the compassion of gratitude, my son.
          Only go forth now and put feet upon your good inten-
          tions that your accomplishment may remember its
          fathering in the memory of this day. Only remember that
          I love you and, when you need my consolation, call.

Interlude

The perfect form of selfishness is unselfishness.

If this be selfishness we have nothing to fear from it.

Canto XI

Delphi: Course of Empire

Time: Circa 1600 BCE

Place: Mt. Parnassus, Oracular Spring of Gases
Delphi, home of Apollo the Dolphin

Personae: Agamemnon, King of Mycenae
A Priest
Oracle of Delphi, 13 years of age

Setting: The Oracle is seated on her tripod
above the spring of Gases

Agam: She is so young. Can she really be wise?

Priest: She is not wise, great king, nor is she foolish. She is innocent. Her power to read the future is natural to us all.
Even your name Agamemnon proclaims the power to
remember the future that we all possess. But philosophy
gone wild has dulled our access to the truth we know.
Thus we must depend upon the uncorrupted innocence of
those untainted by conformity in order to remember
what we already know.

Agam: I would know the course of Empire, that prodigious visitor from eastern climes—Empire that towers with its
shadow, darkening the freedoms we enjoy. Troy, the westward bastion of Empire, guards the approach to the Straits
of Dardanus and to the Boreas Phoros, the gate of the
Euxine Sea that opens upon the ancestral lands of the
Hellenes, to which we desire free access.

Priest: Perhaps, your majesty, I can shed further light upon those
judicious observations before you seek the knowledge of
your fate from the lips of this woman-child?

Agam: Please.

Priest: Empire began at Sumer, the "land between the rivers" in the environs of Erech, and with the reaching tentacles of Ur, whose ships plied all seas, even beyond the Pillars of Hercules. The most recent stage of that history begins with the great flood of Ziusudra that flowed up the Dardanelles against the surface current we see today and drowned the fertile confines of the then fresh Euxine Sea, scattering our common ancestors from sea to sea, and undermining the power of the goddess whose spring this was.

Agam: I have heard some of that.

Priest: Erech sent its messengers to Akkad, before the fall of Sumer, and then to Babylon I in Egypt where the Empire rests today, with Troy its northern bastion. The oracle tells us that one day the power delegated by the gods will cross to the Tigris and go to Nineveh close to the shadow of Ararat where a great nation is arising. Thence it will go to another Babylon II on the Euphrates where the Hebrews, now fleeing from Egypt, will someday be captives. The conveyor language will be Sumerian, from Sumer to Akkad; from Akkad to Babylon I; from Babylon I to Assyria (Nineveh); from Nineveh to Babylon II.

Agam: And all this will carry the ceremony, the language, the culture and the gods of Sumer? And all this is unbroken in our day?

Priest: Yes, and the chain of power will be unbroken for millennia. And those in power, as they are now in Babylon I, will speak the Sumerian language, keep their clay tablets in cuneiform and follow the rituals on the ceremonial way as laid down in the *Enuma Elish*, the story of creation and the *Epic of Gilgamesh* of Erech, the quest for the fruit of the Tree of Life. They will celebrate their rituals in honor of the New Year as the sun declines on the equinox when the day and the night are equal over all the Earth. Not until the triumph of Elam will the tradition be broken.

Agam: Is this our solar myth of awesome power with its four portended crises of the light as the sun's gravity draws our emotions to follow it in its course through the year?

Priest: It seems so to me, your majesty. The Oracle further reveals that when Babylon II falls it will fall to the land of Elam, to be known to us as Persia. In Elam, the Sumerian language and custom will be abandoned. Then a Macedonian will arise on these our shores and bring the Empire into our lands. Soon it will pass over the Ionian Sea to the banks of the Tiber carried by one Caesar, the founder of the Empire in Rome. Then after a millennium and a half, it will pass to the temple of Isis and to a city called Parisis, named after her. And thence it will go to the Druid Isles where Lug the Long will call a city by his name: Lugondinnium. Shortened later to London, it will then pass beyond the Western Sea to dwell upon a shore now inhabited by those who will carry the ways of freedom until its coming. She does not see a world beyond that fateful time. Perhaps it will be the eve of the well of darkness or perhaps the resurrection of freedom.

Agam: Is it my destiny, then, to slow Empire's march beneath the walls of Troy?

Priest: Only the Oracle can answer that, but notice, great king, that the Empire is a presage of an Age of Darkness, when men will see themselves as better than other men, will grow fat upon the life blood of their brothers, claiming to have warrant from a god who once ruled in Erech.

Agam: Can even the gods save us from such a monstrous fate? Could such dire prophesy be mistaken?

Priest: All are fallible when it comes to memory, even prophets. But these proclamations of this innocent girl are far too precise and too knowing to be slightly regarded.

Agam: Are there gods then that favor freedom?

Priest: Oh yes! But the gods we encounter, in fact or metaphor, are no more or less divine than you. Would you know something of their story?

Agam: Yes, but not today. I must urge my quest to know from this girl's lips what fate awaits us beyond the Hellas-pont, or as the Trojans call it, the Bridge to Hellas.

Interlude

A poet lends his voice to the songs of his own heart.
A bard lends his voice to the Manifesting Power.
Shakespeare is a bard.

The unconscious is essentially a means of reconciliation between
the all and the One.

The most consoling of realizations is that immortality is not
learned, it is remembered from the womb.
It is death that is learned.
And which is the music of joy?

Canto XII

A Good Use of Time

Time: Sixth Century BCE

Place: Memphta (Memphis), Giza, Egypt

Personae: Pythagoras
           Priest of Ptah, Egyptian god of creation
           Memnon, a pyramid mechanic

Priest: Are you one of those Hellenes from Borea?

Pyth: Yes, from the Isle of Samos.

Priest: Have you come to compare gods like most of you Northerners?

Pyth: Not exactly, I have come about the power we ascribe to the gods.

Priest: You mean about the motion of the stars? For that you should have gone to Babylon, or Chaldea.

Pyth: Perhaps, but you are closer by, a bit friendlier too, I hear.

Priest: Kind words, and you are right, Chaldeans can be prickly and not so free as ourselves, it seems.

Pyth: Speaking of Chaldea, or Mesopotamia, isn't the god you call Ptah called by another name there?

Priest: I think Enki, Lord Earth, or Ea, Lord of Waters are his Sumerian or Chaldean names.

Pyth: Isn't Enki regarded as the creator of man, but not of the cosmos? And didn't the "creation" happen 300,000 years ago, not just a few thousand? That is, the "creation of man?"

Priest: Yes, but we are coming to see our Ptah as the source of all on Earth and in the heavens that pursued the sun at sunset. Of course the sky came long before man!

Pyth: Something of a leap, wouldn't you say? I understand that Enki conducted some kind of breeding program here in Africa, way past the sources of the Nile; crossed his own sperm with the egg of an Earth woman to produce *Adapa*, the first human some call Adam. Doesn't it mean red?

Priest: I've heard that. I've also heard that Adapa was red because he was a cross between black and white. They say the star people were white and the Earth people black.

Pyth: A Chaldean once said that old clay tablets at Babylon record that *Adapu*, as they call him, was made nearly sterile for fear of overpopulation so his makers could control reproduction, and that they crossed his own seed with an egg taken from his own mother and got the female on the first try.

Priest: There was also something about shortening the life span, for similar reasons. It seems the lifespan of the "gods" was some 300,000 Earth years.

Pyth: Why did they do it, the experiments, that is?

Priest: To provide slaves for the grunt work, I understand.

Pyth: Something about digging gold in South Africa?

Priest: The legends of the far south say there are gold mines in South Africa 100,000 years old.

Pyth: We Hellenes have been under a lot of pressure from the Persians who rule Mesopotamia, you know. We fight them because they want to make us part of their Empire. We are a more democratic people from Druid country. The Persians say they have a mandate to rule the Earth that came from the gods of Sumer, those same gods who gave the Empire to Enmeduranki 3,000 years ago.

Priest: I am sure you realize that the Hebrews were chosen by our Pharaoh to rule our country for 400 years. They had a calendar that sounds exactly like the Sumerians, a calendar they say came from Mesopotamia. Yet they were of the opinion that the cosmos only came into existence 3,260 years ago.

Pyth: A bit short-sighted. I understand that they are promoting their god to be the only one?

Priest: They didn't think that way before they came here, but they gave us priests a bad time with it before they left.

Pyth: You mean that business with Amenhotep IV who called himself Ankenaten, and who gave you priests such a hard time by putting you out of work?

Priest: Yes. Ankenaten put all us priests out of work, took over our temples, broke the statues of our gods, and put their god in place of ours. He called their god Aten, I believe. We put up with that for a while, got tired of being unemployed, and ran Ankenaten out of the country, along with

	the Hebrews. He called himself Moses after that, I think.
Pyth:	What was the name of their god when they came down here?
Priest:	El Hadad. They called him El for short.
Pyth:	But El Hadad was the god of Chanaan, wasn't he? The one with the rebellious son?
Priest:	His son went by the name of Baal.
Pyth:	And didn't El Hadad have a brother?
Priest:	Nannar Sin, I believe. They named Mount Sinai after him. He was the god of Ur.
Pyth	I understand that the ziggurat of Ur is still standing in the desert of Mesopotamia.
Priest:	I have actually seen it. There are four levels: bottom level, black glazed brick; middle level, red glazed brick; top level, blue glazed brick, and the tower, gold glazed brick. Ur, they say, was once the commercial center of the world. We have named the ocean past the Red Sea the Ur-ithryan Sea after Ur. Our history tells us that our civilization came to us over that sea of Ur.
Pyth:	Those people who put you out of work, what did they call themselves?
Priest:	When they came here they called themselves Hebrews. The word is better pronounced Ha-abiru. *Biru* is a Sumerian word meaning "to cross over." *Ha* is the definite article, thus the word He-brew means people who cross over (*biru* or *beru* in Sumerian also indicates an astronomical distance).

The planet of the gods of Sumer is called Nibiru. *Ni* means planet, *beru* means crossing. Thus Nibiru means "planet of the crossing." In the Hebrew story it appears in the idea of Passover. But when they left here, after the 400 years, they were dedicated to El Hadad and called themselves Israelites: Is—man, ra—struggle, el—god.

I understand the story of their departure, the Passover, means that when Amenhotep IV left, calling himself Moses, he escaped from the armies we sent after him by crossing the Gulf of Aquaba on a natural underwater bridge. A lot of our people drowned in the process when Moses manifested a shift in water levels. I hear that the Assyrians took a lot of Israelites out of Chanaan over a hundred years ago and many of the Hebrews are in captivity in Babylon right now.

Pyth: We have seen a lot of them in Italy on Phoenician ships. They call themselves Danites (Tuatha da Dannan). They are considered to be some kind of blessing by the Phoenicians. They name rivers for them. Perhaps they are connected with the Earth goddess Dana.

Priest: They say the Phoenicians inherited the western sea routes of Ur when Sumer was destroyed by a poisonous cloud. The Phoenicians took over Urgarit, called Ugarit in the Levant, and the commerce and ship building that went with it.

Pyth: The Phoenicians have a fine city near Italy called Carthage, no doubt a major stop before the Pillars of Hercules and beyond.

Priest: Did you know that our Pharaohs enjoy psychedelic substances from beyond the Pillars of Hercules?

Pyth: Phoenician articles of trade no doubt. For some of us Greeks the *Amanita Muscaria*, the Death's Cap mushroom, is the substance of choice. However let us return to Ptah. We Greeks have a number, Pi, which I believe we may have acquired here in Egypt. We use Pi to describe the energy of curvature. Is there a connection to Ptah?

Priest: Very much so. This city where we now stand is named *Memphta* after Ptah: *Mem* for "flow" and *Ptah* for "the elemental force of manifestation" in the action of which matter appears out of energy. If you gave it a Greek name you would probably call it Mempi, Memphi or Memphis. It was once called Babylon, the Gateway of the Gods, before the present Babylon in Mesopotamia was built.

Pyth: I believe the number you gave us for the letter Pi is 3.14159....

Priest: Yes, it turns out to be the ratio of a circle's diameter to its circumference. And speaking of mathematics, did you know that the word mathematics comes from the Sumerian word *Meh*?"

Pyth: No I didn't. What is the meaning of the word, Meh?

Priest: The Sumerians call the *Meh*, the *Tablets of Destiny*, a compendium of all the sciences including mathematics. In particular, "destiny" refers to the deterministic orbits of the planets and the speed of their travel. The orbit of a planet as its destiny is analogous to the course of each life being a predetermined destiny, modified by an undetermined fate of the heart. We see the force you call Pi as a certain determinant of the course of flow, a force that makes straight lines curve as the course of the planets curve.

Pyth: You mean Ptah is such a force?

Priest: A more personal reference, I suppose. But yes, a force acting upon a flow, causing straight lines to curve.

Pyth: Could it also act to cause the flow to proceed out of two dimensions into three?

Priest: You're getting beyond me there. Let me call our pyramid mechanic. He can explain it better than I. Memnon, do you have a moment? This Helene asks questions more appropriately directed to you.

Memn: Sure. Thanks for the invitation. I don't meet enough curious fellows hereabouts.

Pyth: We were talking about Ptah and his magic number, Pi π.

Memn: He has several magic numbers, you know, one for curves, one for spins, and one for the Golden Section.

Pyth: Golden Section?

Memn: Yes. The Golden Section is one way of designating a transdimensional journey suggested by the Pyramids. Ptah is said to cause energy to curve—the force of Pi π, a non-rational number 3.141... moving, as it were, from one dimension into two; the force of Phi Φ, a non-rational number 1.618... (The Golden Ratio) moving, as it were, from two dimensions into three in an ascending spiral, (The Fibonacci Series 1, 1, 2, 3, 5, 8, 13, 21, 34, 55, 89, 144...), and Psi Ψ, a series of numbers suggesting a further dimensional change from three into four.

Curiously, you can view the progression in the other direction: beginning at 3 and 5, divide the low number (3) into the higher number (5) and 5 into 8 and so on, and you approach Phi Φ 1.618... By another mathematical process you can derive Pi π 3.141... from Phi Φ 1.618... (the inverse square).

Some have suggested that this is a description of a single force eventuating in an observed three-step journey through dimensional change. Our priests see π as that energy of essential flow, Φ as the same energy as life force, and Ψ as the same energy as consciousness.

Pyth: This was known when the pyramids were built? How many thousand years ago?

Memn: Yes, it was well known by the Sumerians many millennia in the past. Some say they built these pyramids here at Giza. Others say the gods of Sumer built them.

Pyth: Granite base blocks, limestone facing, crystal cap and all?

Memn: That's right. Do you know that the crystal cap is cut and fitted to make four faces out of six? And that the crystal cap sits in a gold socket, and the gold socket sits in a silver socket, and the silver socket sits in a nickel-bronze socket, and the nickel-bronze socket sits against the limestone facing?

Pyth: What's that all about?

Memn: Something to do with granite stones, human bones, and immortality. Human bones are like limestone with a carbon base, and granite stones are like crystals with a silicon base. For life force to run between them they need metals in that sequence.

It is really about the living quality of the stones, along with the immortality of every spirit. The crystal cap is also called the Benben, the "highward fire stone," the "rainbow serpent," or the "violet flame." The cap is called a serpent because all energy spins. The rainbow is produced by the prism of the crystal, which effects a spinning wheel or continuum of "lights" or energies that we perceive as color in the obvious senses (infrared, red, orange, yellow, green blue, violet, ultraviolet). One might see black as the continuum between ultraviolet and infrared. The continuum is called the violet flame, a sort of transition between the manifested and the unmanifested world, or vice versa.

The crystal not only focuses a force of energy flow that some call electricity, it also focuses a more subtle form that can carry messages, and it also focuses an even finer force some call aether which is a vehicle of inter-dimensional travel, such as that which happens when you die!

Pyth: My chosen name seems to indicate what you just

described: *Pyth*, python, serpent, spin; *Agora*, an assembly or a coming together in a vortex!

Memn: The comprehension of the "rainbow serpent" is said by our priests to be a basic aspect of initiation. The purpose of initiation is not to make you immortal, nor merely to remind you that you are immortal. *Initiation* awakens in you the deep awareness that you are immortal and frees you of the fear of death, which shadows the ecstasy of life. It accomplishes this by giving you the experience of the "ecstasy of death" during life, thus removing the fear of death and all the distortions that fear stirs up in us so that we are free to make good use of time by helping other people to achieve this astonishing awareness.

Pyth: The "ecstasy of death" and the realization that life is eternal are the objects of initiation? I see that I must remain in Egypt much longer than I planned.

Memn: You should also see how the above is connected with magic. "Magic," as we call it is really telepathic power. Some say it is a middle power between unmanifested power and manifested power. But this is the "magic of initiation" into the "secret of death," death that is the connection between dimensions.

Pyth: Are you saying that telepathy and mathematics together are the keys to the knowledge of eternal life?

Memn: Maybe we should ask our priest friend about that.

Priest: Thank you, Memnon. This is surely my favorite subject.

Pyth: Would it be possible for me to be a candidate for initiation?

Priest: Before you volunteer for that experience, I must warn you that it is a very perilous experience for which you must be made ready by long preparation.

Pyth: You mean fools rush in where angels fear to tread? Please tell me more about the true object of initiation?

Priest: The true object of initiation is illumination which is to realize the inevitability of eternal life. It is much more than believing in eternal life. Each of us knows that life is eternal, but we have learned to believe in death as the end of life. That belief blocks our deeper knowledge of eternity and results in the disabling, unacknowledged, fear of death. That fear warps our conduct and is in some degree the cause of all of our misconduct and despair. Initiation causes you to experience the "ecstasy of death" and glimpse the eternal life that lies beyond death. This knowledge remembered saves you from your self-doubt and teaches you to make good use of time.

Pyth: Will the instruction take a long time?

Priest: A minimum of ten years, usually longer. And you must first spend a great deal of time discovering whether you are capable of sustaining the moral burden of empowerment. This requires long conversations with a master and frequently requires another ten years. If you wish, I will introduce you to such a master. I cannot guarantee that he will accept you. On the other hand, there are some who immediately remember eternal life and its attendant ecstasy and have no need of initiation in the formal sense. Who knows? Perhaps you are such a one!

Pyth: I accept your kind offer, and though it is possible that I am such a one, I must not presume. This promises me the understanding of the meaning of life, and it is to find that meaning that I have come to Egypt in the first place.

Priest: Your humility commends you. When do we start?

Pyth: I've talked with travelers from Sind (India) who seem to look at things the way that you do. They call the power "the Nameless" and they have clever sayings about it such as, "That is That that is That before That is Who."

Memn: I like That! That That that is that!

Pyth: "The Nameless" is not looked at as personal, but as pre-personal, that is, it precedes anything that is as limited as a person.

Memn: My point exactly.

Pyth: They also speak of "breathing," a kind of metaphorical breathing in which "the Nameless" breathes out the cosmos into what we are and what we see, touch, hear, taste and smell, and then "breathes" it all back in again.

Memn: And us along with it! Now there is a metaphor!

Pyth: Exactly. They say space and time are illusions, though, and so breathing is a metaphor for something that is all happening at once.

Memn: In all dimensions at once I suppose.

Pyth: They see the fullness of "the Nameless" in every part of

	it all, from the smallest to the greatest and from the nearest to the farthest, either in time or space.
Memn:	"The Nameless" is the manifesting power that is every when and every where at once!
Pyth:	They also say if you realize this, more than just think about it, you will always be at home, in a sort of ecstatic state, very quiet, and exciting simultaneously.
Memn:	Sounds to me like we are back to initiation, telepathy and the "ecstasy of death" again. You know Anubis is usually thought to be the god of death who weighs your soul against a feather. You want your soul to be light for Anubis, but it is Thoth whose name *means* death. Note that Anubis has a threatening aspect but Thoth is the essence of benevolence, and it is he who has written what we call the *Egyptian Book of the Dead* or the "book of coming forth by day" that some call the *Torah* and the Egyptians call the *Tarot* the *Taroth*, for *Torath* is the plural of *Torah!*
Pyth:	All masters feel the whole thing is "divine" and all we need to do is get in touch with that and help others who want to do the same.
Memn:	My point exactly.
Pyth:	The oriental masters are very non-hierarchical and say not only is "the Nameless" equally present in all things, but all things have the power to realize that! Inequality arises only in that people achieve the empowerment in varying degrees. Those masters are never critical of others for not using the power nor do they look down on them for that reason—they just have compassion for them and help them out if they ask.
Memn:	Sounds a lot better to me than worshiping gods. I think I have heard some of those people talk in Memphta. They wore saffron robes and called themselves Saca. Are you up to a little play time, you know, being a kid again?
Pyth:	A light heart and an innocent mind are the harbingers of joy! You are only old if you are afraid to be young.
Memn:	Well then, let's spin. Oh yes, spin sunwise. Lead with your left foot and your left hand and spin to the right. That's it. Go round three times, and let your hands go out to where they want to go. That's it. Notice the angle?

Both yours and mine are the same? Know what? Our arms make the same angle to the ground as do the sides of the Great Pyramid. Your first lesson in pyramid mechanics.

Pyth: Isn't that also the angle of the main face of a quartz crystal?

Memn: Bravo, you noticed! If you measure the angle it is fifty-one degrees, fifty-one minutes and fifty-one seconds, 52° for short!

Pyth: And that has something to do with the Golden Section, with the number Phi **Φ** ?

Memn: Exactly, and the Great Pyramid is constructed such that its size is a multiple of a model pyramid with a distance from the center to the side edge of 1 unit and a height at center equal to the square root of Phi **Φ**, yielding a distance from the side edge to the top, of Phi **Φ**. This relationship produces that same magic angle for any size pyramid, as do your arms when you spin.

Pyth: Amazing! So the key is human bones and granite stones, quartz crystals and limestone stone circles, devas and pyramids, lightness of heart and eternal life!

Priest: We would call that telepathic force you mention the finger of Ptah.

Memn: Taken as a metaphor, gods are acceptable. Let's see… the finger of Ptah when it bends is the force of Pi **π** As it moves, it constructs a circle where once was a straight line.

Pyth: Or, to use the ideas of my friends from Sind, "the force used by 'the Nameless' to manifest the cosmos."

Priest: But doesn't Ptah have two fingers?

Memn: Perhaps three, all forces, of course: one to make a circle, one to make a spiral, and one to reflect.

Pyth: Cylindrical spin, conical spin, toroidal spin—all related to each other.

Memn: Well, after the circle goes round and round, the second force makes it spiral upward until it flows at a perfect perpendicular to the plane of its origin, and as the cone escapes gravity and extends into space it becomes a torus.

Pyth: I see three shapes: one a column, one a cone, and one a ring. I see the pyramid as a cone with flattened sides.

Priest: Let's look at another magic: the torus, the ring, the reflection. It seems to me you could look at the three as construction blocks of a living cosmos: a cylinder of energy, a cone of life force and a torus, or doughnut shape, of consciousness.

Memn: Three manifestations of the same force.

Priest: Out of one, many, and out of many, one. It's the ladder to the heavens and from the heavens.

Memn: Spinning up and spinning down, helical and vortiginal, sunwise and countersunwise. Children spinning around a pool of clear water, manifesting the universe within?

Priest: Perhaps there is one God after all, and we are all the gods! Thus beware of egotism, racial or otherwise, for the fullness of the power is in all beings, not only humans.

Pyth: My work with the Druids indicates that they base their ceremonies on water flowing underground. They speak of a rotating column of energy flowing around each water flow. When the flows cross at different levels, they don't mix, but the energies mix and make a cone of energy spinning upward until it goes straight up like a beam. They believe that this beam can be bent with telepathic power and made to intercept a "dragon"—an object from the heavens—and alter its course, causing it to miss the Earth. I would not be surprised to find that these angles are like those of the Great Pyramid.

Memn: Nor would I be surprised to find that if you take that rotating helix of energy out into the heavens, it would become a torus. I have read such ideas in the records of Sumer.

Priest: I begin to fear the gods in all of this. I think we are talking about their secrets, and I am not sure they would approve!

Memn: But God would approve. I mean, "the Nameless" would approve!

Postscript

It should be noted that Pythagoras stayed in Egypt for twenty-five years, from age seventeen to forty-two, and perhaps longer.

Interlude

"The senses see the seeming, not eternal now. The change that's ever teeming is all beneath your brow."	Meditation on Parmenides
"Heraclitus' theory is fiery, *fieri*." (*Fieri* to Become)	Meditation on Heraclitus
"Pythagoras rose to mathematical abstraction."	Meditation on Pythagoras
"Anaxagoras taught that all was the manifestation of mind."	Meditation on Anaxagoras (Heart-mind?)
"All is infinite mind and its infinite manifestation."	Meditation on Mary Baker Eddy (Did she read Anaxagoras?)

Canto XIII

Spin–The Vortiginal Nature Of Manifestation

Prologomena

Early Philosophers, as Jacques Maritain has pointed out, at first, impressed by what strikes the senses, sought to determine the constitutive principles of the world. Seemingly not yet conceiving of invisible principles, they began by assigning some sensible element such as earth, air, fire and water as the universal material out of which all things were formed.
~ Newman Eberhardt – A Summary of Catholic History, Vol. I

Heraclitus, over-impressed by becoming,   Energy
imagined everything in flux (Flow).

Parmenides, concentrating on stability, declared   Matter
everything is immutable being (Focus).

Thus were set the extreme limits of speculation: Spirit
Pythagoras rose to mathematical abstraction.

Anaxagoras suggested a ruling mind.   Aetheric

Time:	Sixth Century BCE
Place:	Island of Samos
Personae:	Pythagoras
	A Druid

Pyth: Did you come from Albion by land or sea?

Druid: Phoenician ships. Is there a better way?

Pyth: Perhaps by air. I have heard that you Druids can bi-locate.

Druid: There are still some who can, but I am not yet so advanced. Druid, or Drus-oois, means the wisdom of the oak tree and implies we can talk to oak trees, in fact to many trees. Have you heard of the Acarusian tree alphabet?

Pyth: Yes, I believe the Phoenicians picked it up in Acarusia near the Bosphorus. They were on their way to the Dnieper River and to the portage of Novgorod and found the alphabet very useful for record keeping.

Druid: I'm glad you know of it. Tell me about your name. Doesn't it have to do with Apollo and his slaying of the python at Delphi?

Pyth: Yes, it has to do with the great dragon serpent, the python, and the power of spin. That's why I have asked you to come. You see, I am interested in the mathematics of spin as it affects the building of a community or a nation. This is why I have chosen my name. *Pyth* is for python and the principle of spin, and *Agora* is for the assembly of the people, thus Pyth-agoras.

Druid: You are a Greek, are you not? Or do you prefer to be called a Hellene from the ancient name of Hellas?

Pyth: Hellene is my preference.

Druid: Did you know that Hellene is a word from *our* language? We spell the word Ha-tklan or *llan* pronounced "hatklan" or "tklan." It is the word for our sacred assembly, called by the Earth! We remember it from the Golden Age.

Pyth: Our ancestors came from Borea, the north, and they were blonde-haired and blue-eyed like your people.

Druid: We are the same people!

Pyth: It seems so. Both *agora* and *llan* mean assembly of people, so where does "called by Earth" fit in?

Druid: Now, this is where the action is and the part that is so

	hard for people to understand.
Pyth:	Why so hard?
Druid:	Because of the illusion of sunrise and sunset.
Pyth:	You mean the sun doesn't really rise? That will certainly be a hard sell against common experience!
Druid:	I know, and there is a harder sell. The sun doesn't move to make the seasons.
Pyth:	Is that the story of the two dragons?
Druid:	The blue dragon and the red dragon? Yes, indeed. The blue dragon is the sun's course by day and the red dragon, is the sun's course by year. We call them Merlin's dragons.
Pyth:	But the sun doesn't move?
Druid:	Well, maybe it moves, but we don't see that motion except by observing the night sky, and then it moves so slowly that few have lived long enough to see it.
Pyth:	Do our senses deceive us, then?
Druid:	All the time. The point is, one spin of the Earth equals a day and twice a year the sun stands still. The Mesopotamians know about this and are willing to tell, but lately nobody listens, except maybe we Druids and our Shamanic friends.
Pyth:	Back to spin again, does every motion concern spin?
Druid:	Pretty much.
Pyth:	And is this about mathematics?
Druid:	Yes, certainly. Ask the Egyptians. Those pyramids tell the story. I'll give you a clue: the Golden Section. But let's get back to how the Earth calls the people together.
Pyth:	Is this another illusion?
Druid:	No more than everything is an illusion.
Pyth:	I realize that spin affects community, but the Earth calling people?
Druid:	You know that we are very involved with stones, don't you?
Pyth:	Yes.
Druid:	We find the places to put the stones by finding water flowing underground. Every flow produces a field of telluric or chthonic force spinning around it. If the flow stops, the field of force collapses. If two flows cross at different levels near each other, the fields mix and cause a vortex, perpendicular to the crossing, as a cone of energy

or spirit. The dowser feels it because he, like each of us, walks around as a similar cone of energy. When the cones match, the dowser marks the place with a stone. It is called by some either a holy place or an unholy place, depending on the spin. It's called holy if the spin is sunwise or clockwise; unholy if the spin is countersunwise or counterclockwise. Both the sun and the moon affect the strength of the spin.

Pyth: So, the spin is the dragon or the serpent energy, like the Python part of my name?

Druid: Yes, and each year these "dragons" call people. Some respond and some do not. Those who do respond are drawn to the "holy place" at the same time. We consider these people to be called by the Earth to choose a singer who will sing the nation for a year. This is how pythons or dragons relate to "intentional community."

Pyth: Do the shamans also know these things?

Druid: Yes, we all remember them from the Golden Age.

Pyth: Excellent! Now that I understand the Golden Age was built around the Golden Section, can you help me with relating that to the pyramids?

Druid: Perhaps. First I must tell you the name of the vortiginal spin coming out of the earth.

Pyth: Is it python?

Druid: That is another name for it, but a name for many other such phenomena as well. This particular kind is called a deva. The word divine and the word devil come from it.

Pyth: So the deva is measured by the Golden Section?

Druid: In a manner of speaking. The Golden Section is derived from a series of numbers: 1, 1, 2, 3, 5, 8, 13, 21, 34, 55, 89, 144, etc. You get the next number by adding the previous two. Look at your word python. It could also be spelled Pi-thon, or Phi-thon or Psi-thon.

That brings us to the triskel, the three rays that are the symbol of all our Celtic nations. The three rays can be described as energy: Pi π life force: Phi Φ; and consciousness: Psi Ψ. Your letter Pi is a trilithon—three stones making an arch. Your letter Phi is one turn of a vortex. Your letter Psi is a trident standing for the series of the Golden Section itself.

If, at any place in the series, you divide the low number into the high number, you get an approximation of Phi. The higher into the series you go, the more accurate that approximation becomes.

Pi is the ratio of a circle's circumference to its diameter. Psi is the ratio of Phi squared to Pi, which turns out to be a perfect square. If we were speaking of gods, you could say it is one god in three persons.

Pyth: So mathematics can describe the process of building an intentional community just as mathematics is intimately related to that muse we call music! How can I thank you?

Druid: You have already thanked me by hearing and even more by understanding. May you live forever young in the "charm of making!"

Interlude

0	THE GOLDEN AGE
1	You shall know the truth
	And the truth shall make you free
1	Breathes there a man with soul so dead
	Who never to himself hath said
2	This is my own, my native land
3	That government
	Of the people
5	By the people
	And for the people
8	Should not perish from the Earth
13	Give me Liberty
	or
21	Give me Death
34	We hold these truths to be self-evident
55	That all men are created equal
	Endowed by their Creator
89	With the inalienable right to
144	Life, liberty, and the pursuit of happiness
	THE GOLDEN SECTION

Canto XIV

Community!

Time: Sixth Century BCE

Place: Memphta, Giza Plateau, the Pyramids

Personae: Pythagoras
                Anken, a pyramid mechanic
                Emrys Mooredune, a Druid

Pyth: A Priest of Ptah has recommended I talk to Anken. Would that be you?

Anken: Yes. Are you Pythagoras?

Pyth: The very same, and this is my friend and associate Emrys Mooredune who comes to us from Albion.

Anken: Are you a Druid, reverend sir?

Emrys: Yes, I am one of those Boreans, northerners, who finds wisdom in the oak tree.

Anken: We are not favored with many trees in our land. I understand that you also seek wisdom in the stones, and we have plenty of those.

Pyth: Well, that's a good start on why I want to talk to you.

Anken: Perhaps it's not really about trees and stones that we want to speak, but about the flow of energy that manifests itself in them.

Pyth: The priest of Ptah, with whom I spoke, told me that you and he have different ways of looking at things because he calls energy spirit and gets mixed up with gods, a thing you fight shy of!

Anken: Yes, I know that priest very well. While we disagree about a lot of things, we really are good friends. While I confess that everything appears to be alive, I would rather not express it in terms of gods because gods are too frightening, and fear messes up reason.

Emrys: Might you say, those who favor the gods, the gods favor? We have that problem too! Energy and Spirit? I may

86

want a three-cornered hat, a *tri-skel*! We Druids have a symbol we call a triskel. It means three rays from one source. We refer to these three rays as energy, life force and consciousness.

Pyth: How would you explain them in other words?

Emrys: Energy is the power of flow, spirit is the flow of life force, consciousness is flow that is aware of itself flowing, or so we surmise.

Pyth: I want to make one thing clear. I am investigating these matters because of my interest in an agora, or intentional community. I am planning such a community in Italy at Croton. I hypothesize that the structure of buildings and the structure of communities have a lot in common and we should be able to use mathematics to examine and illuminate that comparison.

Emrys: I think you Greeks call yourself Hellenes, do you not?

Pyth: Yes, indeed.

Emrys: That word Hellene comes from our word *Llan*, pronounced 'tklan' or Ha-tklan. Llan means a community of people who live in search of unanimity among themselves, Pythagoras. Perhaps you are just reverting to your origins.

Pyth: I would be delighted to discover that that is true.

Anken: So, shall we discuss how pyramids are connected to all this?

Emrys: Certainly, if we can also discuss how devas are connected to the pyramids mathematically.

Anken: Deva? Isn't that a Persian word?

Emrys: I think so. We use it to describe chthonic or telluric energy that spins up out of the Earth in certain places.

Pyth: I would say everything we are talking about relates to spin—heliacal, rising and vortiginal spin—stars, planets, spires and auras.

Anken: And pyramids, I might add. Our pyramids are a bit squared off, but in Mesopotamia they are in spiral form. The Assyrians call them *ziqquratu*, I call them ziggurats, or conical spin pyramids.

Pyth: I am sure you know the Sumerians attribute them to their gods who came down from the heavens, gods who called themselves Anunnaki, those-who-from heaven-to-Earth-came.

Emrys: I am afraid, Anken, that despite our best efforts we will not be able to keep the gods out of this entirely.

Anken: Apology accepted. I don't mind gods in the mix. I just don't like them in terms of ultimate origin. That is my problem with Ptah. These priests want to make him responsible for everything, and I insist he has a more limited role. It seems to me that any name is too small for where it all comes from.

Pyth: So, Emrys, what does your name mean?

Emrys: In my language it means eagle. It also refers to the pattern of the eagle's flight. It seems that eagles are so big they need assistance to reach hunting altitude, so they look for updrafts to get a free ride to where they want to go. Updrafts spin. So you see the eagle riding upward in a spin that gets smaller and smaller as she goes higher and higher. At the top, she waits for a signal from another updraft, flies over on the same level and then up she goes, round and round again. The secret is the signal and her ability to perceive it telepathically. The eagle is a gyrfalcon, a bird of the *gyr* or spin.

Anken: Two questions: Why do you call the eagle she, and how does she "perceive" the signal?

Emrys: We survivors of the Golden Age reverse what Empire people do. Empire people say, "The masculine includes the feminine when both are implied." We say it the other way around, "The feminine includes the masculine when both are implied."

Anken: Remarkable. Do you then see the feminine as dominant, the way we see the masculine?

Emrys: Not at all. We see them both as equals, no dominance. The feminine is mentioned first because it is more "fey," that is, more intuitive. We actually prize intuition over intellect as being more immediate access to the source.

Pyth: I do apologize, Anken, for changing the subject, but I would inquire of Emrys what knowledge he may have of the story of Apollo coming to Delphi?

Emrys: I know of your Apollo but not that story. Please enlighten me.

Pyth: It involves two places, the Isle of Delos and Mt. Parnassus. Apollo the Sun god and the god of Reason was born of Leto together with his twin sister Artemis. As a precocious newborn he ordered his mother Leto, sometimes called Lat, to carry him to a sanctuary of Gaia, or Mother Earth, on Mt. Parnassus. The sanctuary had a sacred spring of gases that gave oracular powers to sibyls. The spring was guarded by the dragon-serpent Python. Leto followed a "river of olive trees" to Delphi. Apollo, who had brought a bow and arrow, leaning back on his mother's breast, shot and killed Python and took possession of the spring. He then went to a deserted place in order to do penance for killing a sacred creature. There, he and Hermes were companions for twenty years. I think the metaphor is obvious: reason replaces intuition as the primary guide to truth. Male succeeds female in priority. Empire succeeds democracy as a form of government.

Emrys: Exactly why we still start with the female. We call our society matrilineal, not matriarchal, because of the hermaphroditic nature of the true cosmos. It is not a question of dominance, but of mutual equality and balance—reconciliation of the horns of contradiction.

Anken: As a matter of fact, we Egyptians speak of the Divine Hermaphrodite as the origin of the cosmos, or at least that is what my priest friend informs me. He also tells me that the gods of Sumer are not fond of the idea and are the ones who originated the patriarchy in which the male is dominant.

Emrys: That does relate to my eagle because it is precisely through intuition that she finds the updraft, but then, so does her mate. Both powers are on both sides. It is a matter of emphasis.

Anken: So tell us more about the whirlwind. It seems there is more to it than spinning air. You imply a co-relative spin of some other more subtle energy—an energy that communicates information.

Emrys: Precisely. That same "more subtle energy," as you so well

	phrase it, is emitted by all kinds of spin: earth, air, fire, water, and the spin of the more subtle energy itself. We see this more subtle energy, spinning, as the stuff of which all the cosmos is made.
Anken:	That's quite a leap, this connection between external and internal energy.
Emrys:	Too much of a leap for most, I suppose, and if it didn't work so practically we wouldn't have stuck with that concept in the first place.
Pyth:	Do you have an example of subtle energy spin?
Emrys:	Yes, the deva. And this is where your intentional community comes in. It seems there are three forms of deva or helix: cylindrical, conical and toroidal.
Anken:	Toroidal? The great bull again?
Emrys:	Yes, it is the shape of a ring. It is the shape that such a spin takes when it is beyond the influence of a strong field of attraction like gravity.
Pyth:	Does this have something to do with megaliths like *Dinas Emrys*, also known as Stonehenge? Interesting, there is your name again!
Emrys:	You noticed. Dinas Emrys means Eagle Mountain. The mountain is the spinning deva and the eagle's spiraling up around it helps you find it.
Pyth:	I'd like to get back to what this has to do with community. Do you imply that a community of stones can help build a community of people?
Emrys:	More than imply. That is the point exactly. It isn't the stones that do it though. It is the vortex of chthonic energy spinning through the stones. Did you ever talk with a Silk Road merchant?
Pyth:	No.
Emrys:	Well, if you ever meet one ask him if there is a character in his writing for water flowing underground. We Druids have an ancient connection to China going back many thousands of years. There is a Chinese character that shows a builder's square over the symbol of flow and it refers to how two crossing streams of water flowing underground at different levels build a deva that extends above ground. The Chinese are dousing their whole country. It's called Feng Shuei.
Anken:	Do you imply that people can also read devas, just like

eagles?

Emrys: I do indeed. We are all "living stones" because our bodies emit a spinning energy that comes to a peak over the top of our heads—our "little pointed heads!"

Pyth: I think I see where this is going. If you put people in a circle, their "devas" join and make a big one?

Emrys: Exactly. And if you are standing around a chthonic deva, the Earth reinforces the experience of unity of thought and feeling of all present in the circle—unanimity.

Pyth: Ah, there is my community and a way to build it.

Anken: I expect my priest friend is going to call that one of the fingers of Ptah.

Interlude

Gnostic Trinity

The Gnostic trinity is composed of two darknesses and one light. It is clearly identified in other traditions:

Chinese:
Mu, The Unmanifested Darkness
Wu, The Manifested Darkness that is the Womb of Light
Li, Light

Celtic:
The Darkness that is
The Womb of Darkness that is
The Womb of Light.
In Merlin's terms: "Mother-Father god of light who comes forth from the double darkness."

Matrilineal Innocence: (as evidenced at Catal Huyuk)
The Prehermaphroditic Manifesting Power.
The Great Goddess, Shekina; the female hermaphrodite of the night sky, the first manifestation of the Unmanifest Divinity.
The Great Bull of Heaven: the masculine principle of the material world, our sun or any star.

Meditation on the Gnostic Trinity
With gratitude to Robert Plant
Darkness, darkness be my pillow
Keep my mind from constant turning
To the things I cannot see
As you turn my heart to yearning
For the things that set us free.

Canto XV

The Greatest Vice

Time   Sixth Century BCE

Place: The Dekkan, Raj Gir, Buddha's House

Personae: Siddhartha, the Buddha
                Ananda, the beloved disciple

Ananda: Sakyamuni, may I trouble you with a private conversation?

Siddhar: Has your cave brought you questions, Ananda?

Ananda: Yes. Perhaps Mara, the tempter, has visited me without a name. I find myself puzzled as to the nature of delusion as opposed to illusion.

Siddhar: I sense there is a particular respect.

Ananda: Yes. Travelers from the west have come here asking questions.

Siddhar: Have they no oracles in their own land?

Ananda: Yes, however it appears that their rulers, or Pharaohs as they are called, have been disturbed and uneasy.

Siddhar: What have these wanderers made you wonder with their questions?

Ananda: About the nature of vice, Sakyamuni. Is there a single cause of all vices?

Siddhar: Greed—the most excessive of all desires.

Ananda: Yes. I recall that teaching now and most heartily agree. However, the westerners say there are a group of wise men called Stoics who live in a place called Tarsus near the western sea beyond the Sea of Ur. These men claim that sexual desire is the root of all vices, counter to their opponents, the Epicureans, who say that it is no vice at all. How does memory serve you, Sakyamuni?

Siddhar: Memory serves me to say that if greed is the mother and father of all vices then sex is relatively fine, but if sex is the mother and father of all vices then greed is relatively fine. I opine that this latter sentiment would serve Mara the Tempter very well.

Interlude

In the recent paedophilia crisis a
layman approached a bishop and said:
"Bishop, is this paedophilia crisis a crisis of faith?"

The bishop replied:
"Oh no, it is far from a crisis of faith!"

The layman might well have replied:
"Then perhaps it is a crisis of trust?"

And an observer might have added:
"And bishop, which do you think is more important?"

And a prosecutor might have cross-examined:
"And bishop what do you think?
Would you agree that betrayal is not so much a violation of faith
as a violation of trust? And furthermore, isn't the ogre behind the
failure of trust the Church's demonization of all sexual behavior?
A demonization that makes it impossible to distinguish what
sexual behavior is acceptable, what is not, and what is monstrous?

My own comment would be:
Clerical Arrogance.

(Clergy is from Greek *kleros* meaning chosen)

Canto XVI

Empire's Destiny

Time: Fourth Century BC

Place: Upper Egypt, Quattera Depression, west of the Nile
Delta

Personae: Alexander the Great,
               following the siege of Tyre
               The Oracle of Amun at Siwa

Oracle: Good morning, Alexander. My dreams showed me you
          were coming, and why! Now tell me what really hap-
          pened at Isis.

Alex: We used the phalanx strategy and charged straight ahead.
          I aimed for Darius and he ran. His army ran as well. His
          generals wounded him fatally, and dying, he wrote his
          will and gave me the Empire, requesting that I marry his
          daughter Statira

Oracle: Remarkable how the fate of mankind turns on such a
          fragile pylon as one man! I understand that the
          Phoenicians at Tyre delayed you a bit, but you made a
          peninsula out of their island and laid them waste. You are
          a determined man, Alexander, and not yet thirty! Since
          we here in Egypt surrendered to you from afar, may I
          know why you did not press on to Babylon and Persepolis
          to take possession of your prize?

Alex: Seer, I think you know my reasons.

Oracle: Yes, Alexander, I do. I have seen the answers to your ques-
          tions. One you will like and the other will move you to
          anger. I fear your anger, Alexander.

Alex: I understand your fear, and also understand your power
          and your reputation for veracity. I have had enough of
          sycophants and desire truth no matter how painful.

Oracle: Your wisdom, Alexander, makes me eschew the role of fool, though he be the only man among the counselors of the king who dares to tell the truth.

As to your first question, no, Alexander, Philip of Macedon was not your father. Your mother, Olympias, tells truth. She was bedded by a god, and you are three quarters divine, like Gilgamesh.

As to your second question, no. Like Gilgamesh you have not inherited immortality. But in compensation you will be allowed to conquer the world before you die, though it be in the flower of your manhood. You will be remembered as the greatest conqueror in all the story of man, and will be the hero of those who will seek to follow in your footsteps.

Alex: My very soul is pierced and my rage at destiny knows no bounds! Oh, blighted blessing! To be shorn of life in the very shadow of immortality. What little solace Empire that demands life's brevity.

Oracle: I will not beg for mercy, being the bearer of such ill tidings. To be slain by you is such an honor as to be worth my life. Strike, Alexander, if my death be any solace to your wound.

Alex: The bloody murder of multitudes lies before me as the task of conquest. Far be it from me to take the life of a man courageous enough to tell the truth at the price of his own demise. I ask only this sacrifice: that you embrace me that I may sob out my sorrow on the template of your beating heart.

Interlude

To those who inherit the reins of Empire:
It is true you have a divine prerogative, but from what god?

Whom the gods would destroy they first make mad with power,
and absolute power corrupts absolutely.

Those who take greed as a virtue will discover sooner or later
that they have chosen bitterness as a companion.

Bitterness of the hardened heart, the fruit of the tree of despair, is a journey into sadness and recrimination. It is frequently the child of greed run amok. It frequently leads to the abandonment of the pursuit of life's meaning and of the quest for illumination, and is the gate of the greybound darkness and the illusion of the permanence of negativity.

Walk carefully upon the weavings of fate, lest, slipping, you should fall into the illusion of nothingness from which, like destiny, there is little escape in this mortal life.

Canto XVII

Astrology, Astronomy and the Roots of Origin

Time   255 BCE

Place: Babylon II, Mesopotamia

Personae: Berosus, Chaldean Priest of Bel
                An Athenian

Athen: Are you Berosus?

Berosus: Some call me that.

Athen: I was told beyond the Hellas-pont that you have collect-
         ed knowledge of former things.

Berosus: I have been curious about the ways of this land, yes.

Athen: I am told that our knowledge of mathematics and the
         stars came from here.

Berosus: I have been told the same, and I am convinced that it is so.

Athen: Your memories of Alexander must be very fresh. Didn't
         he die here about fifty years ago?

Berosus: Yes. He spared Babylon the vengeance he wreaked on
         Persepolis. It was here that he spoke those words of con-
         flict and strife upon his death bed when Ptolomy asked
         him, "Alexander, to whom do you leave your Empire?"
         Alexander replied, "To the strongest."

Athen: Nor was he gentle with us Greeks, though he avenged us
         in the sack of Persepolis. Please tell me, Berosus, do you
         still honor *Marduk* and the gods of Sumer since Cyrus
         carried away the Empire from your palatial city of
         Babylon, where it had rested so long?

Berosus: The New Year festivals continue along the ceremonial
         way where the cool night mist arises from the Euphrates,
         even though Alexander's general, Seleucus, moved the
         capital north to Seleucia. You know the dimensions of
         Babylon, do you not?

Athen: Twelve miles square, with the Euphrates dividing it into
         the old city and the new one built by Nabuchodonosor II.
         Isn't that your Babylon?

Berosus: Yes, although we are now in decline, the old city of Babylon is for the heavenly twelve, the twelve markers of the ages, the signs of the zodiac. It is the twelve days of celebration, the celebration of the creation in the *Enuma Elish* and of the Quest of Immortality in the *Epic of Gilgamesh*. Yes, Marduk, he who stole the *Tablets of Destiny* and usurped the Enlilship in the name of his father Enki, is still here.

Athen: Are the *Tablets of Destiny* about the calendar? That is what I have come here about. Aren't there three calendars?

Berosus: Yes, the calendars are connected to the sun, the moon and the stars, to be exact. The sun measures days and years, the moon measures months and weeks, and the stars measure the ages. These modes of measure were given to us by Marduk and his friends with great precision, more than anyone looking from the Earth could ever have imagined. The tablets are more about orbits than calendars. It is said that twelve is also the number of the aspects of our souls.

Athen: Aren't our gods harnessed to the stars?

Berosus: Not to the stars, but to the courses of the stars. And, to connect star to sun, do you know about the heliacal rising of the night sky?

Athen: I have heard it referred to.

Berosus: Heliacal rising refers to that portion of the night sky that rises where the sun will rise an hour later, or, more exactly, where the sun seems to rise.

Athen: Seems to rise, Berosus?

Berosus: Stars and sun do not rise or set as it seems to us. The Earth turns beneath them. This is what our gods have told us.

Athen: So much for the certainty of sunrise!

Berosus: We live in a world of illusion—illusion that is but a metaphor for reality.

Athen: I believe our Plato suggests this with his *Allegory of the Cave of Glaucus*.

Berosus: In Sind, which you call India, Siddhartha the Buddha has said as much.

Athen: Then the journey of the sun through the year is also an illusion as we follow it through the seasons?

Berosus: Indeed. The sun is more than a jolly jester having nothing better to do but wander around heaven all day, or all year.

Athen: We are much confused by appearances, are we not?

Berosus: Yes. Marduk tells us that the sun is the great stability in our neighborhood of the cosmos. A sun who spins in place, while the planets spin around him.

Athen: As I listen to you, Berosus, I feel you see the stars as somehow sentient like ourselves, or do you only speak in metaphor?

Berosus: I suppose all speech is metaphor. And yes, I see the fullness of the source of being in all beings. That includes sentience in all beings, no matter how near or how far, no matter how great or how small. One might say we are all a metaphor for what we truly are.

Athen: Then our attributing the gods to the stars and their courses is but a shadow of the underlying reality?

Berosus: The Buddha implies such things, though refusing to speak of gods. Those wanderings have brought me such intimations, and my own secret self awakens to vitality in the very thought!

Athen: Come to think of it, the same is implied by the zodiac that populates the heavens with the images of living beings spelled out in the stars.

Berosus: Yes, indeed. You know, don't you, that those twelve signs are the reason for Marduk's twelve days at fall equinox and for our twelve-mile-square city?

Athen: As you have so recently explained! Our year has twelve moons. Is that the reason?

Berosus: By no means. There are thirteen moons in the year, not twelve. Multiply 13 months by 28 days and you get 364 days—a year with one day to go. From the point of view of the Earth's circuit around the sun, we are looking at multiplying eight fortnights by 45 days and get 360—a year with five days to go.

Athen: But what is the 45?

Berosus: We call it a fortnight.

Athen: The Druids, priests of our Hellenic ancestors, say the Stag of Seven Tines is chased out of the unmanifest world by the Hounds of Heaven, and for five days at year's end runs through our world as the pursued "messenger of life."

100

Berosus: We know the Druids. They proclaim the solar myth which I understand to be the true calendar of all mankind.

Athen: So the year is a procession (going forward) of the signs?

Berosus: And the ages are the precession (going backwards) of the signs. But that doesn't change the moon. There are still thirteen months in the year, not twelve. Our gods have told us so, though mortal human wisdom may disagree.

Athen: Tell me more about the wandering stars, those you seem to call by the name planets. Why do they wander, or do they? And why the word planet?

Berosus: Illusion again. The *Meh*, the *Tablets of Destiny*, speak of planets. In fact, they are the primary reference of the term "Tablets of Destiny." The planets have fixed courses at fixed distances from the sun and fixed speeds of transit. All of these are called the "destiny of planets" as proclaimed in the *Meh*. By the way, they are called planets because they move in a sort of "plane" around the sun.

Athen: Do your gods tell you the speed of transit of the Earth around the sun?

Berosus: About 66,000 miles an hour, a thousand miles a minute, the sexagesimal system.

Athen: And all the while we think we are standing still?

Berosus: Another illusion. The Earth is turning on its own axis at 1,000 miles an hour, the daily "path!"

Athen: No wonder we are so confused.

Berosus: Yes, look at this bridge to clarity, which is to see all beings in terms of spin! Now, to get back to your question. No, the planets do not wander. They just seem to wander. It's all in the point of view. The Sumerian *Tablets of Destiny*, the *Meh*, speak of them as follows: The sun is like the center of a whirlpool. The wandering stars are not wandering but have slots like ripples in an ellipsoid pool. Although from the Earth's vantage point we see them "wander," the sun sees them as we see the courses of the fixed stars. The Sumerians say their gods have called the fixed course of any star its "destiny" and so the *Tablets of Destiny* inscribed on precise clay tablets tell us exactly what that "destiny" is.

Athen: Then the Earth has a destiny too, like all the stars, wandering or not, but a destiny like that of all the other "wandering stars."

Berosus: Exactly. All these "wandering stars" are a fixed distance from the sun and relate to each other as the Golden Section relates to the structure of our bodies. Remember that the Golden Section is the mathematical proportion of all things appearing in nature.

Athen: We need to discuss that, but where does the term "mathematics" come from?

Berosus: It comes from the Sumerian word, *Meh*, that we spoke of. *Meh* is another term for the *Tablets of Destiny* which also contain other information, in addition to what we've learned about the stars. The *Meh* is the reason astrology is considered the mother of all the sciences. For as the stars follow very precise law, so does everything else in the universe.

Athen: We have a word in our language, *phoosis*, a word meaning the essential flow of being. Perhaps that is the origin of the word physics. I believe there is a saying of Heraclitus that goes, *"Panta h'rei oudhen menei,"* meaning "All things flow on, nothing remains the same." Some refer to this as the Law of Nature.

Berosus: To quote Parmenides, another of your philosophers, "The senses see the seeming, not eternal now; the change that's ever teeming is all beneath your brow."

Athen: The one and the many, fixity and flow. Contradictory it seems, but reconcilable.

Berosus: All that comes from Sumer too, perhaps modified by the Egyptian sense of grandeur. The *Meh* are inscribed on clay tablets in wedge-shaped characters called cuneiform. We here in Babylon have copied them exactly as handed down. We call some of them *Letters from Erech*. The knowledge in the *Meh* is mainly described in pairs—one for the intellect and the other for the intuition—like astronomy and astrology.

Athen: Astrology and astronomy, aren't those Greek words?

Berosus: Yes, Alexander has not been without his influence here in Babylon. Hellenistic versus Hellenic you know!

Athen: But "astro" means star, "logos" means word, and "nomos" means law or name.

Berosus: I have noticed that the law can't get hold of you without your name!

102

Athen: Good point! This implies that in astronomy we get hold
          of a star by giving it a name, and the star gets hold of us
          by "speaking a word" in our hearts.

Berosus: Very good. The first would be astronomy for the intellect
          and the second, astrology for the intuition.

Athen: I hear that when the Israelites came out of Egypt their
          Pharaoh, Ankenaten, also called Moses, gave them com-
          mandments on two stone tablets. Do you suppose...?

Berosus: Very likely. The Egyptians are much fonder of stone than
          we Mesopotamians.

Athen: As to the stars, you call the intellectual study astronomy.
          That is, finding a name or a law for a star. The intuitive
          study you call astrology. That is, experiencing a star as
          speaking to you, and who can be sure they do not? But
          other sciences have double tablets too: physics and meta-
          physics, chemistry and alchemy, mathematics and
          numerology, and so on.

          In any case, getting back to the wandering stars, we
          have five: Hermes, Aphrodite, Ares, Zeus and Kronos. I
          hear those upstart Romans, who are trying to best the
          Phoenicians at Carthage right now, have different names:
          Mercury, Venus, Mars, Jupiter and Saturn.

Berosus: We have even different names. Back to your list of plan-
          ets, the Sumerians have Earth in the list between Venus
          and Mars. That makes six. The Sumerians also have one
          out between Mars and Jupiter, the so-called asteroid belt
          and the location of the perihelion of the planet Nibiru.
          That's seven. They count the Moon as a planet, that's
          eight. They have three more: Ouranos, Neptune and
          Pluto, also called "Little Gaga." That makes eleven. And if
          you count the sun, that's twelve. They refer to Mars as
          the "way station" between the asteroid belt and Earth.

Athen: Nibiru? What does that mean?

Berosus: It means planet of the "beru." A Beru is a large astronom-
          ical distance. You might find it amusing to know that the
          Sumerians invented beer. For them it was a sacred drink.
          Perhaps they named it for a large astronomical distance,
          which a large quantity of beer can cause you to experi-
          ence!

Athen: I have never heard of many of those planets, beer or no beer. Can we see any of them, that is, beside the sun and the moon and those I mentioned?

Berosus: I suppose we can see them, but we don't yet know how.

Athen: What do your gods know about these other planets other than that they are there?

Berosus: A great deal. They know how big they are, how fast they travel around the sun, how far they are from the sun, how fast they turn on their axis, and what they look like close up. By the way, they count the planets in reverse from the way we count them. We start with the sun, and count Earth as number three. They start with "Little Gaga" and count in. So Earth is number seven! They are very fond of Gaga. You will notice they call it "the outpost" because it is the first planet one encounters when entering the solar system. For them it is a sort of "greeter" that announces their long trip is almost over.

Athen: When they reach the Earth, where are they coming from?

Berosus: Nibiru. They say that Nibiru almost collided with Tiamat, the proto-Earth, out in the asteroid belt, also known as the "hammered-out bracelet." This is the boundary the Hebrews see between the "Waters Beneath the Heavens" and the "Waters Above the Heavens." The "bracelet" is the string of broken pieces of planet left when Nibiru ejected a piece of itself as it passed by Ouranos, Saturn and Jupiter. That piece smashed into the proto-Earth cleaving it in two and sent it reeling into its present orbit. I have seen a book the Hebrews brought here called, in their language, *B'Rashid*, meaning "in the beginning." In Greek it is called Genesis. In that book it mentions *Tohu* and *Bohu* as being around at the time of the creation. *Tohu*, I think, is Tiamat, and *Bohu* is Nibiru. By the way, the Sumerian word for Hebrew is Ha-Abiru, meaning the "people of the crossing."

Athen: So they were coming from Nibiru? But you said the perihelion of Nibiru is way inside of Gaga and all the other planets beyond Mars. How could Gaga be an outpost?

Berosus: Good question. The answer is that when Nibiru knocked the Earth out of the "bracelet," Nibiru was deflected from its course and set up an orbit of 3,600 earth years.

Athen: You mean it is that long between its perihelions?

Berosus: Yes. 1800 years to apohelion (far out) and 1800 years back to perihelion (far in).

Athen: So when they spot Gaga coming in they know they are about to get a sunbath?

Berosus: Yes. And, more important, they are getting close enough to Earth to visit.

Athen: How come we never hear about this?

Berosus: Perhaps because the priests are afraid to ask, and perhaps because the Empire doesn't want to be found out. It could be dangerous to talk about this. You never know who is listening.

Athen: It could make a lot of our religions look like fairy stories!

Berosus: Well, I am afraid they are fairy stories. Did you know there is a word for the King of the Fairies in every known language?

Athen: Why would the emperor care about such fairy stories? And where is the emperor now?

Berosus: It's about Alexander again. Remember? When he died he said, "To the strongest!" and his generals took him seriously and fought it out. Ptolomy got Egypt and Seleucus got all the rest except Greece. "The rest" included Mesopotamia and Chanaan, as well as India and the country half way to China. Antiochus Epiphanes, a successor of Seleucus running his Empire out of Antioch, turned the Jewish Temple into a gymnasium full of naked young men which set off a rebellion. He would just as soon not start any more religious scuffles by bringing up the gods of Sumer. They will come up again sometime but don't expect those monotheistic Hebrews to be happy with them.

Athen: Hebrews again. Who are those people?

Berosus: They were the people who were brought here from Chanaan by Nabuchodonosor and put to work learning banking. When the Persians carried the Empire to Persepolis, Cyrus sent the Hebrews home, but not all of them went and there are still a lot of them here.

Athen: Our big rival back in Greece is Sparta. They claim they are related to the Hebrews through Cadmon and call themselves Lacedomonians.

Berosus: It's possible they're related, yet the Hebrews claim they come from this neighborhood, down south where the Ziggurat of Ur stands abandoned in the desert. They claim to have spent 400 years in Egypt and to have come out of Egypt about the same time the Empire first came to another city by the same name as our Babylon.

Athen: That would have been about the time of our Trojan War, but wasn't that Babylon in Egypt?

Berosus: So I hear, but it seems to me that if they spent 400 years in Egypt they would have very little Mesopotamian blood left by then! One thing is certain. They are running their god as the prime monotheistic candidate. As I told you, I don't think much of monotheism—it sounds like Empire to me.

Athen: Isn't their god El? And isn't El really El Hadad, the brother of the god of Ur, Nannar Sin? How did El graduate to be the source of all?

Berosus: It happened during their time in Egypt, and the Egyptians have grandiose ideas, as I just mentioned. I believe the Hebrews call their ancestor from Ur Abraham, or originally, Abram. That has always interested me because Brahmin are a group from India or Sind. We do a lot of mixing with those people, and they shared a god with Ur, Nannar Sin. Not only is Sind named after him, so is Sinai, down there between Aquaba and the Nile.

Athen: But in Greek *a-Bram* means "not at Brahmin!"

Berosus: Hebrew or not, we must all be concerned for the gods. It is they who built the first cities right here between the rivers. It is they who left us the knowledge of the stars and it is they who moved us from an egalitarian society to a hierarchical society, and they who disempowered us and made us into slaves.

Athen: Did they come to Earth for our benefit or their own?

Berosus: They didn't even know we were here when they came. They had pressing needs of their own.

Athen: Do you know what those needs were? And how do you know?

Berosus: As to the second question, because they told us so. As to the first, they needed the gold. They had run out on Nibiru because their atmosphere was decaying. They

106

needed the gold to make the white powder of gold and diffuse it in their atmosphere—a life and death matter for them.

Athen: Did they need our help to get the gold?

Berosus: Eventually, yes.

Athen: From where were they getting the gold?

Berosus: South Africa, way beyond the sources of the Nile.

Athen: How did they enlist our help?

Berosus: In a word, they enslaved us.

Athen: Why? How? When? Where? Which ones did it?

Berosus: Where? South Africa. When? 350,000 years ago. Why? To get labor to dig the gold. How? By a carefully described breeding program. Which ones did it? The Anunnaki High Council: Enlil, Enki, and Ninti, the three children of Anu, the Father in Heaven, Emperor of Nibiru.

Athen: Father in Heaven. You mean that was a title of a mere god given to one of these beings we named god? Did they ever set us free and give us our independence?

Berosus: The one referred to as Father in Heaven is known as Anu, and no, they never set us free. They did give us a human administrator though.

Athen: Where and when did they do that?

Berosus: At Erech down river from here, near Ur, three thousand five hundred and nine years ago on the day of the autumnal equinox, when Hebrews celebrate the new year. It was done by Anu in his sanctuary, the E-kur, in the presence of his granddaughter Inanna, whom we call Ishtar and the Egyptians call Isis and whom you call Aphrodite.

Athen: A sort of first Independence Day? What was the name of the human Emperor?

Berosus: En-me-dur-an-ki. He was the administrator of Erech. In our language, Aramaic, he was called Enoch.

Athen: What does his name mean?

Berosus: En—Lord, Me—the *Tablets of Destiny*, Dur—bond, An—heavens, Ki—Earth. Or, Lord of the Encoded Information for the Maintenance of the Bondage between the Heavens and the Earth.

Athen: Bondage? Is that the bond of slavery between the gods and mankind?

Berosus: Exactly. Same Empire, different Emperor. Surely, no lack of bondage.

Athen: Tell me again. Why did they establish that bondage in the first place?

Berosus: It was about a labor dispute and a strike down at the gold mines.

Athen: In South Africa? Is there any demonstrative evidence down there that we can see?

Berosus: As a matter of fact, yes, though I don't know anyone who has seen it recently. It's the gold mines. Legend calls them King Solomon's Mines. Some are over a hundred thousand years old and are a thousand feet deep with the equipment still in the bottom. One thing is sure—they are a lot older than Solomon.

Athen: So, what happened?

Berosus: When the gods came here they thought they would get the gold out of sea water, but it was too expensive. Their headquarters were at Eridu, and Enki was in charge. He decided to dig in South Africa because a survey had shown that it was a likely place. For workers he used the crew of his own ship, the one he came in on. There were fifty crewmembers. They went down there to what was called the Abzu, did some prospecting and started digging. Evidence around here shows they were great miners and refiners of metals. You know how to find gold, don't you?

Athen: Doesn't it have to do with quartz crystals?

Berosus: Yes. All gold deposits are the result of gold being taken out of seawater by percolating through quartz. They seem to have had equipment to find quartz. You know that the cap of the great pyramid is quartz, and did you also know that it was set in a gold socket?

Athen: And the gold socket was set in silver, which was set in nickel bronze, and that was set against the limestone.

Berosus: Very good! Something about energy transfer. Granite stones to human bones.

Athen: So, how long did they do the digging themselves?

Berosus: Remember that the gods have a typical life span of 300,000 Earth years. It seems that working here tended to shorten the span. They say they worked 100,000 Earth years before they went on strike and created a mutiny.

Athen: And did they settle the strike?

Berosus: Ah! That's the point. The management committee came down from Eridu. There were three members: Enki, Enlil, and Ninti, the three children of Anu. They met with the strikers and asked them if they had any suggestions as to how to keep the project going without the strikers.

Athen: I suppose that's where we come in?

Berosus: Of course. The strikers said, "There are some people around here pretty much like us. We have tried to get them to work but they don't see any point in it. They get on very nicely without working. It seems they have telekinetic powers better developed than our own. Besides they are hard to catch. Every time we try to catch them they become invisible. We suggest that if you can find a way to catch a female, you could induce pregnancy and breed a worker."

Athen: You mean breeding experiments?

Berosus: Yes. So the two brothers, Enki and Ea, turned to Ninti, their sister, and said, "You are the biologist here. Do you think you could manage that?" "I can try," she replied.

Athen: Do you have written records to back that up?

Berosus: Yes, plenty of them, in cuneiform of course.

Athen: So, how did Ninti carry out her breeding program?

Berosus: She figured out how to catch a female, collected a number of eggs from her, stored them in a cool place and got her brother, Enki, to donate a sperm sample. She fertilized the eggs and planted them in the wombs of fifteen Anunnaki females. They first got monsters that didn't qualify to the conditions Enlil had set.

Their big worry was over-population. First, they wanted a male with a low virility so he could only reproduce with outside assistance. Second, they wanted him to have a 120-year life span like his mother, not the 300,000 years of his father. They had had a dangerous over-population problem on Nibiru and didn't want to go through that again. And lastly, they wanted him to have the more limited telepathic powers of his father, and not the much more extensive telepathic powers of his mother so he and his descendants could be more easily controlled and be more suitable slaves.

Athen: What is your primary evidence for this?

Berosus: Cylinder seals.

Athen: What are those?

Berosus: It is about clay tablets again and the need of signatures. You obviously can't sign your name on a clay tablet. Rather, they made inverse carved cylindrical stones with a special design to indicate the responsible person. Then they rolled it out at the bottom of the tablet in the wet clay.

Athen: And Ninti had a special one for her signature?

Berosus: Yes. It shows Ninti, or Ninharsag the Nurse, as she is frequently called, with her hands in the air. Behind her is the night sky displaying certain planets. Next to her is a table with medical apparatus. And down in the corner is little Adapa with big bulging eyes and his hands crossed over his privates. Ninti is saying, in cuneiform figures of course, "I have created!"

Athen: That sounds like an old Greek saying, "Eureka! I have found it!"

Berosus: Probably Ninti is the original.

Athen: So why the name Adapa?

Berosus: The Hebrews have it as Adam. In either language the word means red.

Athen: Why red?

Berosus: Because if you cross black and white skin you get red. The gods, you see are white, and native humans are black. So if you cross them you get red.

Athen: Why the different colors?

Berosus: Because the Earth has plenty of sun, and Nibiru has little or none. If life develops in darkness it is white, if life develops in sunlight it has to be black to survive. It seems that the gods were very allergic to sunlight.

Athen: Interesting. I understand El, the god of Israel, was afraid of the sunrise, or so their book says. I take it there is more?

Berosus: Assuredly. It's about how they created the female mate for Adapa. They put Adapa to sleep and took a sperm sample, selected some live sperm, took one of Adapa's mother's eggs out of cold storage and got the female on the first try. By the way, the Sumerian cuneiform for a sperm is a bent line. It also means a rib. That seems to have caused a lot of confusion in *B'Rashid*, the Hebrew book of Genesis.

Athen: And these experiments were done in South Africa? Did they keep us there?

Berosus: No. Enki, whose children they were, took "us" back here to Eridu in the E-din (Eden) so he could watch and take care of them. Enki and his brother Enlil were not on the best of terms because of rivalry over who should be Lord Earth (En-ki). Enki thought it was too bad that Adapa and his mate should be deprived of the right to reproduce on their own, given they had been deprived of long life spans. So he took Eve aside and taught her how to change Adapa's diet so they could have children. She got pregnant, whereupon, Enlil came by on an inspection tour and saw her condition. He was very angry that his pesky brother had interfered with his plan, so he sent them back to Africa before they could get the other gift—the long life span.

Athen: I understand that in the Hebrew book *B'Rashid*, the Tree of Knowledge is the tree of carnal knowledge and the other tree is the Tree of Life.

Berosus: Probably so. I think I will bring it up with some of our Hebrew guests next time I get a chance.

Athen: Tell me more about the planet of the gods. Where did it come from?

Berosus: The records say it came from the Dog Star, Sirius. It seems that Sirius is a double star and the stars lined up in such a way that Nibiru, a planet of Sirius, was sort of sling shot into space by that alignment. It came in this direction and was captured by the sun's gravity.

Athen: How long ago?

Berosus: Four billion Earth years. One of the peculiar things about Sumerian mathematics is that it starts with huge numbers like four billion and works down to sixty. That's why it is called a sexagesimal system and not a decimal system based on ten. You know, 60 seconds in a minute, 60 minutes in an hour, 360 degrees in a circle, etc. What's puzzling is that, although there were mold spores, there were no complicated life forms on Nibiru at that time. So how could they have known the age of the planet?

Athen: I suspect it may have to do with the Merkabah and telepathic space-time travel starting after there were more developed life forms!

Berosus: Why didn't I think of that? Thank you!

Athen: So Nibiru brought the simple life forms that it transferred to Earth in the collision?

Berosus: Seems so. Some have likened it to a rape, Nibiru being male and Tiamat female.

Athen: Back home I had some conversations with Libyan people who know of a tribe in Western Africa called the *Dogon*. They tell similar stories about visitors from Sirius they call Joannes. These nine-foot beings scared them long ago when they came out of the sea in strange garb with breathing apparatus above their chests that went snap when they inhaled.

Berosus: Interesting. That word *Jo-annes* shows up in the Sumerian story, too. As a matter of fact it also occurs in the Egyptian story. Since the Egyptians admit their civilization came to them over the sea of Ur, that may explain their reference.

Athen: In Mezraim, or Egypt, there is a temple at Luxor, a great stone temple called Kar-nak, that speaks of Isis in veiled terms as the Dogon speak of Sirius. Do you mind going over some of what you just said again?

Berosus: Patience is the ability to bear suffering, so suffer through this initial discourse with me and I will.

Athen: Maybe we should have a little of that beer right now!

Berosus: (*Taking a deep breath.*) Well, down to about 450,000 years ago the Anunnaki people of Nibiru had never visited Earth. But about that time their volcanoes had cooled to such a point that their atmosphere was deteriorating dangerously. They had discovered that disseminating gold in a high spin state into the atmosphere would stop the deterioration.

Athen: High spin state?

Berosus: Remember, they were accomplished metallurgists. They tell us that the atom is really not the ultimate building block.

Athen: Our philosophers are always arguing about that. Some even say there is no atom, only a monad and that the monad is really a spiral spin of aetheric energy. Could that have something to do with your "spin?"

Berosus: Perhaps. I understand that your Pythagoras got such information from the Egyptians. Apparently there is a low spin state and a high spin state of the "monad" with the low spin state being shaped like a sphere and the high spin state being shaped like a cone pyramid or maybe some other arrangement.

Athen: I understand Pythagoras describes three states: cylindrical helix, conical helix, and toroidal helix, all of them proportionate to the Golden Section. Maybe they learned that from the technology of the gold diggers!

Berosus: Maybe I should have come to see you! You really seem to be ahead of me on some of this! Maybe it's fast, faster, fastest. The cylinder is slowest, the cone is faster, and the torus is fastest. That might even explain the variations in celestial spin.

Athen: High spin state would really be higher spin state, with highest yet to come.

Berosus: Aren't there three Greek letters for that: Pi, Phi, and Psi?

Athen: And Pi Π is shaped like a megalithic trilithon or three-stone arch, Phi Φ is shaped like one turn of a spiral, and Psi Ψ is shaped like a trident of good old Poseidon, the one that contains the other two!

Berosus: Poseidon is Enki-Ea you know, the Lord of the Waters.

Athen: This is so exciting to me I'm afraid I'll get tired and never notice till I collapse!

Berosus: So let's slow down. But wait a minute, "Golden Section?" Could that relate to the white powder of gold? Alright. Let's stop. We'll pick it up tomorrow.

Postscript

Berosus, a native historian of Babylon, was a Chaldean priest of Bel (Bel-Marduk) who wrote three books in Greek on the history and culture of Babylonia. These writings were widely used by later Greek compilers, whose versions in turn were quoted by religious historians such as Eusebius and Josephus. Berosus flourished during and after the lifetime of Alexander the Great, although the exact dates of his birth and death are unknown. It is certain, however, that he lived in the days of Alexander (356-326 BCE) and continued to live at least as late as Antiochus I Soter (280-261 BCE), to whom he dedicated his famous history of Babylonia.

Zecharia Sitchin, in his work Earth Chronicles, has given us much of the material behind this speculative conversation. Not only is Mr. Sitchin a man of courage, more importantly, he is also a man of God.

Interlude

Superstition means to stand above.
Understanding means to stand beneath.
Superstition: As the head stands over the heart.
Understanding: As the heart stands under the head.

The proper use of a written truth is
to stimulate the memory of that truth.
The improper use of a written truth is
to replace a truth remembered.

Probably the ultimate superstition and idolatry
is replacement of the knowledge in your heart-mind
with somebody else's written document.

Truth is a feeling stimulated by a thought.

Canto XVIII

Legacy and Betrayal

Time: Circa 29 CE

Place: Caesarea Philippi, a town on
             the slopes of Mt. Hermon

Personae: Jesus
             Simon Peter
             Other disciples

Setting: Next to a large well

Jesus: Look, Simon. Do you see the dawn breaking over the mountain?

Simon: Yes, master, the cock crowed and wakened me as I slept. I had a troubling dream.

Jesus: Do you see this well?

Simon: Yes, master, megalithic, is it not?

Jesus: Yes, Simon. Now consider the mountain where the snow rests for most of the year. See how smooth its shoulders are, without watercourses?

Simon: Yes, master, why is that?

Jesus: Because it is a fire mountain, a volcano. The rain and melting snow filter through its porous slopes into the earth. Wells, springs like this one, come up all around the mountain's base. They form the sources of the Jordan and the rivers of Damascus.

Simon: Is that why Naaman the Syrian asked why he must wash in the Jordan when the rivers of Damascus came from the same source?

Jesus: Yes, Simon. But look at the stones in this well. They are granite and not basalt like the mountain. They were obviously brought from afar. Notice how old and solid they are. They are *Petra* or *Lithos*, bedrock. The little stones beneath your feet are *Petros*, lava stones, and they crumble under your weight.

Simon: There was something about that in my dream.

Jesus: Yes, Simon, and from this time, I will call you Petros.

Simon: Because of my dream?

Jesus: No, Simon, but because you are weak, though you strive to be strong.

Simon: Because the cockcrow made me fear?

Jesus: Simon Peter, who do people say that I am?

Simon: They say you are a prophet like John the Baptist. They say you are a master, like the Buddha. Some say you are an Anakim come to rule us. Some say you are a messiah like Alexander the Great, come to rule the world as a Jew as Alexander ruled it as a Macedonian.

Jesus: But who do *you* say that I am?

Simon: You are the only son of the living God!

Jesus: Is that what you dreamed, Simon?

Simon: Yes, master. But I also dreamed that I betrayed you before the cock crowed at sunrise.

Jesus: Yes, Peter. You proclaim me by saying that I am a son of God. In this you are correct. But when you say "only son" you betray me and say what I am not. For all humans are sons and daughters of God as much as I am. Yes, I am a master, but so are you, and so is every person born into this world, whether man or woman. We differ only in the degree that we manifest what we are. It is so because the fullness of the Divine One rests entire in every being, no matter how great or how small, no matter how close or how distant in space or time. I have not come to proclaim that I am different and better than you. I have come to proclaim that we are all the same in so far as we are all born masters. More importantly, I have come to proclaim that our real purpose for being here is to help each other discover the masters that we all are.

Peter: I am afraid of so awesome a responsibility!

Jesus: I know Peter, and so are most of us humans, and it is this fear that will cause you to betray me. Do you see this Petra, the curbstone of this well of pure water, water that is as pure as any on Earth? Upon that curbstone of the bones of Mother Earth I will found the gatherings of the people who will come to me in search of their truth.

Gilgal, like Joshua's Gilgal, is a circle of living stones who dance as the stars dance, spinning into one spin, singing in one song, feeling joy as one joy in the power of manifestation.

You, Simon Peter, shall be called Petros, the little stone that causes those who step on it to stumble. Many will come to follow you as one who knew me and they will cause many to stumble in the Age of Darkness that is coming. But do not fear, Peter. Your very betrayal of me will be your salvation, for hope will not die in you. And in the in-time to come and in a dimension beyond your present forms, both you and all those whom you have led astray will find your masters within and will become fellow journeyers on the path to that eternity which the divine breathes out and breathes in as the destiny of every being.

Peter: But Lord, to whom then will you leave the assembly of those who will be your true followers? To your wife, Mary of Magdala, and to your children by her? Or perhaps to your mother's uncle, Joseph?

Jesus: I will give primacy to no one, Peter, because we are all brothers. I suspect that my brother James will be first among equals with those in Jerusalem who understand this is what I mean when I say "poor in spirit." My brother Thomas is most likely to tell my story in a way that people will understand.

Above all, remember this Peter: Beware of the Empire, and call no man father, for we all have but one Father!

Interlude

Blessed are the poor in spirit,
for theirs is the kingdom of the heavens.

~Matthew 5:3

Ebion

Poor in Spirit

Equal

Scribes and Pharisees, hypocrites, you go over land and sea to make one convert and then you neither enter the place that you profess to seek nor allow anyone else to enter.

Could this be a description of those who recite and defend doctrinal teaching in place of finding the truth that is always within them, and helping others to do the same?

Is not conformity to received doctrine
the broad way and the wide gate?
Is not finding the truth within the small gate and the small path to knowing what has always been?

For you shall not be heard for your speaking,
rather for your seeking.

Canto XIX

And Jesus Said

Time: Ash Wednesday, 2004

Place: The Road to Santa Cruz

Personae: Jesus
                Myself

And Jesus said:
I am a savior,
But not as you have been told.

I did not seek to save all,
For many need not saving.

I suffered on the cross,
But not for your sins
Or for the sins of others
And surely not my own.

I suffered to spare the lives of my people,
The people of my time
Who, restive,
Trembled on the brink of rebellion

Not against God,
But against Empire.

Not only that of Rome,
But that of Alexander.

Not only that of Alexander,
But that of Cyrus the Persian.

Not only that of Cyrus,
But that of Babylon II.

Not only that of Babylon II,

120

But that of Assyria.

Not only that of Assyria,
But that of Babylon I.

Not only that of Babylon I,
But that of Akkad.

Not only that of Akkad,
But that of Sumer.

Not only that of Sumer,
But that of the gods of Sumer,
Those colonists
Who enslaved us all.

I came to save my people
From fruitless rebellion
Against the World Spirit of Empire,
Empire that is the enemy of human freedom.

And although I saved them
For half a century,
In course of time
The Empire feasted on their blood
And scattered them to the winds.

I am the son of David,
David the King of a free Israel
Who stood not slave
To any empire
Nor to any human
Nor even to God our Father.
For our Father has no need of slaves.

I came into Jerusalem
Through the Golden Gate
In the eastern wall of the city
That caught the rays
Of the rising sun of equinox.

I came riding on a white beast
As all had been told
That the son of David would come.
I came to save my people

From themselves
And their impatient hearts;
Hearts that had waited too long
For the freedom of their fathers,
When each person followed the self-evident truth
In their own hearts.
Hearts that had waited too long
For that freedom that had vanished
So long ago.

As I rode silently
They cried out,
"Hosanna to the son of David!"

Their priests were terrified.
Their priests remembered
The injunction of Cyrus,
"Return to Jerusalem!
Build your temple again,
But never let the son of David
Sit upon your throne!
For on that day you will rebel
Against the Empire
And on that day
We will come in vengeance!"

The priests remembered
That Alexander had made the same condition;
And when Caesar took
The Empire to Rome
The Romans followed suit.

Judas Maccabeus had founded
The Hasmonean dynasty
To sit upon the throne of David,
A dynasty that still ruled
Through Mariamne, Herod's wife,
And Herod's children by her.

But the Hasmoneans were not the heirs of David
And vengeance did not come.
But now in my time
The people would wait no longer

To raise the son of Zorobabel, the heir of David,
To the throne.

And so the priests cried out to me,
"Tell them to stop!
Don't you know that
If the Romans hear these Hosannas
They will come
And take away our place and our nation!"
But I answered them,
"If I silence them
The very stones will cry out!
For the yearning of my people's hearts for freedom
Is adamantine as stone."

And so I came on,
With branches of the olive,
The white beast treading
Upon the offered garments of my people;
Knowing that it was worth my life
To claim my heritage
In the face of Roman cruelty.

And when I spoke to Judas saying,
"Do what thou must do,"
He obeyed
But with sorrow in his heart;
And betrayed me to
The brutal inhumanity of the Empire
That I might risk crucifixion and death,
For it is indeed expedient
That one man should die
For the people.

But when I came before Pilate
He saw what I was doing
And was grateful.
For bitter man that he was,
He preferred to shed the blood of one man
To the torrents he must otherwise shed.

He taunted the priests
Who did not understand.

"Shall I crucify your king?"
And, terrified by cowardice,
They shouted back in chorus,
"We have no king but Caesar!"
Bearing the bloody crown of thorns,
Weakened by the scourge of lashing,
I carried the cross beam
To Golgotha,
The place of the skull.

I felt the deadly nail in my feet
And the pierced agony of my wrists,
Though the God who manifests us all
Would have spared me
By wakening my power
To send the pain away.

I chose the pain
So the Romans would know
That they had not failed
In their vengeance
Against a rebel king.
But Pilate would not let them
Slay me.
He would not let them break my legs.
They pierced my side so I could breathe
Against the suffocating fluid in my lungs.
Pilate let my uncle Joseph
Take me down
And hand me
Into the arms of my beloved mother
Whose heart was surely breaking.

But Joseph and Nicodemos,
Whose name means "Victory to the People"
In the Greek Language,
Carried me into
That sweet cave in the stone of Mother Earth
Where no one had ever been laid,
A tomb that, at great expense,
Joseph had prepared for himself.

And the people came at great risk
Bearing a hundred pounds of myrrh and aloes
To disinfect my wounds and heal me.
And when I had rested
The guards fell asleep
As Pilate had ordered them,
And my friends took me away
To where my beloved wife,
Mary of Magdala,
Could care for me
Armed with her astonishing
Awakened power of healing.

Do not believe those
Who say that I died that day.
Believe my brother James.

Do not believe that
I resurrected from the dead.
Believe my brother James.

Do not believe that I ascended into heaven.
Believe my brother James.

Only remember that I love you
Because you are human like me.
Only remember that like the Bodhisattva,
I answer those who call.

Only remember
That eternal life is not reserved for some,
But is the destiny of all.

And though the Empire has triumphed
To this day in my name,
Do not believe that the Empire is mine,
Or that I approve its sway.
Rather
I, like you, seek the truth of life
And love most strongly those
Who know the splendor of that quest.

✳

Interlude

Yes, I am the child of God.
And so are you.

Canto XX

Soliloquy

Time:	34 CE
Place:	The Road to Damascus
Personae:	Saul of Tarsus
	Paul of Tarsus

Saul: I am Saul of Tarsus, Tarsus beneath the Mountains of the Bull, the ancient Auroc. I am namesake of Saul, King of Israel. But, I am also known as Paul of Tarsus, namesake of A-pol-lonius of Tyana, hero of the Stoic school of the Cilician Pirates that succeeded Carthage and the Phoenicians as masters of the Mediterranean and as the navigators of Rome, inheritors of the tradition of the Great Bull of the Heavens.

    As Saul I remember David, who supplanted Saul as king of Israel and who stood upon a stone in the wilderness of Zin and proclaimed, "Saul, Saul, why do you persecute me?" I remember Samuel, who mourned the lack of manifest vision and became the first of the Prophets as he was last of the Judges, and how he chose David to replace Saul. And I remember Apollonius of Tyana, who is the hero of the Stoics in conference as the Vates, prophets of the Empire, those philosophers who spoke the philosophy of the Hellenistic world, in the shadow of Alexander.

    I am the man who never knew Jesus, and I am also the man who proclaimed him God. I am the man who was chosen by the Sanhedrin to root out the Followers of the Way in Damascus and see that they troubled Israel no longer.

    Shall I, Saul, speak of myself as Paul or shall I be Paul who speaks to Saul? What is in a name? And which of us is I and which myself? Shall I speak of loyalty or betrayal? Which of my selves is loyal and which betrays? Which shall I choose: Jesus, or the Sanhedrin who hired me? Or is it that I do not know the difference? Perhaps I can find myself if I address myself as the other, so let the play begin!

He turns around and becomes his own reflection.

Saul: Let me ask you, Paul, do you remember the origin of your name?

Paul: Of course. I am the alter ego of A-poll-onius of Tyana. I am not a blood relative of his, but I have adopted his name. I am a Jew through the blood of my mother, but I am also a Mithraist, my father's religion to which no woman is admitted. I was raised as a Stoic child who looks upon sensuality as a bane yet holds no brief against greed. I grew to manhood in Tarsus, beneath the mountains of the Bull of Heaven, the commercial center of the Empire where the Stoics built their dominance upon the repression of the instincts of the flesh. I am half Jew and half Mithraist, but I am neither by inclination. Candidates for the office of God struggle within my soul and my questing made Apollonius my ideal long before I became embroiled with the Galilean who is the stone the builders rejected.

Saul: I am you and you are me but I do not seek that you should adopt me. I am the one who passed to Jerusalem from beneath the cirque of the Mountains of the Bull. I claim my Jewish heritage through the blood of my mother and came into Herod's temple in Jerusalem—Herod, the father of Maccabean sons. I came seeking employment to defend God's Chosen People, of whom I am one, against the plots of those raving Sicarii who would draw down the ire of Rome. Unlike you, I am not confused and I know to whom I am loyal—not to some upstart Galilean but to the royal prerogatives of the God of Israel.

Paul: I remember Annas who hired me in the name of the Sanhedrin to walk the road to Damascus and seek the "street called straight," and upon that street to find the "followers of a way" laid out by a man I never met. My instructions were plain: Confuse them, deceive them and make them trip over their own sandals. Or, bemuse them and praise them and raise their exemplary Jesus to unreasonable heights which no sane man could believe. Then disempower them with the confusion of obedient slavery so they will no longer trouble the followers of Moses and Israel.

Saul: However, if you do that you must engage in a lifetime of deceit, and waste the undoubted talent of your brilliance.

Paul: Know that if I succeed, the emergent Empire of the Romans may find the product of my genius most helpful to avoid the pitfalls of a religion that women may not join, a religion called Mithraism, and the Romans surely control the vagaries of fortune with their mastery of military power.

Saul: So which of us shall take the road to Damascus?

Paul: Let it be me. Your name is clearly Jewish and it is not toward, but away from Judaism, that Annas, the high priest, would have us lead these deluded followers of Jesus, who see him as a Jew to be imitated. I will turn them into worshippers, not of a resuscitated rebel king, but of a resurrected god who will die on the cross for the sins of mankind, be the only begotten son of God and appropriate the god of Israel to be a Goyim god of unimaginable splendor who has lost his interest in the Children of Israel. A god who will replace with Jesus the dying Great Bull of the Heavens who dies at the hand of Mithra, as Jesus dies upon the cross.

Postscript

On the road to Damascus Saul-Paul describes his Manifest Vision.

In the book of Samuel: "There was no *Manifest Vision* in those days." What days? The days of the Judges when every man sat under his vine and his fig tree, did his own sacrifices, and followed the vision, the voice of God that each man heard in his own heart-mind.

Samuel was the last of the Judges and the first of the Prophets. He was called by the Voice at Shiloh where the Ark rested between the horns of the Great Bull of Heaven and while Heli the priest slept. Samuel's ear was open to the Voice from the day of his conception.

129

Since there was no manifest vision in those days, Samuel became the One to Speak for God.

The word prophet comes from *pro-phemi*, one who speaks on behalf of another—in this case God. Samuel, burdened with the power of "vision for the nation," chose Saul to be King to administer the ordinary affairs of life. Saul performed the sacrifice, a task reserved for the Prophet who could waken the ecstasy of death in the victim before the stroke and thus make the act of killing holy. Saul, impatient and unfamiliar with the power of his authority, botched the Sacrifice of the Bull and angered Samuel who replaced him with David.

On the road to Damascus, Saul of Tarsus, of the City of the Great Bull, claimed to have a manifest vision like those in the days of Moses. In those days the people came together on the Sabbath to experience manifest vision, to hear the Voice and see the glory, and to know that they heard and saw the same vision together. They did the same for Aten in the land of Egypt where they reigned as Pharaoh's hand for four hundred years. In Saul's manifest vision he says, "I saw and heard what I saw, some heard and did not see, some saw and did not hear." This is indeed a credential of divine favor, if it ever happened.

Saul of Tarsus knew his scripture well; he remembered Samuel. He describes the process of manifest vision perfectly, too perfectly. He does not favor us with the name of a single witness other than himself!

Interlude

"For God so loved the world that
he gave his only begotten son that whosoever believeth in
him should not perish but have everlasting life."
~ John 3:16

And the Manifesting Power said,
"My friend, that is sheer nonsense made up by
a Master of Deceit.
All beings are my begotten children and
aeternal life is inevitable.

"On top of that I have given no one authority to issue
ration books for immortality. How much did they charge you?"

Canto XXI

The Master Dialogue

Time: Circa 245 CE
Place: The Library at Alexandria, Egypt
Personae: Origen
           Plotinus
           Ammonius Saccus

Origen: Have you seen Master Ammonius lately?

Plotinus: I heard he traveled up river to Luxor and hopefully he
           will be back soon.

Origen: Always on a journey, isn't he?

Plotinus: The Nile is the prime meridian of the gods, you know,
           running south to north, longitude, as the Ganges goes
           west to east, latitude. Either the banks of the Nile or the
           banks of the Ganges will do as a walking space for a mas-
           ter.

Origen: The solar myth again! The solar cross: the "red road" of
           the sunset, the "blue road" of the day, and where they
           cross, the "violet flame." And with it the story of the solar
           hero, whose life story is the life story of all masters
           whether it is their personal story or not. Is there a land on
           Earth where the sun's story is not told, from its death and
           resurrection at one winter solstice to its crucifixion and
           death between two thieves on the Horns of the Bull at
           another?

Plotinus: We must add the tides of life like the tides of the sea fol-
           low the career of the sun, pressing with the insistence of
           grace upon the spirits and bodies of all beings. Those who
           see the sun as a living spirit have a valid point that is con-
           founded by those who see the sun as the "manifestor of
           the cosmos." The sun is but a creature, like ourselves.

Origen: I have encountered that very difficulty among my fellow
           Christians who want to do that same thing to our Jesus.
           The story they tell of his life is surely a combination of
           the stories of those two solar heroes, Horus and Krishna.

132

Speaking of which, whom do you prefer for your solar hero? Perhaps Horus?

Plotinus: No, I prefer Ammonius' solar hero, Sakyamuni, the Buddha. I suppose you still espouse your Jesus?

Origen: Quite so. Though since they call him *Saca,* I am sure Master Ammonius shares your preference.

Plotinus: I am quite willing to acknowledge your Jesus, as long as you don't claim him to be unique. It is my opinion that your Jesus, whose name comes from a Hebrew word meaning "root," just grafted a Buddhist shoot on a Jewish root. The word Buddha comes from a Sanskrit word meaning the bud of a lotus plant whose root pushes out of the mud towards the sunlight—its opening representing enlightenment.

Origen: We Christians have much debate about the uniqueness of Jesus and I am inclined to believe your perspective.

Plotinus: Mesopotamia is a land of two rivers. Egypt has but one, while India has three Holy Rivers: the Indus, the Ganges and the Cauvery. Some flow north-south, some west-east. It seems to me that the Solar Cross proclaims one out of many, and perhaps many out of one, but does not allow for one to the exclusion of any within the many.

Origen: How long ago did your Buddha live?

Plotinus: Five hundred years. I understand that after his death his teachings were carried on by daily chant until the time when Augustus became our first emperor. Buddha's teachings were written down at that time in a dialect of Sanskrit called Pali, however we cannot be certain if the disciples wrote it down correctly.

Origen: Did Master Ammonius tell you that?

Plotinus: Yes, it seems that we disciples seldom get it right. Perhaps you should ask him yourself.

Origen: Disciples not able to write it down correctly has always been perplexing to me, but perhaps it is because I too am a disciple.

Plotinus: Yes, as we all are in the footsteps of Ammonius.

Origen: Although I follow Jesus, and you follow Plato, and Ammonius follows Buddha, and I know many follow you, and they say many follow me. Nonetheless, perhaps we should all follow only the prompting of our own hearts!

Plotinus: Agreed. Masters are not fond of being quoted, and certainly not fond of being obeyed. It seems to me they follow their own hearts and suggest we do the same.

Origen: Did Buddha have disciples?

Plotinus: They say there were five in his company at Raj Gir—the Spinning Mountain—and that each had his own cave of residence below the fumerol and the spring with the little fishes. These five came to *him*, he did not call *them*; nor did he ever send them out to teach.

Origen: Many here in Alexandria say it was the same with Jesus, and that the story of twelve is a myth—the solar myth again—of the twelve signs of the zodiac.

Enter Master Ammonius

Plotinus: Welcome back, Master Ammonius. You are just in time to help us answer a few questions.

What is a master? What do masters do and not do?

Ammon: Let's start with what masters don't do. They never tell you what to do or not to do. They never tell you what to believe or not believe, and most of all they never ask you to believe in them.

What do masters do? They are peripatetic—they walk around meeting and greeting people, as did Jesus on the paths of Palestine, Siddhartha on the Gangetic Plain, and Socrates in the streets of Athens, Lao Tsu by the Hwang Ho River, and the Green Tara over the Himalayas from India to China through Tibet. When a master meets you, he or she looks right into you and sees exactly who you are.

If you are a bitter person who embraces greed as a virtue that will protect you from the fear of death, the master says, "Good Morning" and walks on by. You are too much work.

If you are disturbed by the conflict between what you have been told and what your heart remembers, the master says, "Good Morning, Master."

To which you reply, "Who? Me?"

And the master says, "Yes, you. I have come with a question for you."

"You, master, have a question for *me*?"

"Yes. Do you remember?"

"Do I remember? Remember what?"

"Do you remember that you have 'the power'?"

"The power? What power? Oh, perhaps I do remember that."

"Good. I would only suggest that you should use it. Good-bye.

Oh, and by the way, if you should have questions about how to use it, call upon me, or any other master that you may prefer, and one of us will show up in your heart-mind and whisper the answer in your own voice. Good day!"

Interlude

May we respond in Gratitude
To the One whose fullness we receive.
As we respond in Compassion
To the many in whose emptiness we share.

Canto XXII

Sol Invictus

Time: 324 CE
Place: Nicea, Akarusia, Bythnia (European Turkey)
Personae: Constantine the Great
             Eusebius, Bishop of Caesarea

Eusebius: May I inquire, your majesty, what is your religion?

Constan: "Sol Invictus, the Unconquered Sun," whose victory we remember in his resurrection on the day following the end of the sun stand of winter, December 25th.

Eusebius: Solar religion has many forms to invoke the image of the Solar Hero. May I inquire as to yours?

Constan: Mithraism, the religion of my army which invokes Mithra as its hero as he who slays the "heavenly bull."

Eusebius: Ah! He who is honored in the Mithraeum in Rome, beneath the "Hill of the Vates," also known as Vatican?

Constan: The very same. And, I notice that your story of your Jesus, in the book my mother Helena gave me, is essentially the solar hero story we assign to Mithra.

Eusebius: Yes, your majesty, and my research in the Library of Caesarea indicates the same story is told of Horus of Egypt, Krishna of India, Mabon of Wales, even the Buddha of India, and very many others. I think we all prize the sun, if not as our Divinity who manifests the Cosmos, at least as the most appropriate symbol of that Divinity.

Constan: I see, bishop, that you have a broader view than most of your fellow Christians who seem to insist on the uniqueness of your Christ?

Eusebius: I truly believe that learning leads to broader views, your majesty. We do not encourage learning among our followers. We rather say to them, "I have resolved to know nothing except Christ Jesus and him crucified."

Constan: Is it true that Paul of Tarsus, is, if not the author, at least the editor of the version of your holy book that we have come here to approve and canonize?

Eusebius: Very true, your majesty. Being from Tarsus, where Mithraism takes its origin, it is surely Paul who weaves the solar hero as the life story of our Jesus. Actually, we have no record of the details of Jesus' life.

Constan: But Paul never knew Jesus, or so he says. Doesn't his secretary, Luke, who also never knew Jesus, say he, Luke, was a good investigative reporter in following up the story?

Eusebius: Quite right, yet I am of the opinion that the only witness Luke ever talked to was Paul, and Paul admits he never met Jesus in the flesh.

Constan: I have talked to travelers over the Silk Road to China whose wares the Romans prize so highly, travelers who say there was a wise man who lived along the Yellow River, a man called Lao Tzu who tells all the parables attributed to your Jesus!

Eusebius: I am aware of that, majesty, and I am also aware that our "scripture" is not at all original but is more an anthology of much that has gone before. I am also aware that our bishops, at least the orthodox ones, are arrogant and in denial of that fact and insist not only on the uniqueness of Jesus, but upon the uniqueness of his story.

Constan: You may be interested to know, Eusebius, that is why I am interested in your religion. We Emperors like to be the only one—the one for whom all others should be prepared to die. You know: "Hail Caesar, we who are about to die salute you"? We also favor your one God for the same reason and wish to build Him in the image of ourselves. Diocletian persecuted you for providing another god to worship besides himself. I, like Paul of Tarsus, wish to join you and turn your god to my purposes!

Eusebius: Thank you, your majesty. I had assumed those were your motives, but I would not have been so bold as to accuse you of them. In fact, I myself and my fellow orthodox conspirators are fully aware, as you are, and we seek to be your aristocrats, your administration in ruling the Empire.

Constan: We really do understand one another then! Since we are building a religion to replace Mithraism, we should use most of its symbols. Perhaps we should discuss that further. By the way, I understand that the Great Bull is the male companion of the Great Goddess whom many see as the night sky.

Eusebius: Yes, that is true. At Caesarea we have many records of Mithraism's origin showing it's the rediscovery of the precession of the equinoxes. I believe Hipparchus the Stoic perceived that relationship while measuring the temple of Karnak at Luxor over 500 years ago. And yes, the Chanaanites and Phoenicians were devotees of the Great Goddess, and the Jews still remember her as the Shekina.

Constan: Yes, Rome was founded about a thousand years ago, and the twins Romulus and Remus were suckled by a she wolf, an image of the Great Goddess, whose surrogate, the matrilineal queen, appointed twin kings, each to represent her for 40 moons. As I recall, they were eaten, body and blood, by the queen and her council at the end of their terms; one was the king and the other his tanist. And as I recall, Hipparchus was shocked to find that Aries had pushed Taurus out of center stage during the Heliacal rising of Sirius, another slaying of the Great Bull sacred to the Goddess!

Eusebius: Hipparchus brought that message back to Tarsus, to the Collegium of the Stoics. They were greatly disturbed that someone was moving the courses of the stars, with which the Stoics identified their gods, and that they were thus perceived not to be immortal after all. It started a ferment to find a god behind the gods, a male god of course, who could defend them against the power of women, and perhaps die on a cross.

Constan: Then those Hebrews who were brought out of Egypt by the monotheistic Ankenaten chimed in to say that the one behind the moving of the gods is our Male God of Storms, El, whom we brought out of Egypt a thousand years ago! And didn't they call Ankenaten Moses?

Eusebius: Yes. But they had not been able to sell their god to the rest of us until Jesus came along. Before that Mithra, the solar hero, had the inside track with his Unconquered Sun.

Constan: Then, of course, the Jews didn't appreciate their opportunity and hired Paul to sell their Jesus to the rest of us instead. Meanwhile, they looked for someone else to play Alexander for them. That is, to be their messiah and to make a Jewish Empire. Let us understand, I am just trying to do what Ankenaten was trying to do: become the sole Earthly representative of the true God!

Eusebius: For that, let's look at Mithra's altar. We should adopt the same set-up as Mithraism, without the back wall of the night sky, the night sky that some call Neit or Nud, or Shekina the Great Goddess. As I recall, the back wall shows the constellation of Taurus with Mithra astride the bull plunging a dagger into the Pleiades, right over the Bull's heart.

Constan: I might add that Mithra's altar is rectangular, made of marble with six candles.

Eusebius: We should have the same set-up without the night sky, Mithra and the Bull. Instead of Mithra between the two sets of three candles we should put Jesus on the cross, invoking your vision, Majesty, of *"En to-o Nik-e"*—"In this sign you will conquer"—without being obvious, of course. Another point is that there are six visible stars in the Pleiades and Mithra was the invisible seventh. We will make Jesus on the cross stand for the invisible seventh!

Constan: What symbol do you use for Jesus now?

Eusebius: Two fishes, the sign of Pisces. Have you noticed that as Moses replaced the bull with the ram, we have replaced the ram with the fish? But a bloody crucifixion scene represents Mithra much better.

Constan: Very clever, bishop. You let me keep my symbols and still have molded your religion, meanwhile knowing exactly what we are up to.

Eusebius: Yes, the killing of the bull and the crucifixion of Jesus seem to have a lot in common. Both are about the killing of a sacred being and the will of God. The secret of blood sacrifice is that we feel a little guilty every time we kill to eat, and try to assuage the confusion by believing the creature died willingly. It's all about assuaging our guilt, guilt that Paul disguises as original sin.

Constan: That is the baptism problem. Even though I am a soldier and accustomed to bloodshed, I really think this Mithraist business of hanging the bull up by his right hind foot, while the initiate stands naked under him and the priest cuts the throat and lets the blood run over him—well, it's a little too much, even for me. Yet it does prepare one for battle, and it does represent the matrilineal bull as companion to the Goddess.

Eusebius: Then there is the birthday business. We don't know when Jesus was born, but there is a hint: "The virgin shall conceive." We have exaggerated that all out of proportion to mean his mother didn't have intercourse with his father. Of course, it merely means that he was conceived, probably in the normal fashion, during the sign of Virgo, late August or early September. That makes him born in late May, an inconvenient time for a solar hero who is always born on December 25.

Constan: December 25, Mithra's birthday, and the biggest celebration of the year. We celebrate the birthday of Mithra and that of the sun together. It is a very good time. December 24 is the low tide in the tides of light and in the tides of human emotion. On that night the tide of light turns and starts coming in again. We celebrate the resurrection of the sun that day.

Eusebius: We have a big battle about that resurrection business. The Gnostics, who follow a path of knowledge, say they don't remember Jesus being resurrected, only resuscitated. Frankly, I think they are right, yet those followers of Paul will have it no other way, despite lack of any convincing evidence of resurrection.

Constan: I find that you need to have an outlet for wild enthusiasm available to slaves whose lives are quite stale. So let's keep the resurrection in there. When do you celebrate it?

Eusebius: Spring equinox.

Constan: When the day conquers the night? Good idea. We will keep solstice for the start and equinox for the finish. That will keep them from finding out we just have a modern version of Mithraism here. I am pleased that you are so frank with me, Bishop Eusebius of Caesarea! Maybe we can do business.

Eusebius: Why do you want to do this, your majesty?

Constan: You mean settle your squabbles?

Eusebius: Yes. We haven't been able to settle our disagreements, though Irenaeus tried.

Constan: Wasn't he a bishop in Transalpine Gaul? My mother used to mention him when we lived by the Danube over in Moesia.

Eusebius: Bishop of Lyon, actually. Lyon was the central *castra*, an army camp for the whole west of the Empire. You must have been there?

Constan: Many times. My mother used to say Irenaeus was the man who ran out the Gnostics that you indicated before. By the way, who was the head of the Gnostics in Jerusalem?

Eusebius: James and Thomas. James was Jesus' elder brother, and Thomas was Jesus' twin.

Constan: That must be very inconvenient for those who are attached to virginity. Remember, as I said before, there's something about twin kings in the tradition of the Goddess and our Romulus and Remus were twins.

Eusebius: Also something about a pillar where you hung the bull by the right foot at sacrifice. James is admitted by all to be the central person among Jesus' early admirers in Jerusalem. Thomas, in his account, reports that when Jesus was asked to whom to go after he was gone, Jesus replied, "You shall go to James the Just for whose sake all is made manifest."

Constan: Did they have a name for James' group?

Eusebius: Yes, Ebionites. It's a Hebrew word for poor. In this case it means "poor in spirit," that is, a group of people who regard each other as equals, another condition of Goddess society.

Constan: I don't think we emperors would be too fond of that. There again, Goddess societies were egalitarian and democratic.

Eusebius: Exactly what Irenaeus thought. He invented the word heresy to describe James and his Gnostic Ebionites and condemned each of their beliefs one at a time. Irenaeus was surely no egalitarian.

Constan: I suppose Irenaeus found few things to agree with in the teachings of James?

Eusebius: Practically none. For Ebionites, it was James and Thomas; for Irenaeus, it was Peter and Paul.

Constan: Hmm, a conflict between God and the Goddess, between the orthodox and the gnostic, between Empire and democracy!!

Eusebius: Like you, your majesty, I realize that though Plato's democracy is the best form of government, democracy has no place in an Empire. God and Empire are the ultimate hierarchy and the Goddess is democratic!

Constan: Bishop Eusebius, it seems to me you are indeed a very learned man, and you really don't have much use for what your orthodox Christians believe, am I right?

Eusebius: Exactly right, your majesty. After all, let's be practical. What use would an emperor have for a religion based on the fundamental equality of all beings, a view that Gnostics espouse?

Constan: Is that what your Jesus really taught?

Eusebius: Yes. Freedom, equality and brother-sisterhood. Jesus seems to want to go back to the matrilineal model best represented today by those Buddhists who are everywhere still, especially in Alexandria. Apparently Buddha didn't approve of the Brahmins. The Brahmins were too patriarchal and hierarchical for him. Do you know about the Kaaba Stone?

Constan: You mean Mecca and that big meteorite?

Eusebius: That's it. Do you know what gods have been, and still are, sitting in effigy on the stone?

Constan: No, I don't.

Eusebius: Well, they are in neither Sumerian, Egyptian, Greek nor Roman guise. They are all the gods of India!

Constan: Really? Amazing!

Eusebius: Do you know where the western frontier of India really is?

Constan: No.

Eusebius: It's the Gulf of Aquaba between Arabia and Sinai.

Constan: That close?

Eusebius: Yes. Much of the religious ferment has been brought on by the Buddhists who call their God "the Nameless," implying prehermaphroditic. Frankly their ideas make more sense to me than any of ours. I think the real Jesus had the idea that we are all still innocent at heart and that our innocence is the root of our power. As a bishop I find that very anti-hierarchical and threatening and contrary to the teachings of Paul, and am sure that you do, too.

Constan: Well, you are certainly right about that! We must band together to support Peter and Paul against James and Thomas, especially against the Goddess and those Gnostic Buddhists! What a clever idea you have to create a religion in support of servitude, based upon the teachings of an anarchist who is an advocate of democracy! Eusebius, my friend, let's do it!

Postscript

The Council of Nicea was seen as mediating a dispute between Alexandria in Egypt and Antioch in Syria, both capitols of the partitioned empire of Alexander. His general, Seleucus, acquired most of Alexander's domains from the Aegean to India, while Ptolemy got Egypt. It is said that as Alexander lay dying in Babylon on his return from India, Ptolomy whispered to him, "Alexander, to whom do you leave your empire?" Alexander is said to have replied, "To the strongest!"

The contention between Ptolomy and Seleucus is curiously continued between the monotheist Arians of Alexandria and the tritheists of Antioch (Tritheist meaning three gods). Eusebius worked out a compromise by referencing a Druid concept of the triskel—the three rays that are, for Druids, the three powers of manifestation. The word for "person" was created at Nicea from the Greek word *prosopon*, meaning a mask, hence, "The Masks of God" through which the one God "looks." This resulted in Eusebius' masterpiece at Nicea, The Holy Trinity: One God in Three Persons. Following this decision, both the tritheists of Antioch and the Arian monotheists of Alexandria were regarded as heretics and their works burned.

Constantine never became a Christian, though a bishop baptized him on his deathbed. He also never established Christianity as the religion of the Empire. That was done about a hundred years later by Theodosius, whose name means in Greek: The Gift of God.

Interlude

Is not obedience the virtue of a slave?
And does the Divinity we call God ask us to be slaves?
If so, why has that Divinity made us free to err?
Isn't destiny more logical
Than fate?
Is not fate more hopeful than destiny?

After all
If Jesus is a master
Is he a master of slaves?
Or is he truly a master of life?

Canto XXIII

The Tao

Time: 500 CE
Place: The pass of Bramaputra River through the
            Himalaya below Chomolungma (Mt. Everest)
Personae: Bodhidharma
            A monk who seems a native of the territory

Monk: Good morning, master. I sense in you a Buddha awak-
        ened.
Bodhi: Only one in whom there is awakening can truly sense the
        awakened. And so I say to you also, good morning, mas-
        ter!
Monk: You have come through the monsoon to this thin air, have
        you not?
Bhodi: Yes, to ascend upon the Earth tests mortal powers and
        refreshes the spirit.
Monk: May I presume to ask where you are bound?
Bhodi: To the Tan Gula Shan where the great rivers rise and flow
        south and east; south to Bengal and east to the great sea.
Monk: We sometimes call that island of great mountains Middle
        Earth. It is also known as Shan Gula Tan, which some pro-
        nounce as Shan-gri-la. It is said that the Shan-min, the
        mountain people, still know the ways of the ancient ones
        who inhabited the Earth before the coming of the gods.
Bhodi: I experience the voices of those ancient ones in my
        dreams, as I am told Siddhartha did when he discovered a
        Buddha in every sentient being only waiting to be awak-
        ened.
Monk: Will you return this way to pay homage to
        Chomolungma, that greatest mountain that towers to the
        sky above the sea?

Bhodi: It is not my plan to return, but to go on to the lands of Sian where tribes have wandered below the Yangtze. I follow what I believe is the path of Avalokatesvara, that divine hermaphrodite who appeared as male in India and as female in China, where she is known as Kwan-Yin, or Koan-Yin.

Monk: Do you know his-her story at Nirvana's Gate?

Bhodi: I know something of it. Tell me what you hear.

Monk: The female aspect ascended from the male body and came to Nirvana's Gate where she was addressed by the gate-keeper: "Avalokatesvara, you need not prove your worthiness to enter here. We have long forewarning of your virtue, so much so that it makes our faces shine with the fires of enlightenment. Come, freely enter!" She-he replied, "Gratitude, the reward of the generous, fills me at your greeting, but I must decline. I have come this far only out of respect for your generosity. Now I must return, not to come again until every sentient being has gone in before me."

Bhodi: That is why she-he is my way-shower. She senses the Buddha in every sentient being in the cosmos, and sees all beings as sentient. She will not rest until each being is realized, though it requires her to labor without rest against the illusion of time.

Monk: We are most privileged to have met each other as companions in this quest.

Bhodi: Indeed. I am also curious to learn of the ancient masters on the Yellow River that flows past Shan-tung into the Yellow Sea. I understand they lived a thousand years ago as contemporaries of Siddhartha the Buddha, and my real mission is to see if their teachings reflect those of the Buddha in the image of truth.

Monk: Will you then remain among the disciples of the *Tao Te Ching* of Lao Tsu, the Old One?

Bhodi: That is my intention.

Monk: Then let me regale you with another tale you may not have heard.

Bhodi: Please.

Monk: It is said that Lao Tsu was a civil official in a southern province in his declining years. When his years had passed four score, he cleaned his modest dwelling, locked his door and walked to the city gate that opened westward where the Shan, the mountains, held the red and violet sunset. There was a gatekeeper. Never in his watch had Lao Tsu passed the gate at sunset. As Lao Tsu approached his gate at that unusual time, the gatekeeper asked, "Are you leaving us master?" "That is my intention," replied Lao Tsu, the old one smiling and nodding his head. The gatekeeper sighed slowly, "When you are gone we will starve for the wisdom your presence calls us to remember. Please, master, can you not make us a writing?" "Of course," Lao Tsu replied. Lao Tsu returned to his house, unlocked the door, lit a lamp, picked up his writing brush and began to inscribe those precious characters we know as the *Tao Te Ching*. Then, after four score hours, he came again at sunset to the western gate that opened to the Shan, bowed graciously to the gatekeeper, and smiling wordlessly, handed the manuscript to him. The gatekeeper watched the old master's figure grow smaller as he walked joyously toward the Shan who were the last of Earthly beings to experience the joy of his footsteps and the song of his voice.

Bhodi: It seems to me, brother monk, that you are both the observer and the man—one who knows the woman in himself with joy.

Monk: Most percipient, master, I am also one who knows that Siddhartha and Lao Tsu are more than contemporaries.

Bhodi: Do you know the word *Chuan*?

Monk: I have heard of it. Actually, I come from the sunrise islands beyond the Yellow Sea, the land that we call Ni-Hon or Nippon. In our land Chuan is pronounced as Zen. We surmise the meaning of Zen to be "whole, entire, complete" in reference to the All. We have another word for it, *Matto-suru*, that means to accomplish, to complete, to preserve life and to make whole.

Bhodi: Breathtaking and breath-giving, my friend! I know Chuan, and your wisdom makes it complete indeed. I am inspired by you to surmise that Zen should be the name of a discipline that would show the harmony of the masters and so make its teaching complete indeed.

Monk: Harmony, yes, and does it not also embrace reconciliation, even unity? In my homeland the character for harmony is pronounced 'wa' and it is the symbol of my people.

Bhodi: My brother, I depart from you in the joy of our meeting. The memory of our encounter will lighten my way. May flowers grow in your footsteps.

Interlude

A Child's Garden of Verses of Good and Evil
With gratitude to Robert Louis Stevenson

Good is doing good things for yourself and other people.

Bad is doing bad things to yourself and other people.

The second good is loving to do good things for yourself and other people.

Evil is loving to do bad things to yourself and other people.

Angelic is deciding to spend your life doing good things for yourself and other people.

Demonic is deciding to spend your life doing bad things to yourself and other people.

Canto XXIV

Into the Age of Darkness

Time: Circa 527 CE
Place: Isle of Avalon
Personae: Merlin (Emrys Merlinus Moordune)
               Lancelot, The Best Knight in the World

Lancelot: The mists cling to the lake this morning as messengers of the sea.

Merlin: So early in the morning for a knight! May I ask what draws you at such an hour?

Lancelot: I am called to this mountain often, *always* at midnight when the sun wakens me in the moment of his most distant absence, there where I sleep beyond the river Bru in the fastness of Camelot.

Merlin: A long ride through the enchanted forest then?

Lancelot: Yes. The forest so dark and yet so light to the inner eye. But the barge always awaits me by happenstance on the marge of the River Bru.

Merlin: Does the guardian of the Tor, Gwyn Ab Nud, who is the child of Nud, the Night Sky, not trouble you to set foot on his holy mountain, unguarded by the light of day?

Lancelot: I am often aware of the presence of Guardian of the Gate of the Heavens.

Merlin: There is another gate, you know. It is at the mountain at the end of the world, where the sun bids farewell to the land and to the day before he presses on to the land of the rising sun. There, a whole nation guards the gate they call a window. It is the last earthly entrance to that unmanifested world from which we come forth as travelers into our mothers' wombs. It is also said to be the window through which we pass after our sojourn in this illusion of time. That nation is called Ixtlan and they remember that all men are brothers past all pretense and arrogance. They are the "people of the window" to the present that is aeternal.

Lancelot: How do you know such things, Merlin?

Merlin: We all know them, Lancelot. It is just that some of us have learned how to remember them. Consider the mountain here, the Tor. Do you remember the secrets of its power?

Lancelot: Remember? Perhaps not. I have heard it has to do with water flowing underground.

Merlin: So you've *heard it*, but do you *feel it* flowing, Lancelot? One can *feel* it, you know. This relates to dowsing, and sensing the uses of the force it creates. This same power can waken a healing experience in an ailing person at a great distance in time or space.

Lancelot: Is it the power of the deva?

Merlin: Yes, Lancelot. The word deva is the root of the word devil, and the root of the word divine. For the Divinity is the root of all that is, whether we regard it as nurturing or threatening.

Lancelot: Is it a vortex? Like the one that spoke to Job: "And God spoke to Job out of the whirlwind?"

Merlin: Yes. Everything in the visible universe spins.

Lancelot: So, these rivers beneath the earth are creating a vortex, a sort of breathing?

Merlin: A breathing of the voice of Earth that flows, spinning up toward the night sky. It rises from the crossing of water streams flowing under ground.

Lancelot: Does the same thing occur at Stonehenge?

Merlin: Precisely, but there it maximizes only on summer solstice day. We all walk in such a helix, emitted by the blood flowing in our body where the vessels cross. If we stand together in a circle all our helices join to make a greater one rising from our communion. When I am at Stonehenge my task is to be first among equals as the deva sweeps our combined power up toward the heavens. It is known as the "ladder of lights."

Lancelot: But this mountain, the Tor, is sculpted into a helix by the ancient ones. Is it also such a deva?

Merlin: Yes, Lancelot, it is what draws you here at the midnight hour when the new day is born in your heart beyond the turning of the night sky. Indeed you are awakening to the use of "the power."

Lancelot: Is that what a holy place is? A helix that raises your spirit when you stand in it?

Merlin: Yes. Many of our menhirs, our standing stones, are placed to mark them. And many of our ancestors have chosen to remain behind, in them, to speak the Voice of Heaven and Earth to us, their descendants.

Lancelot: Is this the meaning of All Hallows Eve, as the Christians call it?

Merlin: That day was sacred long before there were Christians. It is the eve of the sign of Scorpio, when winter begins, a time of the severe falling of the life force, when all are in need of help and encouragement against the failing of the light. Thus it is a time to call upon the ancestors.

Lancelot: Don't the Christians attribute such places and thoughts to the devil?

Merlin: Yes, I am afraid the Christians, as we know them, are far from true to their Christ. They are dualistic, and surely there is no religion more dualistic than the one Christians profess. The Christians are afraid our holy places are works of the devil and dedicate them to St. Michael, the warrior of their god. Such a church will surely be built upon our Tor one day.

Lancelot: It seems they will regard our Gwyn Ab Nud, son of the night sky, as a demon.

Merlin: They already do, Lancelot. They liken him to Lucifer, the light bearer who was cast out of heaven for disobedience and for proclaiming, "This above all I will not serve."

Lancelot: So disobedience is the greatest "sin."

Merlin: Indeed. Christians have their god, who is most capable of being offended, giving commandments and requiring absolute unquestioning obedience on pain of eternal hellfire.

Lancelot: But where is freedom then?

Merlin: Nowhere, Lancelot. Like the Emperor of Rome their god has no use for freedom or allegiance and only approves of slavery and obedience to himself.

Lancelot: Is their god always a "he" then?

Merlin: Yes. Any suggestion to a Christian hierarch that their god may be also feminine is greeted with arrogance and rage.

Lancelot: That is the exact opposite of all that our own culture tells us.

Merlin: Exactly! For us darkness is holy, feminine is holy, low is holy. Not that light and masculine and high are not holy, it is just that they are equal and we place darkness, feminine, and low as the first mentioned among equals.

Lancelot: Will we heathens who dwell in the heath ever get along with these Christians?

Merlin: I'm afraid not. Their only interest is in having us become their slaves and keeping our mouths shut.

Lancelot: It seems the Christians are custodians of an Age of Darkness—even the word darkness they do not see as we do.

Merlin: If I were a prophet, I would say that it is so.

Lancelot: Will there be an end to this oppression?

Merlin: Again, if I were a prophet, I would say yes, but not for two thousand years. When the Romans killed twenty thousand of our Druids on the Island of Mona our day was ended. As they died some Druids were heard to say, "You may kill us all, but we will return in a hundred generations as your descendants."

Lancelot: What do the Christians say about such an event?

Merlin: They speak of it as the "second coming" of their Christ; when he will come as the judge of the living and the dead, send all the "sinners" or "goats" to hell and take all of the sheep to heaven that they might obediently stand on streets of gold and sing the praises of their god forever.

Lancelot: What do you foresee in this regard?

Merlin: There will be a sudden change someday, and it will be a day when at the same moment in the darkness of the night, or in the light of day, all will transform miraculously, simultaneously, like blades of spring grass. The awareness of self-evident truth will arise in the heart of every being and each of us will recognize ourselves as one with all the others in our unity with the source of being, the source of all that is.

Lancelot: But is that not always true, even now?

Merlin: Of course, Lancelot, we need only recognize it and help others to do the same. Do so, however, only if they ask.

Interlude

Merlin is within the stone, waiting for the call.

A myth is not a lie, but a metaphor.
It only becomes a lie when taken literally.

Masters never grant authority to anyone.
Emperors grant authority.
Authority is never needed when the author is present.

Canto XXV

Merlin, Slayer of Dragons

Time: Circa 530 CE
Place: The Convent at Amesbury, Wiltshire
               Stonehenge
Personae: Merlin
               Gwynevere

Scene 1: The Convent

Gwyn: Master Merlin, to what do I owe the privilege of your vis-
         itation? I see that I was quite misinformed concerning
         your passing from this world.

Merlin: My lady, whose name means whiteness, my inner voice
         has whispered that you have need of me. As for my pass-
         ing, you are not quite misinformed. I have, literally,
         passed from this world, but remain to be called in vision
         by those who have need.

Gwyn: Your inner voice, as usual, is correct and your heeding of
         its call awakens my gratitude.

Merlin: To be grateful for your gratitude is surely the presage of
         joy. What ponderment of the heart stands origin to your
         call?

Gwyn: My love of Lancelot, Lord Merlin. I know not whether to
         seek its diminishment, thus disarming my guilt, or to let
         it grow and find feet in conversation's course.

Merlin: Concern yourself only with whether your love is firmly
         rooted in the reality of your spirit, for even though
         attended by lust, love experienced as "spirit to spirit" is
         not a brush to taint yourself with guilt.

Gwyn: Has not this overweening affection between myself and
         Lancelot been a sea-cradled rock of destruction, a danger
         to the holy vessel of Camelot and the bonded fraternity of
         its brotherhood?

Merlin: You are generous of heart my lady, but you need not bear
         the burden of that guilt. Camelot was the guardian of the

156

"ancient order of affairs," an order compelled by destiny to recede before the onslaught of an Age of Darkness. Though our actions affect our fate, no action no matter how well-intended, can warp the demands of destiny.

Gwyn: Is there nothing I can do but await the flood of that disaster that engulfs us?

Merlin: My lady, raise your eyes and look westward to where the sun will set. What do you see?

Gwyn: The standing circle of the trilithons some know as Stonehenge.

Merlin: Has it ever been brought to your attention that those trilithons bear within them the secrets of the lightsome burden of the "ancient order of affairs?"

Gwyn: How does that burden find relevance to the lightening of my heart?

Merlin: More relevance, my lady, than has entered into the mind of man to imagine. Do you know that I am truly the Dragon Slayer?

Gwyn: What do you say a dragon is Merlin?

Merlin: It is a stone, not of Earth, flying through the heavens at blinding speed, a grievous danger to any object it may encounter.

Gwyn: Is the Earth then itself a dragon, being an object of encounter?

Merlin: She, the Earth, in this telling, is our fair maiden in need of rescuing. And I myself as the Dragon Slayer am at her request, her rescuer.

Gwyn: What is the use then of the trilithons?

Merlin: They are the instrumentality of my power, but do not be dismayed. It may surprise you to know that I am the rescuer not only of the maiden, but of the dragon as well! Come, walk with me to the monument.

Scene 2: The Monument.

Merlin: You see, my lady, that we come from the east. Observe carefully just how the monument greets us. Look there beside you. That stone is called the Heel Stone. It marks the summer solstice sunrise that casts the stone's shadow onward to that trilithon straight ahead of us. Beyond that trilithon do you see a u-shaped structure of trilithons opening toward us? There in the middle is a rounded stone with its shoulder just above the ground. That is an ancient dragon fallen into the grasp of the deva of this site.

Gwyn: Deva? Grasp?

Merlin: Your pardon, I move too fast. A deva is a spinning energy flowing upward from the crossing of streams underground. Dragons have such spinning fields of energy and they are drawn to similar fields in the Earth like this one.

Gwyn: What is your role in all this, Merlin?

Merlin: I am the "First Among Equals" who gathers the people here when the dragon is sighted to blend their powers together with the power of Earth, spinning upward until it rises straight up into the heavens in a sort of beam. I, then, by my own power, bend the beam to strike the dragon, change its course and make it miss, thus saving the Earth and the dragon.

Gwyn: Do the Dragons come often?

Merlin: There are always many of them nearby; near misses occur constantly. We call them stardust, and when they are larger, shooting stars. The great ones are a way to measure what we remember as the boundaries of ages of the Earth.

Gwyn: Then the great dragons can be both the cause and the harbinger of the Ages of Darkness, such as the one that so tragically impends?

Merlin: After a fashion.

Gwyn: Could that have to do with what the Christians call the "End of the World?"

Merlin: Indeed.

Gwyn: Then you are a savior, are you not?

Merlin: I have played that role.

Gwyn: Then my beloved Merlin, you must *not* go!

Merlin: Do not fear Gwynevere, I am not the only one so chosen. You have the power, too, as do all humans. It is just that the power lies sleeping, waiting for the call.

Interlude

First Among Equals is but a temporary office and,
most importantly, a shared responsibility.

Responsibility is not a burden,
but simply a matter of our equal potential or ability
to respond appropriately to the needs of the situation.

For the dragon dreams of other stones
That fly the ways of night
And work their magic darkly
To become the wombs of light.

Canto XXVI

Summa Theologica

Time: Circa 1220 CE, Fall Equinox
Place: The Monastery of Monte Cassino, Italy
             near the village of Aquino
Personae: Thomas Aquinas
             Jesus
             Raymond of Pentafort

Scene I: Thomas sleeping on his cot beneath an open window; Moon and Venus are visible. His desk is piled with vellum manuscripts. Jesus suddenly appears in vision and speaks.

Jesus: Thomas, we need to talk.

Thomas: Is it really you, Lord?

Jesus: Yes, may I sit here in your chair? No, please don't get up! We can talk just sitting facing each other. It's not as if I were God or something, no matter what they have told you. We are all equals. We are only unequal in the way we realize what we are, and what we know.

Thomas: But my tract on the Trinity…

Jesus: That is what I have come to talk to you about. I am afraid there is no Trinity, not at least as you have been taught.

Thomas: But theology…

Jesus: I am afraid there is no theology either, at least not in books. Theology means the Word of God.

Thomas: But my life's work there behind you on the desk is…

Jesus: Thomas, it is a brilliant work. It will never be matched in the history of the world. Your research is impeccable, your syllogisms are brilliant, every one.

Thomas: But…

Jesus: (*Smiling broadly*) I am afraid your sense of humor is abundantly lacking. The fact is that nothing serious should ever be said unless it is with a humorous touch! You see, if things are stated too seriously, very few people

160

ever read them. Unfortunately, the Bible is another good example of humorlessness, especially the New Testament that Paul put together. He fills it with blazing shafts of glory and monumental speculations, but, unfortunately for him, he never consulted me and most of his speculations about me are not only humorless, they are just plain wrong.

Thomas: But in my syllogisms Paul supplies most of the major premises.

Jesus: Oh, yes. Major premise, minor premise and conclusion.

Major: All crows are black.
Minor: This bird is a crow.
Conclusion: Therefore, this bird is black.

But Thomas, where do you get your majors?

Thomas: From you, Lord!

Jesus: From me, or from what people have written about me?

Thomas: Oh, I see what you mean.

Jesus: Thomas, you assume they know what they are talking about.

Thomas: I guess that is faith.

Jesus: Faith is of two kinds—believing what you are told and believing what your heart tells you. Trust is more important. If you trust, isn't it a good idea to know whom you are trusting?

Thomas: Do you mean that Paul isn't trustworthy?

Jesus: Would you trust someone who betrayed you?

Thomas: Not if I could help it.

Jesus: You have heard that Judas betrayed me. Peter betrayed me three times in the same night.

Thomas: That is what the book says.

Jesus: But you have never heard that Paul betrayed me, have you?

Thomas: No, never.

Jesus: Have you ever wondered about the story in the book of Acts where it says Paul was hired by the Sanhedrin to scatter my friends?

Thomas: Yes, honestly I have and I always felt guilty for wondering.

Jesus: Do you think I am opposed to curiosity, Thomas?

Thomas: No, Lord, it never occurred to me to wonder about that.

Jesus: And why is that, Thomas? Could it have something to do with the fact that you have been threatened with going to hell if you have the slightest doubt about what your teachers tell you?

Thomas: I guess I wouldn't even dare think about that!

Jesus: Ah, I sense a touch of humor, Thomas. Now we are getting somewhere. If anger is one half of risibility, what have you said is the other half?

Thomas: Humor?

Jesus: Let me quote you to yourself: "The risible impulse can eventuate in anger or humor and wisdom requires an effort to choose the humor," or words to that effect.

Thomas: Are you telling me, Lord, to question the major more often?

Jesus: Exactly, Thomas, because your majors are just as questionable as your minors and in this matter even more so because you are founding your majors on the testimony of an untrustworthy person. After all, theology means the Word of God, not what somebody tells you God said.

Thomas: Where, then, shall I seek the Word of God?

Jesus: In your own heart, Thomas, where God speaks to all of us.

Thomas: Are all the voices that speak in my heart God's voices?

Jesus: In a sense, yes, Thomas. Because all things come from God whether we like them or not.

Thomas: How can I know to which voice to listen?

Jesus: Hear them all, Thomas; only learn which ones to listen to.

Thomas: How do I identify a voice I should hear but not listen to?

Jesus: By the shouting. Goodness never shouts.

Thomas: And how else?

Jesus: By the orders. Goodness never gives commandments.

Thomas: No commandments?

Jesus: Didn't you ever notice, Thomas, that even in the New Testament written by Paul I am never quoted as giving a single commandment, that is, except one?

Thomas: You mean "A new commandment I give you, that you should love one another as I have loved you?"

Jesus: That's the one. But notice the humor: most of Moses' commandments tell you what not to do.

Thomas: And you tell us what to do.

Jesus: Actually, I didn't even do that, because masters never give commandments of any kind. What I actually said was, "I suggest that you should bless one another whenever you meet by saying something like, 'May you be a blessing in the heart of everyone you love.'"

Thomas: That gives me chills of joy, Lord, thank you!

Scene 2: Half an hour later in the corridor of the monastery

Ray: What was that? At 2:00 in the morning? Who would be walking the corridors?

Thomas: It's only me, Raymond. Maybe you could help me with these manuscripts?

Ray: Manuscripts? That is a lot of vellum! What are you doing with such a lot of them at this hour of the night?

Thomas: I am taking them down to the furnace room to burn them.

Ray: (*He picks up a page of manuscript.*) But, Thomas, this is your life's work. This will become a synthesis of the faith for at least the next millennium. What do you mean, burn it? (*He snatches the manuscripts away.*) Thomas, why?

Thomas: Raymond, I have seen the Lord, the real Lord Jesus, and all of this is nonsense!

Postscript

It is said that on the following day the writing crew turned up for work as usual. Thomas sent them away with these words: "There will be no work today." When asked why he had stopped writing, Aquinas replied, "I cannot go on. All that I have written seems to me like so much straw compared to what I have seen and what has been revealed to me." The work never recommenced.

Thomas Aquinas' most famous dictum in Latin is: *Tabula Rasa. Nil in intellectu nisi prius insensibus.* Translation: At birth the brain is an erased blackboard. Nothing enters the brain unless it comes through the five senses.

This statement denies the existence of the sixth sense and the telepathic function which is the essence of spirituality. With his *Tabula Rasa* Thomas establishes the radical materialism that gave root to the modern form of worship in the Western European Christian Church and modern science.

It is said that he recanted this error after his vision of Jesus and wished to burn the *Suma Theologica* which is the foundation of the synthesis of the Christian Church. Remember, this was 300 years before the Reformation. An astonishing thirteenth-century alchemical treatise *Aurora Consurgens* is reputed to be the last work of Thomas Aquinas. The author's revelations show how to transcend the materialism of *Tabula Rasa* through the embrace of Sophia, the Gnostic goddess of wisdom and alchemy with its mysticism and reconciliation of opposites.

It should be noted that the original name of Egypt is Al Chem. Alchemy is Egyptian theurgy.

The Philosopher's Stone of alchemy is said to be a catalytic substance that will convert base metal into gold. This is a metaphor of the conversion of material consciousness into spiritual consciousness. Both Thomas of Aquinas and St. Augustine became alchemists before they died. Most of the books in Isaac Newton's library were about alchemy.

Interlude

Lightness of heart
is the fountain of youth
and the doorway of eternal life.

Nothing is more serious
than lightness of heart
and nothing is more frivolous
than unrelieved sorrow.

Canto XXVII

And The Truth Shall Set You Free

Time: Sunrise, May 1, 1214 CE
Place: Assisi, Umbria, Italy
Personae: Francis of Assisi
             Jesus, speaking from a vision
Setting: Cave where St. Francis went to meditate

Francis emerges from the cave.

Francis: Good morning, brother sun! May I sing you my song?

       Good morning to the rising sun.
       Good morning, feel the rivers run.
       Good morning, life has just begun.
       Good morning to my brother sun.

       And what, brother sun, shall we help each other remember today? Do you call my attention to this mountain named after spring, Monte Alverno? Do I feel it call me to its top? To stand upon the altar of Mother Earth and feel her flow to the heavens through my heart?
       He climbs the mountain via a spiral sunwise path. The mountain is in its flowering splendor of spring. It is the time of Beltaine. There is an abundance of red Flanders poppies. He sings as he reaches the summit and spins honoring the four directions. Suddenly he stops in amazement. There is a cross with a man hanging on it. He realizes it is a vision.

Jesus: Do you know why *they* did this to me, Francis?
Francis: They told me *you* did it to die for my sins, is that true?
Jesus: No, Francis, I would never do such a foolish thing. I did choose to suffer on this cross. But I do not wish to be remembered for it, at least not in the first place. I did suffer, not because of sin, but because crucifixion was the Roman punishment of rebellion designed to maximize the suffering of those who rebelled against the Empire.
Francis: Are you God?
Jesus: Yes, Francesco, I am. So are you and so is everything. All

166

comes from the same power and the source is fully within every being, however great or small. I am no more or less God than you are.

Francis: Are you the Messiah?

Jesus: No, Francis, there is no Messiah. Before Babylon II there was no Messiah tradition in Israel. It all came about because of Alexander. Judas Maccabeus thought that if a young Macedonian named Alexander could conquer the world, so could a young Jew. It was a mistake—a mistake that has cost my people much misery.

Francis: Well, are you the son of David?

Jesus: Yes, Francesco, I am, and there you have it. That is why they crucified me.

Francis: I don't understand.

Jesus: You see, when the people were taken away to Babylon II because they didn't listen to Jeremias and threw him in the well, Nabuchodonosor made Judea a province of his Babylon and kept the heir of David captive. Later, when Cyrus conquered Babylon II, he made Judea a province of Persia. Still later, when Alexander conquered Darius at Isis, his general, Seleucus, made Judea a province of his Empire. When Rome conquered Greece, Judea became a dependency of Rome. At no time could the heir of David take the throne because that would be a rebellion against the Empire, whosesoever the Empire was. The Macabees started the Hasmonean line of kings, but that was allowed because they were subservient to the Empire, not descended from David.

Francis: And you are?

Jesus: Yes, Francesco, I am—right back through David to Jesse, his father, from whom I got my name.

Francis: I read that you came into the Holy City and the people sang Hosanna to the Son of David?

Jesus: Yes, Francis, and I let them. They told the truth. But the priests knew the danger to their authority and cried, "Tell them to stop! Don't you know what the Romans will do if they hear this? They will come and take away our place and our nation." I answered them, "If I stop them the stones will cry out!"

Francis: What did you mean by that?

Jesus: I meant that as the Law of Moses is written in stone, so

167

the freedom of King David is written in the hearts of our people. What the heart knows remains as the stones remain.

Francis: So they crucified you for being a rebel?

Jesus: Just like Spartacus and those who followed him.

Francis: Why did you do it?

Jesus: To stop a rebellion that was about to happen. Thousands would have died if I had not preempted the revolt.

Francis: But, why didn't they kill you?

Jesus: Pontius Pilate was no fool, nor was he kind. He appreciated my saving him the trouble of a full-scale revolt. So he put on a show of punishing me, upon my promise to leave the country. The Romans, you know, are always cruel, even if they secretly admire you.

Francis: Are you the only way to God?

Jesus: No, Francesco, I am not. There are as many ways to God as there are beings who seek "the way." Some humans can help show others the way. I am one of those humans and so are you.

Francis: You mean after I am gone many will find the way in their own heart because of me, as many have found that way because of you?

Jesus: Yes, Francesco. After all, the way to God lies within every being; it needs only to be *found* there.

Francis: What do you call a person who helps others find that way?

Jesus: A Master, Francis—a Master of The Way.

Francis: Are there many Masters?

Jesus: Very many, Francesco. In fact there is a Master in every human ever born. However, for a long time now people have been prevented from knowing who they are and of what they are capable by people whose greed knows no bounds and who disempower others to make slaves of them. When someone changes my story and uses it to do that, I am very saddened, especially when they use my crucifixion to justify themselves.

By the way, did you know that my twin brother Thomas has written the best book about me?

Francis: I have heard there is such a book, but no one knows where it is.

Jesus: Someday it will be found again, even though the church

	of Peter and Paul has burned every copy they can find.
Francis:	Can you tell me what Thomas wrote?
Jesus:	Not "seek and ye shall find," for that is a commandment,

and masters never give commandments.
It was more like this:

"Those who seek will find, and that is a promise.
Those who find, will find the truth in their own heart.
And those who find that truth will be disturbed because
of the conflict between what their heart tells them and
what they are being told by others.

Those who are disturbed will wonder and ponder, and
at last they will choose the truth in their own heart.
They will then become masters of themselves and
become truly human, which is the best thing any
human can be."

Interlude

For you shall know the truth and the truth will make you free.
~ John 8:31-37

When you have left us, to whom should we go?

You shall go to James the Just
For whose sake all was made manifest.
~ Gospel According to Thomas

Canto XXVIII

Original Innocence

Time: 1215 CE
Place: Damascus
Personae: Giovanni Bernadone (St. Francis of Assisi)
             Grand Vizier of Jerusalem

Vizier: I see, young man, by your mode of prayer, that you are not a follower of our prophet.

Francis: I have come seeking the Grand Vizier of Jerusalem whom they say Saladin of Tikrit has removed to this city as a place of sanctuary.

Vizier: Then you have found your man, for I am the person honored by the generosity of my Lord Saladin.

Francis: I have noticed that this city, though said to be the oldest on Earth, is fair indeed. Its beauty is watered by the rivers that flow down from Mt. Hermon that stands in the window of this house. Before I leave this holy land, I want to visit the Springs of Jordan that they say flow abundantly beyond Hermon's snowy cap.

Vizier: A most gracious sentiment. Tell me young man, why have you sought me?

Francis: I have come to make peace.

Vizier: I have been told that Allah alone makes peace though we may be of assistance.

Francis: I have also come to express my sorrow and regret over the way in which my Christian comrades have inflicted so much oppression and destruction on Allah's children in the name of our God.

Vizier: Such sentiments cause me great delight. Would you feel such compassion if our Saladin of Tikrit had not ousted Guy de Lusignan from the Holy City twenty-eight years ago?

Francis: If Guy had bested Saladin I would have been even more mortified.

171

Vizier: As you no doubt know, Jerusalem *is* the Holy City of the three faiths of the book: the Holy Koran of our Prophet, the Bible of the Christians and the Torah of the Jews. Three faiths of which our prophet approves as the faiths of the true God though he be known by a different name to each. You may be aware that we held the city in trust for six hundred years until the Christian Crusaders seized it for their own. We continued to carry the torch of learning, which has flickered low in western lands.

Francis: In our book, the Bible, there is a promise that the day will come when we will study for war no more.

Vizier: Personally, that is my hope. I do confess, however, that it was by force of arms that Allah's armies swept from the Nile to the Pyrenees to be stopped by Charles Martel at Tours near the River Loire. Was that not 732 according to your calendar?

Francis: That sounds about right. And from Charles came his grandson Charles the Great. He subdued Italy and founded the Holy Roman Empire on Christmas Day of the year 800 by giving Pope Leo a deed to western Europe with a request to let that seven-foot Charles rule it for him!

Vizier: Alas, we are all too fond of killing one another in the name of God!

Francis: In truth, gentle Vizier, may we not speak together about how we may find a commonality, even a unity, among the religions of the Book? If we can agree here and procure the approval of Lord Saladin, I think it is possible that our grand vizier, Pope Innocent III, might also agree.

Vizier: I hear he is a fierce man and that even now he has sent an army under Simon de Montfort to crush the Cathari in southern France, the Cathari being descendants of the Buddhists of India. What the Cathari call self-evident truth, the papal throne condemns as heresy.

Francis: It distresses me greatly, but we all have our overzealous partisans. I understand Muslim armies are even now sweeping the Buddhists out of India. But let me tell you of a remarkable event—something that happened to me at Rome that showed me another side of our Pope Innocent.

Vizier: It would greatly console me to know that he has another side!

Francis: When I returned from a crusade to Assisi where I was born, it came to me that our God and your Allah are the same. Indeed, the same Divinity is known to all creatures great and small and we are all relatives. Many people came to the ancient church at San Damiano that I had rebuilt in memory of more ancient times. Unfortunately, my bishop was not pleased and his army closed the church and even killed a gentle soul who would have prevented him. I journeyed from my home in Assisi, in a district known as Umbria—the shadows—south of Rome itself, to inquire of his Holiness why his bishops slew the innocent.

As I entered the great splendor of his court barefoot in the company of my barefoot brothers, I saw Innocent III on a golden throne half way to heaven at the top of a long flight of marble stairs with a great mural of our Jesus, large of eye and gracious of mien, displayed in golden radiance behind and above him. Two corridors of censors were swung to fill the air with redolent scent and crowds of cardinals, bishops, princes and kings attended him.

I must admit, the scene overwhelmed me, and then I heard my name called to speak as a petitioner. I quite forgot myself and began to recite the many mercies of our Lord from the sacred book. I felt tears in my eyes as I spoke and heard passion in my voice, which grew louder despite my efforts to control it. Suddenly a voice cried, "Heresy! How dare such a pitiful creature preach to us! Take him away!" But it was not the voice of His Holiness. I could not stop speaking. Two Swiss guards picked me up by the elbows, dragged me backwards and threw me out, as I continued gesticulating and imploring.

My brothers in their bare feet and peasant dress were terrified, and gathered round me in concern. The doors closed and we took counsel with each other as to what to do and what might impend.

Then, the same doors opened and I heard the voice of His Holiness, "Where is he? Where is that man? Bring him back!" The guards reappeared, raised me up, because I was still where I had fallen, and escorted me back into that awesome chamber.

As I stood on the floor looking up at His Holiness, seeing my beloved Jesus as a frame around him, he rose from his throne in his white and golden garments and raising the hem, stepped carefully down the stair while the regal multitude held their breath. He came up to me as I stood barefoot in rags. He said to me, "My son, what is it that you want from us?"

I was surprised to hear myself speak to him, for I was terrified, tearful and confused. "Your Holiness," I asked, "Why? Why must we argue and harmspeak one another? Is not the way of our Lord simple and plain? Is it not something children and our friends the birds and the beasts understand without explanation? Why are we so unkind to one another? I do not understand. Perhaps I am in error."

The Pope was silent for a moment. Then his eyes filled with tears and he said the most astonishing thing. "Error, Francesco, will be forgiven. We here are corrupted by privilege and power. But you, Francesco! We have paid so much attention to Original Sin that we have forgotten Original Innocence. Go and carry your message to all who will hear. And if none will hear, speak with the birds and the fish and your brother, the sun, and your sister, the moon!"

And then the Pope truly astonished me. Putting his hands on my head he whispered, "A blessing upon your head." His fingers touched my hands and he said, "A blessing upon your hands," and he looked down at my muddy feet. He knelt on the floor. Bending down he said, "And on your feet." Startled, I felt his lips as he kissed my feet. Then he rose silently, looked at me and, wrapped in his pontifical robes, was ushered away to ascend his throne as the chorus broke into the *Te Deum*.

Vizier: You see tears in my eyes also, young man. Indeed there is hope. Let us speak together about how we are all brothers and sisters in the compassion of Divine innocence—no matter how divisive our quarrels!

Postscript

Francis worked out an agreement to reconcile Islam and Christianity, and he procured Saladin's approval. When it was presented to Innocent III for his approval, the Pope refused.

Interlude

Brother sun, and sister moon
I seldom see you, seldom hear your tune
Preoccupied with selfish misery
I seldom see the glory around me

But I am God's creature
Of God I am a part
I feel God's love
Awakening my heart

Now brother sun, and sister moon
Now I do see you
Now I hear your tune
So much in love with all that I survey

~ Donovan

Canto XXIX

The Venetian Oligarchy

*"In Xanadu did Kubla Khan a stately pleasure dome decree,
where Alph the sacred river ran through caverns measureless to
man, down to a sunless sea."*
~ Samuel Taylor Coleridge 1772-1834

Time: 1295 CE
Place: Venice, Palace of the Doge
Personae: The Doge of Venice
            Marco Polo

Doge: Welcome home, Marco! How long ago did you leave us?
Marco: Twenty-four years ago. I was just seventeen.
Doge: I understand you were well received in China and even
        honored and employed by Kubla Khan.
Marco: All of us were—my father Nicolo, my uncle Maffeo and
        I.
Doge: I understand you traveled the Silk Road through Saracen
        lands as far as Samarkand.
Marco: Yes. In spite of the crusades raging there, we encountered
        little hostility.
Doge: Did you find the road from Samarkand to Sian well
        guarded?
Marco: Yes. Especially that portion along the Gangsu Corridor,
        below the Altai Mountains, past the Taklimakan, where
        we approached the Mongolian border. Kubla Khan has
        made that protection a priority to ensure the safety of
        traveling merchants. He realizes how important it is to
        make the Silk Road safe since the Romans developed a
        taste for silk even before the Punic Wars.
Doge: Did you know your trip was initiated in response to an
        invitation directed to us by Kubla Khan?
Marco: Yes, Kubla Khan told me that himself.
Doge: Tell me, do the Chinese ideas of Empire seem similar to
        our own?

Marco: In large degree. There is evidence that the Empire came to them from the west, as we westerners see it coming from the east.

Doge: A Middle Eastern origin then?

Marco: So it seems. Nippon lies beyond Cathay to the east. I learned that they also have an Emperor. Interestingly, their word for Emperor is *Sumeragi*, which they say means Spirit of Sumer.

Doge: The Egyptians told us that their civilization came to them "Across the Sea of Ur from the Land of Sumer." Perhaps there is more to Mesopotamia than we have yet remembered.

Marco: Please tell me, how has my beloved Venice fared in my absence?

Doge: Very well indeed. You know, don't you Marco, that since we occupied these marshy islands five hundred years ago, the power, especially the commercial power, of Rome has been here and not in Rome?

Marco: My uncle Maffeo told me that. Didn't it come here from Byzantium?

Doge: Yes indeed. You know, don't you, about Tarsus?

Marco: You mean the city where St. Paul was born?

Doge: Yes. Tarsus was the commercial center of the Roman world after the Punic Wars when Rome beat out the Phoenicians and Scipio Africanus plowed up Carthage and shouted, "*Cartago delenda est!*", "Carthage is no more."

Marco: That was before Rome became an Empire, wasn't it? Where did the Empire come to Rome from?

Doge: Greece, Hellenistic Greece. Actually from Julius Caesar's boyhood hero, Alexander.

Marco: But the commercial center stayed at Tarsus? Why?

Doge: Because the Romans were bad sailors, poor navigators, and even worse ship builders. They never learned. They called the people of Tarsus the "Cilician Pirates" because they always extracted the last coin knowing the Romans had no other access to maritime commerce after the Phoenicians were wiped out.

Marco: Wasn't Paul of Tarsus the major architect of Christianity?

Doge: Indeed. Actually, we here in Venice are aware that the Pope's "Christianity" is largely pretentious and much at variance from the teachings of Jesus. However, since we are the custodians of the money-making aspects of Empire, we support and control the Church in order to control the Empire, just as Constantine fashioned the Church to do. We realize that Constantine, not Jesus, founded the Church as an instrument to control the Empire, an Empire from which we continue to profit handsomely.

Marco: You mean that Venice is the heir of the Roman Empire, not Rome or Constantinople?

Doge: Yes, Marco.

Marco: Are you the Emperor then?

Doge: Oh, no, Marco. That would be too obvious. We here in Venice have a sort of democracy of the privileged few—a mercantile democracy, if you please. Plato referred to our form of government as an oligarchy.

Marco: Oligarchy?

Doge: Plato's succession of governments in *The Republic* went like this, beginning in the Grecian Golden Age: *Democracy*—where all people are equal; *Republic*—where the representatives of the people are equal; *Aristocracy*—where the land owners are equal; *Oligarchy*—where the aristocracy becomes permanent and exclusive, reinforced by primogeniture; then *Tyranny*—or what we call Empire, where the only true equal is the Imperator or Emperor. Then, Plato says, "Comes the revolution!"

Marco: So you prevent the revolution and the return to democracy by stopping with the oligarchy?

Doge: Well said, Marco! Of course we can never publicly admit what we are doing and if you accuse us of it, we will be insulted and deny it. If you persist, we will come after you secretly.

Marco: A masterful deceit then?

Doge: Yes, Marco, a tightly-held and ancient conspiracy.

Marco: And you control the Church?

Doge: Yes, indeed!

Marco: But you don't believe in it?

Doge: Of course not. None of us hold any allegiance to any organization or system of belief except our own oligarchy!

Marco: This has been going on for five hundred years?

Doge: Yes. And we have no reason to believe it will not go on for at least another thousand.

Marco: Why do you trust me with this information?

Doge: Because your family is one of us, and your uncle, Maffeo, has asked me to invite you to join us now that you are forty and grown to a man's estate.

Marco: Are we "masters of deceit" then?

Doge: An excellent way of putting it, but there is more to being a "master of deceit" than you might imagine!

Interlude

Wide is the gate and broad is the way that leads to destruc-
tion and many there be who go in thereat,
but narrow is the gate and straight is the way that leads to
salvation, and few there be that find it.

~ Jesus, Mathew 7:13-15

As papal infallibility
Is strangling the Catholics
So biblical infallibility
Is strangling the Protestants

As Koranic infallibility
Is strangling the Moslems
So infallibility of the Torah
Is strangling the Jews

The infallibility of the Pali Canon
Would strangle the Buddhists
But they seldom claimed it was infallible

A pragmatic sign
Of a master of deceit
Is that he claims to be infallible

Or as Jesus says,
Jesus who never claimed to be infallible,
"The devil is a deceiver from the beginning."

Canto XXX

Primal Encounter

By the shores of Gitchie Gumie,
By the shining big sea waters,
Stood the wigwam of Nikomis,
Daughter of the Moon, Nikomis
~ Henry Wadsworth Longfellow
– *Hiawatha*

Time: Circa 1322 CE
Place: Big Sur Coast of California,
             an Island in the River of Time
Personae: The Esselen Girl
             Her People
             The Bear

She woke
With a deep foreboding,
A lucent memory
Drifting,
A floating island
Spinning on a dark stream,
A celestial counterpart,
A vortex
In the river of time.

This sea margin
Where great crumpled mountains
Made dizzying plunges
Into a morning-shrouded sea
Would someday bear a name,
A name taken from the language of her people,
Sargenta Ruk.
It would be named again
In distant future suns
Big Sur,
River of the fecund south.

She stirred and felt a tingling in her toes
A longing to touch the Earth
To feel the Earth Spirit spiral upward
Spinning upward through her
Toward the lightening sky.

Far out in the flowing sea
She remembered islands,
Islands her eyes had never seen,
Islands as real to her
As this bright land
Where volcanoes still smoked
As they once had in the land beneath her feet.
Hava Iki Iki
Land under the Inner Eye
She savored the name
As it mingled
With the memories of her own ancestors
Who visited in her dreams.

They had crossed these seas
To find this land
That welcomed her each morning
As her feet touched the Earth.
Then in her waking
The sweet odor of the wind
Touched deep delight
A gentle ecstasy of welcome
Familiar yet mysterious
A wilderness of home.

She rose
In the sleeping circle
Of her beloved people
On this high place
Where the circle of the horizon
Moved her to turn,
Slowly
Moving in a sunwise circle
As she felt herself bless her people,
And her people still sleeping bless her.

She felt again the oneness
The oneness that was never absent
The one spiritedness
Breathing as one breath
And yet respectful of her
As if she were the only one.

The foreboding
She had felt before
A sort of pathos
A sweet sorrow
Evoked by a sweetness like the wind
Which though gentle
Spoke of ecstasy
Mingled with primal fear
A fear that would not leave
Though it could not dominate
She had come to know this fear
As her constant companion
But also as her friend
As long as the ecstasy accompanied it
Locking it in a vortiginal embrace
That made her heart light.

Then she saw him.
He was standing very still
Not fifty paces away
So still he was like the stones
That motionless
Seemed to whisper the secrets of timeless time.

He was fixed upon her
As if he had watched her before she was born
And just from over there
Where the sun would set
Between her and the singing sea.

She looked back at him.
Was he human after all?
Beneath that great-nosed
Small-eared hairiness?

184

One could not be sure.
The shamans were known
To wear his coat
When they danced upon the foot drum
Or waited by the trails
To bring the sudden ecstasy of death
To passers by,
Not to kill
But to leave the frightened one
To savor the sweetness of life.

Still
He was motionless
As his gaze now locked with hers.
Was he calling her to come to him
To cross the great river
To the realm of the ancestors?
He seemed to promise the sweet ecstasy of dying
That awaits those who do not flee.

A gentle wind
Bearing the sweetness
Passed over him,
And mingled with his gamy male scent.
It wafted to her
And made her feel desire.

Was he her lover after all?
She who had never known
A man's embrace?

She almost danced toward him.

He rose up
Extending his straight clawed
Clutching arms toward her.

Then, turning suddenly, he was gone
As if he had come
From the rose land of sunset
To help her greet the dawn,

The rose dawn.
Her eyes turned skyward in surprise
Half disappointed by his going
Half delighted by her deliverance.

She saw the blue road of the sun
And turning saw it cross
The rose road of the dawn. And they flowed together
In the violet flame
The violet flame of the ancestral rose
That lay spinning upward
From her whirling, whirling world.

Interlude

May the heart of Earth flow to the heart of heaven
through my heart and through all our hearts together.

And may our hearts be the heart
of every sentient being in all the universe.

~ Mayan Shaman's Prayer
Chichicastenango

Ixtklan

This is not North America, it's Turtle Island.
And only a Turtle Islander may truly live here
All others are just visiting.

But anyone is a Turtle Islander
Who feels themselves moved
By a Turtle Island Heart and a Turtle Island Spirit.

And, if you feel yourself so moved,

Welcome home!

~ Little Bear, Esselen Shaman

187

Canto XXXI

The Long Voyage Home

Time: Circa 1322 CE
Place: Tahiti, in southern Polynesian
               (Kahiki, in northern Polynesian)
Personae: A boy 14
               His people
               The Kahunas

Kapu, Forbidden + Huna, Secret =
Kahuna, Keeper of the Forbidden Secret

His people were the nation of the remembered dream, a dream of
voyaging from the north-western shores of Africa when the Sahara
was still green five thousand years ago.

He had heard the dream recounted since he could first remember.
Everyone knew the dream. It was spoken of often. The Kahunas
would say, "A nation is a dream, a dream that will fail for lack of
dreamers. If you are a member of this nation, it is your sacred duty
to truly dream its dream, for if you do not, you will cause our
nation to begin to die."

He was fourteen and the rites of puberty had prepared him so
that now he was a man—a man who knew how to cope with his
deadly inclinations and to hold them in balance with his gentler
side.

The dream had happened long ago, nearly two full ages ago,
counted by the wheeling stars, nearly five thousand years ago. It
was the longest memory of his people, now so long wedded to the
sea, and to the markers that are the stars. His favorite star was Al
Pharatz. His people, the dream declared, had spent a thousand years
in Egypt after crossing those many flowing rivers that reached "the
sea in the middle of the land" from the south. He often dreamed
about the abundance of the animals of which the dream spoke.

At the time of the dream they had lived on the leeward side of the
mountains that later the Greeks had named after Atlas, who held

the orb of the heavens on his shoulders. Rivers had flowed from the Atlas Mountains into the great Sahara, making their world a paradise.

Their leaders did not demand obedience, rather the people offered their allegiance. Their governing councils were two—one for women, one for men—and both proceeded by unanimity. One made the decisions for the group, and the other carried them out. Unanimity was sometimes called communion, especially on those regular occasions when everyone participated. These were the assemblies of empowerment—out of many, one. In them, the joy of oneness was the goal, a joy that made all experience their oneness with all others. The primary celebrations were twice a year, when the day and night were equal over all the Earth, and his people experienced oneness with all other beings on the planet.

On one occasion, when the two councils were in joint session, the "voice" was heard in the heart-minds of all, quiet but in a tone of warning: "An age of darkness is coming upon the Earth. You should gather your spirits together as one spirit (a spirit-vehicle later called a Merkabah) and search the Earth for a place to keep the Huna, the secret, safe against that Age of Darkness when all truth will be in peril."

They did what the voice suggested and found the islands to be known as Hawaii, unoccupied in the Pacific. They first saw the islands at dawn from the west and made clear note of the silhouette of dark islands against the dawn as the night sky wheeled westward.

The creation story told of a long journey from the Atlas Mountains of Morocco to Egypt, from Egypt through Chanaan to Mesopotamia, from Mesopotamia through Iran to India, from India by sea among the Islands of Indonesia, across New Guinea and out into the Pacific to their present refuge islands.

They would later call those islands Far Kahiki. The voyage had seen long stays, centuries in certain places, especially Egypt, Mesopotamia, and India.

One day the boy had asked a "secret keeper" to tell him the story again:

> One day the council of the wise
> That made decisions then
> In the flow of unanimity
> Had gathered in their accustomed way
> Both the women's circle and the men's circle together.

They had joined to seek the oneness of heart-mind
That was their nation.
They had played the drums of the heartbeat of Earth
When suddenly they coalesced
In the passive state of hearing
And a voice was heard as if all were one hearer.

"Take heed!
An age of darkness is coming
In which all knowledge will be at risk.
The power that bonds you all will be threatened.
Take flight in the ancient way,
As a group explore the Earth
Eastward toward the rising sun
And find a place
To keep the Huna safe against the "powers of the dark"
And when you find the place
Call it
Hava Iki Iki
"land under the inner eye."
Then return and lead your people toward that place.
You have been chosen for this crossing.
When your hearts grow faint
Call me."

That was the kernel of the dream. The wise ones responded, took flight, and sought the place of safety, traveling together over land and sea. Finally, they saw in the light of dawn, far over the greatest sea, an outline of islands, farther from inhabited or uninhabited shores than any place on Earth, and with joy they cried out as with one voice, "Hava-Iki-Iki, land under the inner eye!"

Returning to their people, the council said, "We have found it—the place to keep the secret safe against the Age of Darkness."

They were a star people and had watched the moving stars in the wells of their native land. They had traveled with the moon and knew how she pulled the tides of human emotion along with the following sea. They had greeted the sun each day, rising in joy to greet another rising sun. They had let the sun count days and years; to the moon they assigned the months in the knowledge of the menstra, and the stars counted the ages. They knew the "great year," 26,000 sun years, where the ages precessed backwards against the zodiacal journey of the sun through the year. They knew the constellations and their heliacal rising an hour before sunrise. They knew the "sun stands" and the "days of equal night."

The time of the dream was the heliacal rising of the constellation of the Great Bull with his deadly rider. The Ram would follow, somewhere in Mesopotamia or Iran. The Ram would be pursued by the two fish, the Age of Pisces. They had learned to call it the Kali Yuga in India, the threatened Age of Darkness. Beyond Pisces lay Aquarius, when the secret would be safe again.

So, his people began their physical journey, ever eastward toward the rising sun, across the great Sahara, not yet a desert, but a land of many rivers, filled with the abundance of life. At last the Nile, its civilization already old, and a long stay in Mezraim, Egypt. Then, around the Fertile Crescent to Mesopotamia, a rich and thriving land filled with astronomical wisdom and with a sense of the presence of the gods. Onward through Iran and India. Two thousand years in India. Then, following the maritime trade routes of Sumer to the tin mines of Malaysia, they passed into the great archipelago of Indonesia, reached New Guinea, and then outward at last into that great ocean where their goal lay... somewhere.

In the twilight of the breaking dawn he set out with his people, the great adventure of his fourteenth year. The twilight was dark that morning in Far Kahiki. Dark, not only because of the earliness of the hour, but also because of the black lowering clouds that clung to the horizon. The days before had been tumultuous because it was a choosing time.

For thousands of years they had moved on, ever faithful to the dream. As they had moved into the great ocean, from island to island, tending northward to the Sisters and the Drinking Gourd, the strictures of space had necessitated cruel measures when an island grew too small to support them all. At such time there was a choosing by lot of who would stay and who would go. His lot, the lot of one who would go, had been imprinted with six clustered stars, the Sisters of the *Pleiades*—north.

His people knew much of the stars and their courses. It was a knowledge that had grown greatly in their long ancestral stay in Chaldea, Sumer, "the land between the rivers." Chaldea was the homeland of cities, writing, commerce and all the sciences, where the knowledge of the stars was far greater than in any land on Earth—a land that knew the secrets of the gods and whence they came.

On this morning, the sun had not yet risen and the typically red road of the sunrise was still gray beneath the fading stars of night. A little wind was fresh with the promise of rain. Along the beach were many dugout canoes being filled with coconuts, with breadfruit plants, with chickens, and calabashes of fresh water. There was chanting and song and Aku Aku (Holy, Holy) was everywhere—the awesome sense of mingled fear and ecstasy that welled up in all their hearts from the great unknown.

Then, as the sky lightened beyond the Heiau (temple) of the holy Mauna (mountain), where to move a stone could be a fatal act, a great procession of Kahunas came bearing gifts and spreading the wounding magic of blessing among the people. As they passed the boy, one of them stopped, and with great ceremony presented him a breadfruit tree in trust for the day he would plant it in the new land beyond the northern horizon.

As he received the sprouting breadfruit, as it touched his outstretched hands, the blessing that came with it opened his mind like a great knife to reveal a vision of another land, one far beyond the promised destination, beyond the treasured Hava Iki Iki.

He knew it was not Hava Iki Iki because, like all his people from his youngest days, he had known the creation chant that described the journey in soul travel of the Kahunas, the great journey that had found the islands nearly 5,000 years ago. Very precisely, and with one mind, they had seen the islands black in silhouette against the long red horizon of the yet unrisen sun.

What he saw in this almost blinding vision was not that silhouette, but a long chain of mountains falling steeply into the sea. It was as if he himself was a great bird flying from the land of sunset to the land of sunrise. He saw the long chain of mountains grow larger as he soared upon the following wind, larger, until he could feel the Kona wind of the western sea flow upward from the mountain faces and spin him in sunwise motion above a certain peak whose golden head was raised directly above the sea.

Surely it was a sacred mountain in a land of dream vision. He could see a circle of people sleeping with their heads together. The common power of the one dream they dreamed together drew him down until, just before he touched the Earth, he felt himself no longer a bird but a great shaggy beast with a great nose. He found himself standing stock still between the sleeping people and the sea, staring toward the dawning red sky.

There, her eyes wide with wonder, stood a girl his own age staring at him with a longing that pulled him like a magnet. She began a sunwise spin between him and the dawn, dancing toward him. He felt a great hunger, great enough to devour her. He felt himself rise on shaggy hind feet and extend heavy arms with straight claws to embrace her. Then suddenly a lightning bolt of unbearable pain seared him, and he turned and awoke among his people, holding the breadfruit, ready to embark.

After many days at sea the paddlers were beginning to tire. The tradewinds moved with the sun westward from rising to setting, and their course required but little deviation from the north.

The paddlers divided into shifts, three hours on and three hours off, by day and by night. The children and the animals were restless and scarcely a shift passed without a rescue, though so far none were lost.

A sharp eye was kept on the fresh water, even though at first it rained a little every day and seabirds still followed. There were fish caught in circular throwing nets even though they could only lower them in the open sea. The women sang counterpoint to the base drum of the paddlers' voices as they sank their paddles deep in the sea in perfect time, moved more by an inner connected unanimity than by the coincidence of the beat of their voices.

There was joy in their voices—the joy of promise and anticipation, for the creation song had foretold their leaving Far Kahiki and the next landfall would be Hava Iki Iki. Still, two thousand miles of open sea intervened.

After one full moon had followed another and half again, they began to fear. What if they were off course? Beyond Hava Iki Iki the Kahunas were told there were no more islands, only open sea for thousands of miles where it was said no one had ever gone, and where tales told of great walls of water cresting, great heavings of the Goddess Pele, thousands of feet below. What of the great waves that would carry outriggers up until they stood upon their sterns, until they were released by Pele's sister, the sea, and fell back upon their crews left struggling boatless in the waves? Where would the hope of the Land Under the Inner Eye be then?

Fear came to them then from the land of dreams. The paddlers began to grow faint, afraid of shadows by night and oppressed by the fearsome heat of the day. Doldrums. Instead of sea birds, Mano, the shark god, thrust up his fin behind them, the god of eternal love calling them to the ecstasy of death beyond the moon paths on the midnight waters. Children whimpered, animals groaned. The women were silent and the boy of vision felt nothing but quiet sorrow, where no joy could enter. It was as if the threatened Age of Darkness they had come to prepare against had come to block them from their promised refuge and to steal their hope.

They had now crossed that mysterious invisible line where the spiral spin of wellness reversed itself, a line known to others as the equator. South of that line, countersunwise spin brought joy and fair weather and clockwise brought a sobering, a tendency to illness and rain. In Far Kahiki it had been so. But now as they moved toward the Sisters, the spinning had turned again so that countersunwise winds brought the saving rain.

On a particular night wet winds began to blow from the south. All were parched. They had been on scant rations of water for days. The breadfruit plants were beginning to wither, and already some birds had died. The wind rose before midnight and the waves washed higher, then higher still, until they nearly swamped some of the outriggers as the paddlers tried to keep them pointed into the wind. The waves grew higher still and they remembered the legends of the great walls of water that could destroy them all. Very little fresh water could be saved in such a maelstrom.

Then suddenly, three hours after midnight, the wind stopped and a steady gentle rain filled their empty calabashes. It lasted until just before dawn when the rain stopped and a star was seen directly over them. The skies cleared steadily and soon the full and brilliant heavens covered them from horizon to horizon, though the moon was down.

Their spirits rose as the sea quieted to a gentle lapping, driven by a scarcely perceptible north wind. The Sisters beckoned and the Drinking Gourd pointed to the polar star.

With unanimous joy the people began to sing together—the deep heartbeat of the paddlers' bass against the woodwind voices of the women with whom the children joined, as if all were one instrument.

Then they saw it. The dawn had crept upon them, the eastern horizon still dark gray and the stars still brilliant from the apex of the vault to the places of their setting. There, against the rose dawn that was just beginning to blush, was the silhouette. The very one promised by their ancestors so long ago—the homeland to keep the secret safe against the Age of Darkness. Hava Iki Iki—Land Under the Inner Eye!

They all saw it at once, and were struck dumb. The paddlers stopped stroking, paddles suspended. There was no sound for a long minute. Then their voices rose as one person:

Ale! Ale! Ale!

Mahalo

Aloha nui nui

Their prayer of gratitude echoed across the sea to reach the ears of Madam Pele and her fiery island-building heart, and to call Maui, the god who long ago with his fishhook, pulled from the sea Haleakala, the House of the Sun!

Interlude

Entering the circle
Is entering the spin
Awakening the heart-mind
Together we begin.

Canto XXXII

Do Indians Have Souls?

Time: 1540 CE
Place: Valladolid, capitol of Spain
Personae: Charles V, Holy Roman Emperor
            His Chamberlain
            Bartolomeo de las Casas, Bishop of Chiapas
            Sepúlveda
Setting: The pre-trial conference

Charles: Who is this Bartolomeo who comes to trouble us from the Indies?

Chamb: He was a planter, your majesty, from Santo Domingo, you know of the place. He was fond of his native slaves, treated them as equals, and even sat down for dinner with them on Sundays.

Charles: Not an outrageous practice. But why is he here?

Chamb: Better ask Sepúlveda, your majesty. I am really not sure.

Charles: Sepúlveda. Now there is a very troublesome fellow. I am not sure I like him very much. Very like Torquemada, the Inquisitor, I am afraid, out to kill the heretics.

Chamb: That's the man. They say he has brought every theologian in Europe here to back him. He has the backing of all those planter-conquistadors from New Spain after Bartolomeo's scalp for being a revolutionary and radical by claiming the Indians are people just like us, with rights.

Charles: Well, bring them in. Let's see what they have to say.

Enter Bartolomeo & Sepulveda

Charles: Bishop de las Casas, where is your diocese?

Barto: Chiapas, your majesty, down between Mexico and Guatemala. I serve the Mayan people.

Charles: Very good. Why do you trouble us with this trial?

197

Barto: It grieves me to trouble your majesty. I am most grateful that you have chosen to hear this matter yourself. I come to ask your help for a great many of your loyal subjects.

Charles: And who might these loyal subjects be?

Barto: The native peoples of the New World, your majesty, who have accepted our Lord and Savior Jesus Christ as their savior.

Charles: What is their grievance?

Barto: Not with you, your majesty, but with the planters who treat them very badly and claim they have no souls and are not fully human.

Charles: And you, Bishop, do not agree with these opinions?

Barto: Not only do I not agree, your majesty, but I am sure future generations will not agree and that they will be thoroughly incredulous that any Christian person could have harbored such an opinion.

Charles: I take it, Señor Sepúlveda, that you also are not in agreement with the Bishop's opinion?

Sepul: By no means am I, your majesty. I am confident you will find the opinions of the august theologians I will call to testify are thoroughly in accord with my conviction that these "American Indians" are not only savage, but brutal, and have no claim to be human like ourselves.

Charles: Remarkable. May I ask, Señor Sepúlveda, have you ever visited America and seen these natives for yourself in their native land?

Sepul: No, your majesty, I have not.

Charles: And have any of your "august theologians" made such a journey?

Sepul: No, your majesty, they have not.

Charles: On what evidence, then, do you base your remarkable opinion?

Sepul: On the evidence of the opinions of many gentlemen of quality, settlers of the New World, who have an abundance of personal experience with the natives.

Charles: Do I take it that these "gentlemen of quality" have also benefited greatly from the labor and toil of these natives, and that they are among those who are here accused of abusing them?

Sepul: They are so accused, your majesty, but if these natives are but animals, why should we be held to account?

Charles: Perhaps not legally, but morally, are not even animals proper beneficiaries of our kindness? Especially those who contribute to our needs and desires by their daily toil? Well, let us proceed! Bishop de las Casas, do you have an opening statement?

Postscript

Charles V decided that the American Indians were "people like ourselves" and "fully human." His decision was never accepted by the planters, who continued their abuses. Charles V, Holy Roman Emperor, and perhaps the most admirable of them all, is largely responsible for the greater survival of natives under Spanish dominion than English.

The English never asked the question whether Indians "had souls" and assumed they did not. They extended this opinion to the black Africans who replaced the Indians when their numbers were decimated. The English developed the motto: "The only good Indian is a dead Indian." This policy had its origin in Ireland where the first "reservation" was that part of Ireland west of the Shannon River. If an Irishman crossed the river, he was a fair victim of a "fox hunt."

An interesting corollary to the Irish situation is Wounded Knee Creek in Shannon County, South Dakota. It has only been in recent years that the death penalty has been repealed for American Indian Shamans who practice their form of spirituality. In the United States that repeal came in 1970. However, in Guatemala it was not repealed until 1995.

One might also note a tableau that occurred in Colorado around 1878 when an Arapaho Shaman was caught in the act of performing ceremony. The general lined him up to be shot but, following protocol, asked him, "Do you have anything to say before we shoot you?" Arapahos are very tall people. He looked down at the general and said, "Yes, general, I do. You can kill us all, but we will be back as your grandchildren."

Interlude

Satan never had a fall.
He never was at all.
And if you look within,
There never ever was a sin.

Canto XXXIII

At Last!

Time: Middle 16th Century CE
            Winter Solstice, Sun lying "dead" in the tomb
            300 years after Francis of Assisi
Place: Rome, Italy
Personae: Michelangelo Buonarroti
            A voice

Rain was pouring down the windowpane as he lay on a cot in a small room on the second story. His family name was Buonarroti. They called him Michael the Angel. The rain kept him awake. He turned over, just missing the fifteen-foot high block of marble towering over his bed. It had been there for years.

His chisel lay on the table. What secrets would it find in the marble block when he struck his hammer to it? He had to know before he struck the first blow. It had been years since the Bridge Builder, Pope Julius II, had sent him the block. Hard man, the Bridge Builder, but he favored Buonarroti and wanted Buonarroti to build his tomb as a tribute to stand for all eternity. He was away at war just now, fighting to keep what he claimed as his; what was his from the Empire, inherited from an emperor a thousand years ago.

Buonarroti reflected on the huge slab of marble, then turned a little on his cot and heard the voice. He slept, but he didn't know for how long. He dreamed, and the block's voice spoke to him, "When do I get out?" it whispered.

"What's your name?" Buonarroti wondered.

"David," said the voice. "You heard of me?"

"Yes, but how?"

"Ask your chisel!"

He woke up with a sharp jerk and sat up. The rain had stopped. The moon emerged and touched his chisel. He reached out and put his hand flat against the cool marble block.

"At last!" he said.

Interlude

To what shall I liken the gnosis?
The gnosis is like the root of the tree of knowledge
Accessible to every sentient being
Through the exercise of the power of consciousness
And perceptible through the ecstasies of life force
Eminent through the essential flow
Expressible through the experience of self-evidence
As the essence of Experiential Truth.

Jeshua ben Joseph		Jesus Christ
Thomas & James		Peter & Paul
Gnosis	vs.	Doctrine
Knowing		Believing
Allegiance		Obedience
Freedom		Empire
Equality		Hierarchy

Canto XXXIV

The Pope's Order

Time: 1510 CE, just before the Protestant Revolt
Place: Rome
Personae: Michelangelo Buonarroti
            Pope Julius II

Julius: So, this is your David, Buonarroti. Marvelous! David must feel honored as far away as heaven. Seeing this, he would know at last why Jonathan loved him.

Michel: So, you are satisfied, Holiness, with who was hiding in that stone you gave me?

Julius: More satisfied by your genius, Buonarroti!

Michel: Didn't I tell you about the voice? We are encouraged to listen to it, you know.

Julius: I know, I know. The voice told you to ask your chisel. I am not quite sure who you are, Buonarroti. I am not even sure I like you. But I am sure that I truly love whoever it is that talks to your chisel.

Michel: Am I the one you want to make your tomb?

Julius: I am getting in a big hurry. The French are giving me a bad time, and one day soon I may not come home.

Michel: Yet you keep winning in your fight to run the foreigners out of Italy.

Julius: Perhaps, but they keep slipping back over the mountains, and I am afraid my time is nearly up. Actually, Buonarroti, it is not my tomb I want you to work on first, it's my ceiling.

Michel: You want my chisel to work on your ceiling?

Julius: No, no, Buonarroti, not your chisel. Let your paintbrush's inner voice reveal my ceiling's future.

Michel: Paintbrush! I am no painter, I am a sculptor. Why don't you get Raphael? He's a painter.

Julius: Because I want you, Buonarroti. You are not the only one who hears the voice, you know.

Michel: Who or what do you want to inhabit your ceiling, Holiness?

Julius: Well, I've thought of God and Adam, Buonarroti.

Michel: What about Jesus?

Julius: No, Buonarroti, not Jesus. But you can put him on the wall behind the altar if you want.

Michel: Isn't that where they used to put Mithra, on the reredos? Do you want a Mithraic Jesus?

Julius: You will have to guess what I want Buonarroti, just do it!

Interlude

The senses see the seeming, not eternal now.
The change that's ever teeming is all beneath your brow.

Canto XXXV

Buonarroti's Code

Time: Now
Place   Here
Personae: Any person hearing Michelangelo speak within

I, Buonarroti, had dreams of the Creation.
I painted them on the Sistine ceiling
Of the Bridge Builder Julius II.
Adam lies innocent
A child in a man's body
As God reaches out to touch his finger.
Breathing in the Breath of Life
The very sight of His finger moves all who see it
To remember the resplendent miracle
That is life
Flowing from the Well of Being.
But I knew that it was not so simple.
I knew what Empire
Had done to that Innocence,
That Power.

So I painted another picture
On the wall behind the altar
In the chapel of the Bridge Builder.
On a wall called the reredos
I fashioned a picture styled after Mithra
Who slew the great Bull of the Heavens.
Mithra, whom Constantine replaced
With a Jesus of his own making,
A Jesus of the last judgment
Sending the damned down to hell
With an imperious wave of his right arm,
While compliant sheep gathered on his right
Looking on approvingly.
I, Buonarroti, do not approve of that Jesus.

I painted him as Lucifer
An angel of the light
Populating his hell
With the ignorant and the helpless.
A code
For those to decipher,
Who have the eyes to see.

Stop!
I say, Stop!
This Empire you serve
In the name of God
Serves another master,
A Master of Deceit.

Days will come and are now here
When people will abandon this Empire
By the millions,
Finding where True Divinity dwells
In the heart of every being:
The Truth that is Self-evident.
Then we shall escape the lies of books,
Books that claim to set us free,
Books written to enslave us.
Look upon this Lucifer
This image of the Emperor
And know that such enslavement
Is foreign to this Earth.
Know that the true Jesus is a master
Who abjures all hierarchy
And proclaims that he is equal to all beings
Because of the indwelling of the Divinity,
All beings that are breathed into life by the true God,
That he came to do what all real masters do:
To help us remember that in all that matters
We are not only equal but originally innocent,
And that by seeing that splendor in each other's eyes
And in every being in the universe,
We will do what we were made to do!

Postscript

Thus speaks Michelangelo Buonarroti. His awe-inspiring code still lies unbroken on the wall of the Sistine Chapel, just as Leonardo's code lay unbroken in his *Last Supper*. Leonardo's code, discovered in that painting, has stirred much controversy. Truly that painting and its code are motivated by the same doubts of orthodoxy that motivated Leonardo's contemporary, Michelangelo Buonarroti.

Leonardo's brushwork suggests the humanness of Jesus' face, his rabbinical marriage and the burning of those gospels that portrayed him as married. These suggestions are revealed in the *Gospel According to Thomas*. John's gospel was most likely written to refute. John's gospel makes Jesus alone God. Thomas would have him fully human, a master among many masters, a brother of Thomas and of James the Just.

Thomas' Jesus says not that he is a Messiah, the anointed Christ come to die on the cross to save us from our sins, but that he speaks as a master to help us find the master in ourselves, to find the power to discover the self-evident truth in our own hearts.

Buonarroti goes further to suggest that the Jesus of orthodoxy in his judgmentalism is no savior at all, but Lucifer, a wolf in sheep's clothing, bent upon punishing the guilty.

The *Gospel According to Thomas* was not discovered until 1945 when Carl Jung was among those archeologists who confirmed the find at Nag Hammadi. Its existence had always been legendary.

Interlude

He Who Saves by Answering Those Who Call

Jesus the Nazarite
was born a Messiah
the heir to the empire,
servant of the god s on Earth,

But he chose to be a Jeseus
an alchemist of Al Chem
learned in the way of the Essenes
who saw the fullness of the presence
of the Manifesting Power
as the essence of every being.
In all the universe
including himself
and who dedicated his life
to awaken the awareness
of that presence in all
whom he encountered
and like the Bodhhisatva
he answers those who call.
The treasure of the alchemists
the Philospher's Stone
is the key to the true treasure
of the alchemist:
the Manifesting Power
who is found by those
who look within.

Canto XXXVI

Concordat

Time: Middle 16th Century CE

Time: Middle 16th Century CE
Place: Florence, Tuscany

Personae: Leonardo da Vinci
             Michelangelo Buonarroti

Scene 1: The Ponte Veccio bridge over the Arno River

Leo: Hey, Buonarroti!

Michel: Leonardo, is that really you?

Leo: Been a while! What brings you up to Etruscan country? Don't you have enough trouble in the Eternal City?

Michel: Perhaps I am fishing.

Leo: Am I the fish you are sent to catch?

Michel: You have heard of my good fortune, I see?

Leo: A few things. Quite close to the Bridge Builder, are you?

Michel: Perhaps too close, but, yes.

Leo: He's looking for heretics?

Michel: Not at all. He's too busy playing soldier to toy with dogmas.

Leo: Toying with soldiers too, is he?

Michel: Probably, cat's away and all.

Leo: Build his tomb yet?

Michel: No. He keeps me busy at other things. What about you? I hear you are dreaming up machines that fly and boats that swim like fish.

Leo: A thing or two. What I really like is this Greek Revival—livens up the place.

Michel: You mean Homer, the second Moses?

Leo: Yes, and all those attractive gods the Romans stole from the Greeks. Very phallic you know.

Michel: Phallic indeed. I hear you have a fountain here in Florence with Pan and the Nymphs in all his naked, horned, goat-footed glory, ripe grapes and all.

Leo: Yes, the brass is already green on most of the fountain, but many thumbs keep the phallus shiny.

Michel: Not very abstemious, I would say, but then Rome isn't very abstemious lately either. More orgiastic, I would say, perhaps in memory of the Great Goddess Lat.

Leo: I hear you finally let David out of his marble casket and sent tongues wagging and heads shaking.

Michel: Yes, and I hear you have brought Mary Magdalene down from Arles and put her almost in Jesus' lap at the Last Supper.

Leo: Sure you're not fishing?

Michel: The only fish I am liable to catch is me.

Leo: You up to something, like me?

Michel: I think I've gone way beyond just a married Jesus, Leonardo.

Leo: Really? I've had inclinations to suspect that our allegedly orthodox Lord is really a secret Gnostic. You have proof?

Michel: Enough to paint it.

Leo: Not a sculpture this time?

Michel: No. When I made an innocent Adam on the chapel ceiling it was a good start. I have little use for Paul's original sin, you know. There may be sin, but there is nothing original about it!

Leo: You are worse than I am. I think I could even get to like you! Tell me more.

Michel: Let's get a back table for a little vino somewhere, or you and I will be tried for conspiracy. Too many witnesses on this bridge, and I am sure there are orthodox conservatives here, even in the freedom of Etruscan country.

Scene 2: A small backstreet bistro

Leo: Let's get back to it. It's quiet here. A friend of mine runs this place, knows his customers, too.

Michel: Well, the real piece is not the ceiling that everybody's looking at, it's the reredos.

Leo: Hid it on the back wall, did you? Nobody's told me about that.

Michel: Yes. It's Jesus at the last judgment—not a very popular theme with all those paedophilic Popes, you know.

Leo: "Millstone around the neck" time you mean? Matthew 18:6?

Michel: Yes. "If anyone scandalizes one of these little ones, it were better for him that a millstone be hung around his neck and he be cast into the sea."

Leo: That reminds me of a story from Iceland about Amlodhi's (Hamlet's) Mill. It seems that Hamlet's Mill is the zodiac grinding little ones out of big ones, while the signs dance backward around the Pole star.

Michel: That's the deep sea indeed. No wonder the Romans killed all those Druids on the island of Mona!

Leo: Yes. That Francis of Assisi fellow was very fond of Druids and Cathars, as you know. Brother sun, sister moon and all that. It's a wonder Francis got out of Rome alive when he went there to ask Pope Innocent III leading questions. Gave them all quite a sermon, I understand.

Michel: Yes, like you and me, an egalitarian in a lion's den of heresiarchs.

Leo: I am an armchair anarchist myself, Buonarroti, as I am sure you know.

Michel: Many of us are. Artists and poets are fond of finding their own truth and make bad followers.

Leo: As do painters, but especially they would behead sculptors like you—iconoclasts to the scalp.

Michel: Cleansing the Kaaba Stone and all. They say the gods that Mohammed buried were a fine collection of statues of all the gods of India.

Leo: I've heard that. Best not stray south and east in search of commissions, Buonarroti.

Michel: Yes. Let's stay in Italy a while. The Islands of the Western Sea, as the Hebrews called it.

Leo: By the way, did the Hebrews like your Moses?

Michel: More or less, but they are not too fond of the horns.

Leo: You didn't!

Michel: Yes, I did. And I put them on that judgmental Jesus, too.

Leo: So, that's it? You painted the judgmental Jesus as Lucifer, the angel of light, populating his hell with goats? Splendid! Why didn't I think of that?

Michel: Well, Leonardo, we've had our disagreements, but it seems we have more in common than we thought.

Leo: I'm still not sure how much I like you, Buonarroti, but maybe our quarrels are behind us. Arrivederci!

212

Interlude

Moses! Take off your shoes,
the place you are standing is holy ground!

~ Exodus
(The burning bush to Moses at first encounter)

Was the fire of the burning bush spinning? Why wouldn't it give Moses its name? YHWH means, "I AM THAT I AM" but probably what Moses heard was "It's none of your business, Moses! I am not telling you my specific name." In that culture, at that time, it was understood that if you knew the name of a spirit, you could control it. Moses was not so favored by this particular spirit that Moses would be given that control. It does seem to admit it did have a name and would be vulnerable if Moses knew it. Consider that the burning bush is much like a deva or ahura of Earth energy flowing in a vortex up through Moses' bare feet and heart to enkindle, revealing the "voice" in his brain. (With shoes on, he could not hear so clearly what it had to say.)

Consider also that this "voice" was not entirely benevolent. It seemed fond of getting angry and was found frequently giving orders. On one occasion it shook the Earth and swallowed a whole line of priests who acted contrary to its inclinations. The Egyptian Abraxis was a god of both good and evil, and there has been much speculation that the Old Testament god acted like that: a sort of dualistic, even schizophrenic god, like Zoroaster's Ahura Mazda and Ahura Man. Ahura Man, who became Ahriman, the Christian antichrist of whom Fundamentalist Christians are so fond.

Could "burning bush" have a double meaning? Ahuras and devas are the same experiential spin of Earth energy that is capable of influencing human perception. If the spin is clockwise it is a blessing, if the spin is counterclockwise it is a curse—at least in the northern hemisphere. Have we lost the ability to distinguish good from evil?

Canto XXXVII

Democracy and Empire

Time: Autumn, 1775 CE
Place: Philadelphia
Personae: Benjamin Franklin
            Thomas Jefferson

Franklin: Had a frost yet down in Virginia at Montecello?

Jefferson: Not yet, but the nights are cool.

Franklin: Are there still slaves at Montecello?

Jefferson: Yes. But like Bartolomeo de las Casas, I consider them my equals and we have Sunday dinner together.

Franklin: How about your neighbors?

Jefferson: They do not approve of my egalitarianism, but neither do they reprove me as the conquistadors reproved Bartolomeo.

Franklin: Egalitarianism's the right word, Thomas. I left Boston because my egalitarianism was more radical than my neighbors'. In Boston you are a peer if you own your house, though it be small. The only true egalitarians are the Indians we dispossessed.

Jefferson: Yes. I remember how the French we drove out of Canada took ideas they learned from the Indians back to Paris. Rousseau honored our Indians as the "Noble Savage."

Franklin: Yes, Thomas. The French are closer to their Druid roots than we of English parentage. They remember better the true egalitarianism of their ancestors before the Romans came with their Empire, their hierarchy, and their male gods.

Jefferson: I noticed the ferment in the soirees; even the aristocrats feel the pressure to abandon hierarchy.

Franklin: Yes, unfortunately the merchants, who are the greatest force for change, believe equality means substituting commercial property for real estate as the basis for aristocracy.

214

Jefferson: I noticed that. At least the landed aristocracy have some sense of *noblesse oblige* which inclines them to want to relieve the plight of the disempowered. There is little sign of this sense of obligation among the merchants. I fear the immanence of a wave of indifference among the emerging ruling class toward those less fortunate.

Franklin: My point exactly. In my opinion the Boston Calvinists are not better, but worse in this respect.

Jefferson: Isn't it ironic that both Rousseau and Calvin are Frenchmen? Yet they represent polar opposites—what we feel is best and what we feel is worst in human nature?

Franklin: Unfortunately, Thomas, you and your adversary Hamilton seem to be similarly contrary in your positions.

Jefferson: Thank you, Ben. I never saw that so clearly before!

Franklin: For Hamilton, greed is a virtue. For you and me, greed is the mother and father of all vices. I fear his influence on the future of this nation, which is aborning in our hands.

Jefferson: Isn't it coincidental he bears the name of Alexander the Great, who brought the Empire over the Hellas-pont from Persia?

Franklin: I understand that Julius Caesar, as a young man in Spain, adopted that same Alexander as his "Patron Saint." And it was that very Julius Caesar who brought that same Empire westward to Rome?

Jefferson: Wouldn't you say we face that same Empire in our struggle against England and the tyrannical majesty George III?

Franklin: Well, as Plato said, the republic follows democracy, aristocracy follows the republic, oligarchy follows aristocracy, and tyranny follows oligarchy.

Jefferson: Then comes the revolution!

Franklin: We stand upon that threshold. I fear democracy is a fragile flower in a world where Empire is rampant.

Jefferson: And Christianity founded by a Roman Emperor is no help. It is clear that Constantine founded Christianity entirely for his own benefit, with little concern for the followers of the true Jesus.

Franklin: I agree with you. Haven't you written a book about that? I am sure the true Jesus was an egalitarian who never claimed to be the only one. And I am also sure that Paul is the hierarch in the lot who gave us the Church we struggle with today. That is why I am a Deist and believe all being comes from the Divinity. We do not confuse the Divinity with the god the Christians have made in their own image.

Jefferson: Ben, do you really hold that the Divinity is fully present in all men, no matter how great or small?

Franklin: I am much more of a radical than that. When I was last in Paris I met a Frenchman just back from Pondicherry in India. He told me that an old Indian master called Buddha proclaimed that the fullness of the Divinity, which he called "the Nameless," is fully present in every sentient being in the universe, and all beings are sentient.

Jefferson: Well, that makes my head spin! I am afraid we will find few takers among the Christians, and certainly none among the addicts of Empire, that is if there is any difference between the two.

Franklin: Tom, I think the only real difference between any of us is the degree to which we realize the presence of that ubiquitous Divinity in every being, especially humans. Perhaps all true education should be directed to realizing that end.

Jefferson: Ben, I think there may be a lot more to this. I read the Bible a lot and I have found several quotes in there I like.

Franklin: Just so you realize that you are dealing with three people: the author, the editor and the publisher, and you try to figure out who each of them are, and what the differences are in their agendas. I am a printer and publisher, after all.

Jefferson: Those things considered, one quote goes like this: "If today you should hear the voice, do not harden your heart against it as did your fathers in the desert of bitterness."

Franklin: We all hear voices—it's just a matter of which ones to listen to.

Jefferson: My Iroquois friends say all voices are the voices of your ancestors, but you have to watch out for the horse thieves.

Franklin: Well, since we started out here listening to the Iroquois, maybe we should listen to all of their ideas. They are surely a lot better than Hamilton's.

Jefferson: I am sure the merchants would never agree to that.

Franklin: Merchants, it seems, have never heard of *noblesse oblige* and are therefore dangerous candidates to become the ruling class.

Jefferson: Do you really believe that the self-evident truth is present in the heart of every person?

Franklin: Yes, I do, Thomas.

Jefferson: I see now why the French love you so! Are there any people on Earth so jealous of personal freedom as the French?

Franklin: Not that I know of, and I suspect the reason is that seldom has a greater tyrant emerged on Earth than Louis XIV. Next to him, our George pales in comparison! Nothing makes a better democrat than life under the heel of the Empire.

Interlude

Instead of a Deist, was Franklin perhaps a true Gnostic?
Or is Deist a synonym for Gnostic?
Did he choose to live in Philadelphia rather than his native Boston because the Quaker Meetings of that City of Brotherly Love proceed by unanimity as opposed to the tyranny of the majority?

... and that government of the people, by the people and for the people should not perish from the Earth.
~ Abraham Lincoln

We hold these truths to be self-evident, that all men are created equal, endowed by their creator with the inalienable right to life, liberty and the pursuit of happiness.
~ Declaration of Independence

When an ancient truth is rediscovered, it is first greeted with ridicule, then with violent opposition, but finally it is held to be self-evident.
~ Schopenhauer, courtesy of Noam Chomsky

All government should be exercised at the lowest possible level. Only thus can it serve first the needs of the governed. At other levels it serves first the needs of the Governors.
~ Principle of Subsidiarity, John XXIII

Canto XXXVIII

Priestly Power—The Forbidden Secret

Time: Summer, 1927
Place: A park in Vienna
Personae   Sigmund Freud
               Carl Jung

Jung: I cannot believe my good fortune. Dr. Freud, I believe?
Freud: And who might *you* be?
Jung: A fellow analyst, C.G. Jung.
Freud: Oh, yes, now I recall, the man with the "collective uncon-
           scious."
Jung: In a manner of nomenclature, yes.
Freud: What brings you to Vienna?
Jung: Its charms surely. Actually, I have come to ask to speak
           with you. I have just arrived by train and was on my way
           to inquire as to your whereabouts.
Freud: Well, I guess you have come to the right place.
Jung: I don't wish to inconvenience you. Perhaps another time
           would be better?
Freud: It is a good time. As you see, I am not occupied. A little
           good conversation is appropriate on a Sunday afternoon.
Jung: I certainly admire your work in psychoanalysis. It has
           taken the analytical world by storm.
Freud: I understand that you have had some success in the
           analysis of dreams and have traveled widely to inquire
           into the mythologies of many peoples.
Jung: Yes, I have come to many conclusions similar to yours,
           particularly the hypothesis of the triune nature of the
           human psyche—id, ego, and super ego.
Freud: Have you found parallels to them in your own research?
           And where, particularly?
Jung: To answer the second part of your question first, particu-
           larly in Hawaii.

219

The Hawaiians have a similar "trinity" to the one you put forward: *Unihipili, Uhane, Aumakua*. These words seem roughly analogous to the archetypes that you suggest. However, by studying the way Hawaiians use these words, I found subtle, but important differences. The first term *Unihipili* is the Hawaiian word much like our word geist, ghost or spirit. *Nihi* means sigh, and *Pili* means feel. We should note that, past all expectation, the Hawaiian language may come from the same roots as Indo-European languages.

Freud: Is this sequence, perhaps, part of the basis of your terms: individual unconscious, conscious, and collective unconscious?

Jung: I believe so. *Unihipili*, which means in Hawaiian touching, laughing, crying, feeling spirit, is comparable to the unconscious. The *Uhane* or the conscious mind is the part of the human that is conscious of its own existence and has the ability to reason. In the third term, *Aumakua*, *Aum* sounds similar to the Indian *Oum*, the trilateral most sacred form of Hindu chant. *Akua* is related to the word "acute" but in the sense of "focus." *Aku aku* means Holy Holy, as in the Hebrew *Kadosh, Kadosh*. So the root meaning of Aumakua might be, "Focus of the sacred OUM." The Hawaiian creation chant directly asserts that in their long migration from North Africa to the Pacific they spent 2,000 years in India.

Freud: That certainly expands the mind far beyond the limitations of a Christian Europe, or a Jewish Palestine, for that matter.

Jung: I had that problem, and still have to some degree. The most interesting part for me, and that related to my term "collective unconscious," is this: the petroglyph for aumakua, an image carved in stone, is usually eight stick-men standing in a circle. That suggests to me the old master formula, *E Pluribus Unum*—out of many, one, which is found on the great seal of the United States. It further suggests a Druidic coven in which people gathered together to achieve a common consciousness. The Hawaiians seem to perceive the other half of the master formula, *Ex Uno Plures*—out of one, many. That indicates that we all come from a sort of collective and are motivated to return to experiencing the collective from which we came.

Freud: Is that the basis of your term "collective unconscious?"

Jung: I am not sure, but it's *probable* that's it.

Freud: I see immediately that Jewish, Christian and Moslem theologians are going to make a pagan out of you for dividing up their god!

Jung: I fear that has already happened.

Freud: You mean the hateful mail and the threats, the hang-ups and the anonymous calls?

Jung: Yes, but at least, so far, nobody has come after me with a gun.

Freud: So far, those fellows have only come after me with ridicule. Perhaps I should count myself fortunate. Of course, I have not divided up their god; I have merely accused them of making their god in their own image.

Jung: Perhaps your truth is more self-evident than mine. Schopenhauer's quote sums it up nicely, "When an ancient truth is rediscovered, it is first greeted with ridicule, then violent opposition, and finally it is held to be self-evident."

Freud: This all sounds very refreshing to me after all the ponderous, logical and theological arguments and mumbo jumbo we Europeans get involved in.

Jung: Well, here's another controversial subject: what is a priest? The Greek word from which priest is taken is *presbuteros*, meaning elder. The Latin word, *Sacerdos*, is more helpful, a giver of sacredness, but the Hawaiian word is more practical still: it is *Kahuna*, meaning, Keeper of the Forbidden Secret.

Freud: What might that secret be, and why forbidden?

Jung: It took me a long time to find out, but I now surmise the secret involves how to use the power.

Freud: And what power is that?

Jung: For the Hawaiians it seems to mean the telepathic power to bless and to curse. The Hawaiians have a prayer called the "death prayer" that explains that. You only have to go to a hospital in Hawaii to see how effective the Black Kahuna curses are.

Freud: I take it you have done that?

Jung: Yes. I had only to mention the "death prayer," and the staff refused to speak to me further and asked me to leave. When I later asked a Hawaiian why, he laughed and said, "That is because there are still a lot of people showing up in the hospitals who have been cursed and they always die because the hospitals don't know how to treat them." I asked him if he knew how to treat them and he smiled and said, "Sure, it's easy, just go find a good Kahuna to talk the invading spirit out of the victim."

Freud: That suggests that the reason the power is forbidden is that it can be misused.

Jung: My conclusion exactly, and that causes me to wonder how many of the authorities in our part of the world are misusing it?

Freud: Well, if they are, one thing is certain, the Church seeks a monopoly.

Jung: A monopoly they acquired from the Roman Empire in large degree. I have learned a term for our bad Kahunas: Masters of Deceit. Just because you are a master of the power doesn't mean you will use it properly; you can also use it improperly.

Freud: Do you suppose that is what brought on the dark ages?

Jung: The Hawaiian creation myth suggests as much. They say their Kahuna coven was warned 5,000 years ago that an "Age of Darkness" was coming upon the world and that they should find a place to keep their secret safe during that time. They found the Hawaiian Islands standing unoccupied in the Pacific, but they didn't get there until at least 3,500 years later.

Freud: A remarkable discovery. I shall have to think about that.

Jung: On a different but related note, have you heard of the Buddhist revival in Germany?

Freud: I have heard of it but have not paid much attention. As I'm sure you know, I am very suspicious of all religions and especially of religious controversy of any kind. They all seem to be arguing about which lie is more unbelievable than some other lie. What do you think?

Jung: After seeing what being a Lutheran minister did to my father and what following his teachings has done to me, I have concluded that Christianity is the illness that we are.

Freud: You can add Judaism and Islam to that list as far as I am concerned. But what illness are we, to put it in analytical terms?

Jung: Schizophrenia, I opine, and in all three of its "incarnations."

Freud: You mean bi-polar, schizoid and schizophrenic?

Jung: Clearly.

Freud: You know what they say: a bipolar person can curse you, a schizoid can maul you, and a schizophrenic can kill you!

Jung: How many people has Christianity killed for disagreeing with their dogmas?

Freud: Many millions, and surely Islam is no better, and in their time of power, neither were the Jews.

Jung: I am afraid you and I would not be welcome in church, mosque or synagogue.

Freud: That is certain. So tell me more about your Hawaiian trinity, Unihipili, Uhane and Aumakua. Didn't the Druids have something like that?

Jung: Yes, come to think of it. The signet of all the Celtic nations is the *triskel*—*tris* is three; *skel* means ray, combined, it is the three rays.

Freud: Any idea what the rays are or what they do?

Jung: Yes, I think they are about one power that has three aspects in manifesting the cosmos—the force aspect, the life aspect, and the awareness aspect.

Freud: From my study of Greek, I think I read something in Pythagoras about that: Pi, Phi, and Psi.

Jung: Very interesting. Pi—the flow of energy, Phi—the quality of life, and Psi—the reflection of consciousness. That seems to be very nearly my trinity as well: individual unconscious, individual conscious, and collective unconscious. It could also be stated Unihipili—individual unconscious, Uhane—individual conscious, and Aumakua—collective unconscious.

Freud: Perhaps there's also a connection to my idea of id, ego and super ego. It seems to me we are all on the same track, but none of us has the entire picture.

Jung: If we are trying to be whole and less schizophrenic, perhaps that is what "wholiness" is about.

Freud: There you go on that religious business again.

Jung: I take it you've had enough of the Holy Roman Empire?

Freud: Indeed. I was very relieved when they sent the Hapsburgs packing after the last war, but I'm not sure I can go along with you on this "collective" business that you attach to my super ego.

Jung: That is what I have really come to see you about, but perhaps we tax a Sunday afternoon too dearly, especially on such a fine day. Shall we adjourn and speak again?

Freud: By all means! I have heard there was an American who said, "I may disagree with what you say, but I will defend to the death your right to say it!" Tomorrow morning at my place then?

Jung: So gut! Bis morgen, mein herr!
(Very good! Until tomorrow then, dear sir!)

Interlude

A coven seeks the unanimity of bonding.

Empowerment comes from the union with the Manifesting Power.

Canto XXXIX

The Illness That We Are

Time: The next day
Place: The parlor of Freud's home
Personae: Sigmund Freud
            Carl Jung

Freud: Good morning, Herr Jung, very prompt I see.

Jung: I trust you slept well?

Freud: Do you mean dreamed well?

Jung: I would not presume to ask.

Freud: Why not? You've asked everyone else you know, haven't you?

Jung: Remember Hamlet? "The dream's the thing in which I'll catch the conscience of the king?"

Freud: You mean Uhane I suppose? Seriously, I did dream about your Aumakua, just don't ask me what. What was it, Unihipili, Uhane and Aumakua? And you liken them to my id, ego and super ego, and to your individual unconscious, individual conscious and collective unconscious?

Jung: Yes, and there is another story about this "trinity" that may interest you. It seems the Hawaiians agree with you that the ego is the problem. They say the Uhane is very proud, and refuses to admit that the Aumakua exists because nothing could be higher up than the Uhane. He is willing to admit Unihipili exists because he is obviously inferior. So Aumakua talks to Unihipili and teaches him very intelligent games—children's games. Uhane notices the games and realizes there must be someone else around. Whereupon Aumakua suggests that he is that someone. If Uhane can keep from denying that, they all begin to communicate and live happily ever after. If, on the other hand, Uhane bolts and goes into denial, the man may die separated.

Freud: That seems more acceptable than hell and purgatory. Does it open a door to reincarnation?

Jung: That seems to be what is implied in some sense.

Freud: Would that make the unconscious the mediator between the collective unconscious and the ego?

Jung: Brilliant! I had never looked at it that way exactly. Surely the ego or conscious is not much of a communicator, except for the purpose of establishing its superiority over the other. And surely it is through the individual unconscious that the collective unconscious communicates with the conscious.

Freud: I see possibilities there. Let's look at the separation. Let's start with the word schizophrenia. It comes from the Greek verb *skizo*, pronounced 'skidzo.' It means to divide.

Jung: Are you aware that the original meaning of the verb *skizo* was to divide into twelve parts?

Freud: The twelve signs of the zodiac, do you suppose? Something to do with astrology, that bugaboo of the scientists? Perhaps it also suggests twelve as the usual number of multiple personalities?

Jung: Could we not also hypothesize that the function of the collective unconscious is to unite, so the function of the individual conscious is to divide? The intuition asserts, the intellect denies. Is that denial scientific doubt?

Freud: Perhaps one could say that the intuition works primarily through the id, or individual unconscious, or the Unihipili, while the intellect works primarily through the conscious, or the ego. The super conscious, or collective unconscious or Aumakua communicates the intuition to the id.

Jung: It seems that the conscious is like Michelangelo's chisel, that chips away the great inspirations into a shape that the senses can comprehend.

Freud: It is also probable that the word *skizo* and the word *conskio* are originally identical, one in Greek and the other in Latin.

Jung: That would have to do with individuation, the means by which the individual perceives himself as separate from the collective.

Freud: We are clearly not dealing with dualism here, a term perceived as a negative, but with duality.

Jung: Exactly, unity and separation, though clearly correlative opposite terms, are not to be regarded as opposing one another in a moral sense.

Freud: Then schizophrenia, perhaps an extremely negative term, achieves its negativity not because of its essential function, but because of exaggeration.

Jung: Though not so obvious, I would also suggest that reconciliation, an essentially positive term, can also become a negative term by exaggeration.

Freud: I am afraid we dare not publish such discoveries for fear that no one will understand them.

Jung: I propose we should publish them anyway because some people will understand them, and the understanding of the few can catalyze the perception of the many.

Freud: Let us speak more about schizophrenia. Are you suggesting that present-day Christianity is the major cause of the schizophrenic epidemic in the world, particularly as expressed in America?

Jung: Yes, I trace schizophrenia to Calvinism. My father was a Calvinist, albeit a Lutheran Calvinist. I watched his anguished attempts to reconcile his religion with his truth. That conflict destroyed his life.

Freud: Being from Catholic Vienna, I have not had much experience of Calvin. Was he Swiss? I understand he ruled Geneva for a long time.

Jung: No, he was French, and he studied to be Roman Catholic priest in Paris during Lutheran times. Calvin's teachings remind me of a radical school of Islam which holds that there is no fate in Islam, you know, only destiny. That is, all is the will of Allah and no matter what you do, you can't change it. It's called *kismet*—no free will at all. Destiny can't be changed, but fate can.

Freud: Doesn't that relate to the Greek myth of Arachnia, the spider woman, who spins a web in which the material of the web is destiny and the spaces are fate?

Jung: That's the one. In truth, it is the mystery of freedom. Logically it cannot be resolved. How can God know all, past, present, and future and yet leave you free to change the future? Destiny may be more logical, but the social consequences can be disastrous—if you can't change the future, why bother trying?

Freud: Yes, and those who don't bother trying are slaves.

Jung: My opinion exactly. Belief in destiny can pave a road to despair, bitterness, schizophrenia and a death wish. Your only defense is not to think about it, but it will still push you into what I call schizophrenic denial. And please understand that I am using the word schizophrenia according to the etiological meaning of the word and not the accepted clinical definition.

Freud: So is this what John Calvin preached in Geneva?

Jung: I have seen copies of sermons delivered by Calvin in the Cathedral of Lausanne on the north shore of Lake Geneva. If you go in there you will see pews with scratches all over their backs, and signs in French, German, Italian and English. They read: "It is said that these scratches were made by the fingernails of those listening to John Calvin preach."

Freud: Why?

Jung: Here is a sample of his type of sermon: "We are a *Massa Damnata*, a damned mass, we are all born sinners and corrupt, and not even God can change it. We are all doomed to go to Hell and suffer for all eternity.

    "But God is lonely, and like King Saul, needs people to console him, people to stand upon the streets of gold before his throne in the Holy City and sing his praises. Therefore, God has chosen some of us for this privilege. Of course we are evil and God can't change that, so he will cover his elect with a white garment to conceal the evil that we are.

    "You may ask, then, why are we here? We are here to find out whether God has chosen us or not. How can you tell? You get rich! Only the rich go to heaven, everyone else goes to hell."

Freud: Astonishing! In that case, greed is the primary virtue!

Jung: To conclude the litany, "Greed is a virtue; murder in pursuit of Greed is not a crime; and the end justifies the means as long as you get rich!"

Freud: I assume your father didn't get rich?

Jung: No, he didn't. I am also sure that no one has ever been so wrong as John Calvin.

Freud: Didn't Calvin have a Scotsman as a fiery apostle?

Jung: Yes, John Knox, the one who cursed Mary Queen of Scots as her Catholic majesty arrived in Scotland. He also tore down the cathedral at St. Andrews with his bare hands. Madman is too kind an epithet for him. Wouldn't you call that schizophrenia?

Freud: Didn't he found the Church of Scotland, the Presbyterian Church, and didn't that Church form the basis of Christianity in America?

Jung: I am afraid so. I have heard that America has the highest rate of schizophrenia in the world, and that a majority of schizophrenics in America are women.

Freud: No doubt because women find themselves more naturally opposed to such negativity than men.

Jung: That is what I surmise. I also fear that America will soon lead the world, and that the leadership of America will become completely Calvinist.

Freud: Then we may expect America to follow the lead of Pope Innocent III at Bezier in his famous reply to Simon de Montfort as he besieged the Cathars, "Kill them all, and let God sort them out!"

Interlude

The co-relative opposite of schizophrenia is integrity.

Canto XL

In Hoc Signo Vinces:

In This Sign You Will Conquer

Time: 1927, the Reign of Pius XI, Achille Ratti
Place: Rome, near the Vatican Hill
Personae: Francesco Pacelli, Brother of Eugenio Pacelli,
Vatican Delegate
             Domenico Barone, Delegate of Benito
             Mussolini
Setting: Negotiations precedent to the
             Lateran Pact of 1929

Barone: I have heard that your brother Eugenio may be Pope
         some day!
Pacelli: There are such intimations, but our respect for his
         Holiness Pius XI, Achille Ratti, restrains us from such
         speculations.
Barone: Ah, true. *Romani-ta* I understand. Is not Pius XI of the
         same family as Michelangelo? I believe his last name was
         Buonarroti.
Pacelli: Perhaps, Florentines all, but, though similar, the names
         are probably not the same.
Barone: Signor Pacelli, could you help me to remember the histo-
         ry of *fasces*, since our good Benito Mussolini, who boldly
         ordered these talks, has chosen to use it in the name of his
         party, "fascist"?
Pacelli: It is a very old word indeed, and very much involved in
         the origin of the Roman Empire, which Il Duce wishes to
         restore as Master of the Mare Nostrum (the
         Mediterranean), with himself in the role of emperor.
Barone: He speaks often and publicly of such aspirations.
Pacelli: We must go very far back indeed, perhaps a thousand
         years before the birth of Our Lord, when Rome was but a
         pagan village in the plain of Latium. Are you familiar
         with the word faggot?

232

Barone: Of course. It's a bundle of dry sticks tied with twine found in the Roman village three thousand years ago, is it not?

Pacelli: Precisely. Such faggots are still used to feed cooking fires in most of the world where people lack axes for larger wood.

It is said the Romans were very democratic and ruled by covens of women. Their towns had no walls and no wars, a situation in common with the Etruscan territory on the Arno River. All went well until raiders came riding on horses out of the north and began to help themselves to the goods of the villagers who had no means to resist.

Barone: The Alps were porous even then?

Pacelli: Apparently so. At some point the Romans, tired of being helpless, called a meeting to decide what to do. Someone asked, "What are we going to do?" Someone else answered, "Get horses!" It probably took a generation to get the horses and another generation to learn how to use them. Horses, you know, are late-comers to the Mediterranean. King Saul had no horses, only donkeys. Horses came into Italy as they did into Palestine, from the north and east.

Barone: Riding on horses? I understand the Chinese have a character for that.

Pacelli: The word for horse in Latin is *equus,* from which comes our word equal. A patrician was originally someone who owned a horse, a plebian did not. Horses made Rome a patriarchal, hierarchical society.

Barone: Remarkable! Might not one say all horses are equal, but some horses are more equal than others? We adopted such a premise in meetings of the fascist party.

Pacelli: I would not recommend you bringing that up at a meeting of bishops.

In any event, there was another meeting, a meeting of horse owners, one from each *gens.* A gens is a sort of extended family.

Barone: *Nostra famiglia.* Are you sure you are not from Sicily?

Pacelli: I don't think so, but in those days perhaps all Italy looked south to Magna Graecia, of which Sicily was a major part. Back to the meeting, the presiding person had brought two battle-axes left behind by the raiders. He asked someone to bring him a faggot. He untied it and handed a stick

233

to each participant. Then he ostentatiously broke the handle of one axe over his knee, held it up and said, "See? Useless. Now bring me back those sticks!" He tied them together around the handle of the other axe and held up the result. "Now let's see if anyone can break this *fasces* over their knee." There was a broken knee or two, but no broken handle. He held up the axe and proclaimed, "From faggot to *fasces*: *In Hoc Signo Vinces*. From now on, in this sign we will conquer."

Barone: As I recall, a soldier called a *lictor* carried a *fasces* with the motto before every Roman legion wherever they marched, a *fasces* in silver effigy.

Pacelli: Yes, and Constantine reported seeing that motto in Greek, *In to-o Nik-e*, written around a cross of crucifixion. He saw it in the rising sun sometime before winning the battle of Milvian Bridge, up the Tibur River from here.

Barone: Was Constantine ever baptized? I understand he was a Mithraist and his god was *Sol Invictus*, the Unconquered Sun. Isn't the chief Mithraeum down under the Vatican hill here?

Pacelli: Signor Barone, mercy for the sake of *Romani-ta*, please!

Barone: An Italian, especially a Roman one, should know that diplomacy is the art of telling the truth with all the benefits of lying. A thousand pardons, Signor Pacelli.

Pacelli: Does this story sound familiar to you?

Barone: As a matter of fact, Il Duce tells the same story himself. He has no *gens*. Instead, he has our Italian corporations. He intends to bind the corporations around himself as sticks were bound around the battle-axe and restore the Roman Empire.

Pacelli: Since the Church is the mother and father of all corporations I suppose we are here to make the Church one of his faggots?

Barone: Precisely, Signor Pacelli. The Church will serve as his principal faggot, and he will make it worth your while and worth ours, as well.

Pacelli: How will he do that?

Barone: By pacifying the spirit of Pio Nono, Pius IX, who is said to moan about St. Peters at night, lamenting Garibaldi's theft of the Papal States. Il Duce wishes to make the Vatican a sovereign nation and to give you a billion lire to boot in government bonds, contributed by the corporations, of course.

Pacelli: Perhaps we can do business. It seems you have made us an offer we cannot refuse.

Postscript

Before the end of his life, Mussolini said in a public speech, "I should not have called it fascism. I should have called it corporatism."

Interlude

Essence is implicit in existence
As consciousness is implicit in all unconsciousness.

Or

Consciousness is implicit in unconsciousness
As essence is implicit in existence
Because sentience is implicit in what appears as insentient
Because the Manifesting Power is fully present in all manifestations.

So behold the Manes, the spirits of those who have gone before.
They are our assurance that immortality of the spirit is inevitable
in every being,
As time and space are illusions in the ubiquity of now.

Canto XLI

Self-Evident

Time   Circa 1930
Place: New York City
Personae: Justice Benjamin N. Cardozo
              Justice Oliver Wendell Holmes

Holmes: I appreciate your giving me this time.
Cardozo: I am sure, Justice Holmes, that by any scale your time is more valuable than my own!
Holmes: Jurisprudence! That most neglected and yet most vital aspect of the law. That is why I have come to speak to you.
Cardozo: My experience of law school was identical. Like equity, jurisprudence was treated with reverence but never adequately defined to my satisfaction. Much time was spent on Constitutional Law, yet I don't recall ever having any discussion of the relationship between jurisprudence and Constitutional Law.
Holmes: Nor I. Maybe we need to go back to Mr. Blackstone and the Common Law of England.
Cardozo: Remedies! My favorite course in law school!
Holmes: Mine too, and, as I remember, most of my fellow students found it superfluous. Perhaps it is the poet in us that is fascinated by the law as metaphor.
Cardozo: Or perhaps the bard is truer to that which is larger than his own voice. It always seemed to me that history is better sung by Homer and Shakespeare than told by historians preoccupied with war and religion.
Holmes: Bravo! Then let's look at Shakespeare's time. In those days, law was for the King's Court and equity was for the Church Court.
Cardozo: And the purpose of equity was to examine the judicial decisions—to see whether they violated standards of "fundamental fairness" by considering "subjective factors," even *spiritual* ones, as well as strictly legal principles. It was a broad appeal process that looked for more

237

than errors in the legal process. It also looked at jurisprudential considerations.

Holmes: Precisely. Now that we have separated church and state, the courts have combined both processes as "courts of law and equity."

Cardozo: On top of that, the codification process has steadily eroded the judicial process by narrowing the scope of judicial discretion, an unanticipated negative side effect of "government of laws and not of men."

Holmes: Ah, yes, the "positive law" as opposed to "common law." The positive law is what the emperor said it was or now, what the legislature says it is. Common law is what everyone remembers, unwritten law, tribal authority, an attempt to mitigate the Roman law or positive law. Should we speak of the negative effects of positive law? And which is the law of nature?

Cardozo: That reminds me of the noble obligation problem, which is well stated in the Grosvenor's motto: *Virtus non Stemma*, "Only those who do by nature what *noblesse oblige* requires are truly noble." And is it not noble to listen to your heart before you pronounce the law?

Holmes: Indeed. So, who is more likely to listen to lobbyists—the legislator thinking about the next election, or the judge who remains until removed?

Cardozo: And who is more likely to be motivated solely by greed than a lobbyist? Perhaps you are familiar with what Erasmus said at the beginning of the *Enlightenment*, "For the Lord Jesus, contrary to the opinion of many, came to restore the Law of Nature as opposed to Natural Law."?

Holmes: Whereas the Church sees Jesus as establishing the Natural Law rather than serving the Law of Nature!

Cardozo: Should we restate the difference between the two?

Holmes: With a bow to a sense of humor, I'd put it like this: The Law of Nature is how things work, and the Natural Law is how the Church says that Jesus says that God says it works.

Cardozo: Very bardic, Mr. Justice Holmes. Both Homer and Shakespeare would be proud of you.

Holmes: It seems that though you can separate church and state by keeping the bishops out of secular government, you can't separate religion and politics. Since the law is mostly about contracts, bonding between promises, and religion is about bonding in general, we really have a conundrum here.

Cardozo: In my fraternity at college there was a rule that at the dinner table you could discuss anything but religion, politics and sex, the fear being that dinner would likely be interrupted by a fist fight if you did.

Holmes: I think the problem is really the difference between faith and knowledge. Faith is far more uncertain and fragile because you have to believe what you are told. Knowledge is much more solid in that it is based on what you personally remember.

Or perhaps there are two kinds of faith: one is the usual faith in what you are told, and the other faith is in your own power to know the truth in your own heart.

Cardozo: Such knowledge is a lot more humble, as a rule, because most of us are willing to acknowledge we might be wrong. But doesn't the Church arrogantly claim to be infallible? And do they not require you to believe them and not your own heart?

Holmes: The Church has a lock on that, especially since the time of Garibaldi and Pius IX who codified infallibility for himself by nefarious manipulation of the Council.

Cardozo: The Protestants are no better off since they have replaced the Pope with the Bible as their infallibility and are quite willing to kill those who disagree with them, at least in former times. Faith in charlatans is even more dangerous, and more productive of fanatical conduct.

Holmes: All of which points out why all the founding fathers, especially Ben Franklin, styled themselves Deists and not Christians. A Deist is really a Gnostic, and Gnostics, it seems, are not so prone to fanatical conduct, at least nowadays.

Cardozo: Deists shy away from the term Gnostic because to claim oneself so was the heresy of heresies among Christians, as defined by Irenaeus of Lyon in the second century.

Holmes: As I recall, when Jefferson handed the draft of the Declaration of Independence to Franklin, who was the Grand Master of the Philadelphia Masonic Lodge, he crossed out a word which Jefferson had used and inserted "self-evident." The revised document then read: "We hold these truths to be *self-evident*, that all men are created equal, endowed by their creator with the inalienable right to life, liberty and the pursuit of happiness."

Cardozo: Very Gnostic, indeed. That is the very essence of Gnosticism or Deism: "Every human being is capable of discovering the self-evident truth in his own heart."

Holmes: Whereas orthodox Christianity insists that if there is a conflict between their stated beliefs and the truth in your own heart, you must believe what they tell you and not what you remember, or you'll go to hell in a hand basket.

Cardozo: I see now that Positive Law and orthodox faith have a lot in common.

Holmes: As do Common Law and Gnosticism.

Cardozo: The Law of Nature is Gnostic, and Natural Law is Orthodox.

Holmes: Do you see other aspects of the present legal system that are mostly Gnostic?

Cardozo: Two, immediately—judicial notice and the jury system.

Holmes: How so?

Cardozo: Well, judicial notice means that the principle involved is self-evident and the judge must acknowledge its truth without evidential proof. The jury system requires unanimity in certain cases and not tyranny of the majority.

Holmes: Mr. Justice Cardozo, this nation is in a lot of trouble. We are in the process of losing every trace of democracy and returning to that very tyrannical absolutism of Empire from which our founding fathers sought to separate us.

Cardozo: I agree, Mr. Justice Holmes. Democracy is based upon the principle that all of us are equal and able to find the truth in our own heart, especially by perceiving it through unanimity in an assembly. Or, as once was said by Sam Terman, "If most people were not by nature above the law, there would be no law."

Holmes: And without such understanding we will relapse into a tyranny that is likely to be more absolute than the one we rebelled against.

Cardozo: Looking across the Atlantic to Germany, Italy, Spain, and Russia I see the process of tyranny advancing there as well.

Holmes: I fear tyranny will be our fate unless our people are educated once again to dream the dream our founders passed on to us at the cost of so much personal sacrifice.

Interlude

A nation is a dream, a dream that will perish for lack of dreamers
to dream the dream that the nation is.

So what is a true patriot?
Someone who dreams that dream—and not just sometimes.

E pluribus unum
Out of many, one
Out of many dreams one dream.

Ex uno plures
Out of one, many
Out of one dream many dreamers.

Out of many dreamers with one dream—a true nation.

Canto XLII

Supercalifragilistic
Androhermaphrogenous Expialidosious

I have never coveted affluence and luxury and even despised them a good deal. I have always had a high regard for the individual and have an inseparable distaste for violence and clubmanship. All these motives made me a passionate pacifist and anti-materialist. I am against any nationalism, even in the guise of mere patriotism. Social equality and economic protection of the individual appeared to me always as the most important communal aim of the state. Although I am a typical lover in daily life, my consciousness of belonging to that invisible community of those who strive for truth, beauty and justice has preserved me from being isolated.

The most beautiful and deepest experience a man can have is the sense of the mysterious. It is the underlying principle of religion as well as the senior endeavor in art and science. He who never had this experience seems to me, if not dead, then at least blind. I sense that behind anything that can be experienced there is something that our mind cannot grasp and whose beauty and sublimity reaches us only indirectly and as a feeble reflection; this is religiousness. In this sense I am religious. To me, it suffices to wonder at these secrets and to attempt humbly to grasp with my mind a mere image of the lofty structure of all that there is.

~ Speech of Albert Einstein to the
German League of Human Rights – 1932

Time: October 1938
Place: Zurich, Switzerland
Personae: Carl Jung
               Emma Jung
               Albert Einstein
Setting: Kussnacht, residence of Carl and Emma Jung

243

Carl:	Sunday! The day of the Solar Hero.
Emma:	Carl, we have much to celebrate.
Carl:	Emma, what I wish to celebrate today is my gratitude to you for your patience all these years.
Emma:	I'll confess, it has not been easy, Carl. But, I suppose, being married to a true holy man never is.
Carl:	Dear Emma, it takes one to know one. And if I am holy it is largely because you were there before me.

Doorbell rings.

Carl:	The doorbell! And at nine o'clock, who could it be?
Carl::	Let me find out.

Opens door.

Carl:	You look familiar. Have we met?
Albert:	Long ago. Albert Einstein here.
Emma:	Dr. Einstein, my husband will be so pleased!

Einstein enters as Carl Jung approaches.

Carl:	What a surprise! How delightful! I had understood you were in America now.
Albert:	Maybe I am bi-locating! No, I'm just home to Basel on a visit. Great affairs are moving across the German border, affairs that bode ill for the peace of the world; affairs for which people of my persuasion are very threatened indeed. I am not here for that reason. However I do need your counsel on another matter.
Carl:	No better way to start a week than to be asked for counsel by the world's greatest living genius.

They shake hands and embrace.

Albert:	As a preliminary, Carl, I understand that beginning with your travails concerning your father you have diagnosed Christianity as "the illness that we are." Is that correct?
Carl:	Very much so, I regret to say.
Albert:	Would you extend that diagnosis to Judaism?
Carl:	I would not presume, being brought up by a Lutheran father with grim Calvinist leanings. Since I've heard it said, "Roses are reddish and violets are bluish and if it wasn't for Jesus we could all be Jewish," perhaps I could hypothesize a similar diagnosis.
Albert:	And what about Islam?

244

Carl: Since the Koran has made all three fellow religions "Religions of the Book," a similar hypothesis could extend in that direction.

Albert: Now, since we are all tarred with the same brush and inheritors of the same virus that produces "the illness that we are," would you be so bold as to say what that illness might be called in psychiatry?

Carl: Schizophrenia.

Albert: Ah! Just what I thought. That is why I am here.

Carl: Really? I hope you don't take this too personally.

Albert: Since you obviously take it personally, my dear Carl, could you really object if I do also?

Carl: Thank you, I suppose not! Is there another reason, Albert?

Albert: Yes, we are all getting on and people are beginning to wonder about what they call "my genius." I have been asked by some prestigious medical people in America to allow my brain to be dissected when I die to see if there is something physically unusual about it.

Carl: A bit ghoulish of them. So how did you respond to their request?

Albert: I said, "Yes, but would you mind telling me what you are looking for?"

Carl: And what did they say?

Albert: I imagine you've heard about the hypothesis of the bicameral mind?

Carl: Yes, of course. But what is the relationship between genius, schizophrenia and the bicameral mind?

Albert: Actually, Carl, they now hypothesize that it may be a tricameral mind.

Carl: You mean the frontal lobes? Right brain, left brain and the corpus callosum connecting the right brain to the left?

Albert: Yes, exactly. The right brain connected to the left hand and the left brain connected to the right hand and the corpus callosum connecting the right brain to the left!

Carl: So, they want to check you out to see how big these lobes are in your head?

Albert: Something like that. It seems one of their researchers has hypothesized that the most important lobe is the corpus callosum. It is something like Taoism, on which, I understand, you've done a lot of work. Yin, yang, Tao—yin

245

being right brain, yang being left, and Tao being like the corpus callosum. That is, Tao is more, much more, than yin and yang combined, having, as it does, the power to balance opposites.

Carl: Did you ever think about the word Is-ra-el in this respect?

Albert: Strange that you should say that. Yes, because as you are suspicious of dogmatic conformity in Christianity, so am I suspicious of such conformity in Judaism.

Carl: For that reason I offer the story of Jacob wrestling with the angel as an apt metaphor. In my view it is Jacob's struggle with himself, his left brain grappling with the right. I see Jacob, the man, as the left brain; I see Jacob, the angel, as the right brain; and the struggle is in the corpus callosum—Ish-Ra-El or "*Man-Fights-God.*"

Albert: Carl, my friend, I confess I have thought of that, but my unacknowledged orthodoxy would not let it come clear. Thank you! Now, let me see if I recall correctly. The angel said to Jacob, "Let me go for the sun is rising." And Jacob replies, "I will never let you go unless you bless me." Whereupon the angel kneed Jacob in the groin and dislocated his hip so that he limped the rest of his life. He then added, "Oh, all right. I will no longer call you Jacob, the supplanter, but Is-ra-el, because you have fought with God and prevailed."

Carl: And how prevailed? Because the left lobe, through the work of the middle lobe, has chiseled the massive insight of the right lobe into a concept workable in the manifested world. Tell me Albert, how large do they think your corpus callosum is, or do they say?

Albert: What they expect to find is that my left and right lobes are normal size and that my corpus callosum will be up to four times normal size.

Carl: In other words genius is not so much in the capacity for infinite attention to detail as it is in the power to reconcile apparent opposites.

Emma: If I may interject, are there differences between men and women in these respects?

Albert: Yes, but let me just remark first that the reconciliation of apparent opposites sounds something like the cure for schizophrenia to me.

Carl:	As Winston Churchill would say, "Bully!"
Emma:	May I speculate that the right brain and corpus callosum tend to be larger in women and the left lobe larger in men?
Albert:	That is precisely what I have heard.
Carl:	This awakens in me what I have found in the analysis of 70,000 dreams and in the examination of many of the surviving mythologies of the world, on site—the prevalence of the ideal of the Divine Hermaphrodite!
Emma:	I was talking the other day with our friend, Irma Klopfer, about how we women must deal with our men, because our men are so afraid of the feminine in themselves. She said to me, "Emma, I think it's because we all know in our hearts, whether we are a man or a woman, that it is the feminine part of us that is more intuitive, and therefore, as a man, you fear that power and are in denial of that fear. This plays havoc with the honesty that alone is the support of honor."

I replied to her, invoking the Divine Hermaphrodite of which you speak as the ideal of our perception of ourselves: "We should not fear what we are; we should only be circumspect of how we put our power into play."

Albert:	In the last century we used to speak of our wives as our "better halves." It would have been *better* if we had acknowledged that even though our wives might represent our better half, the feminine half is as surely in us men as it is in you women. Unfortunately, our own feminine power has been suppressed by our very fear of it.
Carl:	In those societies that survive still as representatives of the Golden Age so commended by Plato and Pythagoras, I have found examples of nations in which this balance is not only honored, but forms the very basis of the society itself.
Albert:	Then if my right brain and my left brain are the same size, perhaps my corpus callosum, after a fashion, maintains the balance between them. So, perhaps, the larger the better!
Emma:	If I may be so bold, Dr. Einstein, do you ever attend movies in America?
Albert:	Seldom, but occasionally.

Emma: Have you ever heard of a movie called *Mary Poppins?**

Albert: Yes, I have actually seen it. Why?

Emma: Well, that Disney movie was based on a book written by a woman of my acquaintance who is familiar with the uses of telepathic power. What did you think of it?

Albert: It was delightful and appealed to what I like to call my innocence.

Emma: Do you remember the catch phrase, "Supercalifragilistic Expialidosious?"

Albert: Doesn't everybody?

Emma: Did you ever decipher that as a code?

Albert: No, but now that you mention it, I almost did.

Emma: Super-cali-fragilistic means "super fragile, breaks easily." Expiali-dosious means "a dose of expiation." It's about expiating your fragility.

Carl: Remarkable, Emma! That certainly is how to deal with that primal fear that disorients and disempowers us men.

Emma: Yes, Carl, but there was another word, one the editors took out: androhermaphrogenous. It went like this: Supercalifragilistic Androhermaphrogenous Expialidosious. Or, super fragility is expiated by access to androhermaphrogenous power.

Albert: So that is what my corpus callosum is, androhermaphrogenous? But, being a man, I am shy about using it?

Carl: Let's see, *Andros* is Greek for man; *Hermes* is the male god of love; *Aphrodite* is the female goddess of love and *gyn-e* means woman—all Greek words. A very incarnation of the Divine *Herm-aphrodite* in which all powers are reconciled.

Albert: This is all quite fascinating, but I must return to addressing the purpose of my visit. The maniac across your northern border is trying to build an atom bomb; I have to convince our president, Mr. Roosevelt, to beat him to it.

* *This is an anachronism as* Mary Poppins *was released in 1964.*

Interlude

The quester is the fool   34
Who seeks the truth in the world outside   21
But who fails to find it there   13
Until she finds it in himself   8
And thus she is changed   5
Into what he always was   3
While the world opines   2
That she has become
A fool.

Canto XLIII

Myth and Spirituality

Time: 1950
Place: A Stanford University lecture hall
Personae: Professor
           Students

Prof: Good morning, class. Today we're going to discuss the vast concepts of myth, spirituality and the Manifesting Power. Carl Jung, in his *Secrets of the Golden Flower* writes: "In so doing he, Wilhelm, has given me the courage to write about a Chinese text, which, though belonging, in essence, to the mysterious shadows of the oriental mind, at the same time—and this is important—shows striking parallels to the course of psychic development in my patients, none of whom is Chinese. In order to make this strange fact more intelligible to the reader, it must be mentioned that just as the human body shows common anatomy over and above all racial differences, so too does the psyche possess a common substratum."

       What do you think Jung is saying? Could he be saying it is probable that the "common substratum" lies within the psyche of every sentient being in the manifested universe?

Pupil: This is something like the relationship between "quantum" and "relativity" that I'm studying in physics.

Prof.   It is, but one must tread carefully here. Terrestrial manifestation is clearly a comparison, a metaphor, for some underlying principle. Western mindset looks primarily at the dualistic, material side of reality as primary emergence.

       There is a great controversy as to which comes first as cause in the universe, matter or spirit. Conventionally, matter is assumed to be cause of spirit. Upon reflection it is quite clear that matter is the effect and spirit is the cause even though it is also true that matter is also cause of what might be called a secondary spirit.

The oriental view is that matter is a manifestation of spirit or energy, spirit being matter personified. Today, quantum physics impels us to this recognition and to take the oriental view very seriously. It is also very confusing to us because our received doctrine is largely based on materialistic assumptions.

Pupil: You mentioned a metaphor earlier. Would you define metaphor, please?

Prof: A metaphor is a comparison, an implied comparison. Metaphor is the major component of myth. A myth is a handed-down tale, a story designed to illustrate an underlying principle. A myth is only a lie if taken literally.

Pupil: Okay, so maybe the myth can't be taken literally, but do you believe some mythological characters existed in real life?

Prof: The heroes of myth may be real historical persons, or fictitious ones. Their physical existence is not essential to the value of the myth. Not the symbol, but the thing symbolized, the "unmanifested principle," is the point of the myth. The Bible is essentially a book of mythology. We have evidence of the existence, such as Herod the Great, Alexander the Great, Augustus Caesar and Nabuchodonosor. Others are fictitious, like Job.

Pupil: You say the Bible is essentially mythology? Does that mean you don't believe the Old Testament is an historical account?

Prof: The Bible is considered by many to be an accurate literal record of history. While the history it records may be largely accurate, all of it is not. The purpose of the Bible, up to the time of Christ, was not to record history. Its purpose was to support the current world view of the people of the time or times in which it was written regarding the origin and purpose of a certain nation. Traditional Hebrew metaphors make no effort to distinguish real and historical persons from fictitious ones. All are treated and spoken of as actual persons.

We must realize that the authors, editors and publishers of the Bible were primarily concerned about the fundamental message and not what we today would call historical accuracy. Most likely the Bible had little literal meaning or significance to its editors and publishers. At best it is a well-intentioned metaphor and at worst it is a Masterpiece of Deceit drawn by persons of suspect motives in regard to our freedom.

Pupil: I've heard a reference once before to the Bible as a Masterpiece of Deceit. This source said there are people who keep ancient secrets alive. Do you know anything about that?

Prof: Yes, there have always been people holding the ancient wisdom. A Kahuna is a Hawaiian keeper of the forbidden secret. What is the secret? How to use The Power—the telepathic power of blessing and cursing.

Bless and do not curse,
for by what blessing you bless you shall be blessed
and by what cursing you curse you shall be cursed,
and therefore bless and do not curse
that you may become the blessing
in the land the Lord has given you,
and not the curse.

Empowerment to use The Power comes with no guarantees. We are free to use The Power or misuse it. We must beware of in whom we awaken the power, the secret, lest we empower a Master of Deceit.

Pupil: This source also said there are sites that hold those same ancient secrets. Is that true?

Prof: Yes. One such place is beneath the altar of Chartres Cathedral. There lies buried in the earth an ancient asteroid called the Black Virgin. It is the ordination stone of the Druids. A student Merlin (Merlin is the title of an office) studied for ten years before he was allowed to descend the sacred well, enter the cave tunnel and touch the Stone of Empowerment. It protected itself against those who would misuse The Power. If a person with "Straight Eyes" touched the Stone, he would become empowered to recite the "Charm of Making." If his motives were clouded, even a little clouded, he died on the spot. Many bodies were taken from the Well of the Charter. Chartre is French for charter, and charter is another word for covenant.

A covenant is a bond between spirits, as a contract is a bond between minds, and religion means to re-bond. We are bonded by birth; we are re-bonded by free choice. Bonded to what? Bonded to the Source of Being.

Pupil: What is the Source of Being?

Prof: In my opinion the Source of Being is best described not by what it is, but by what it does. What it does is to manifest the universe, and therefore I call it the Manifesting Power. Manifested is the so-called physical world, the appearance of energy in material form, and the energy itself that lies within the material appearance. Unmanifested is the aetheric force that manifests in the energy that composes the material world.

    The theological word transcendence may be seen as expressing the relationship between the manifested and unmanifested force or energy. We must realize that the principles of transcendent force (aetheric) are analogous to, but dimensionally different from, the principles of manifested force—the best example perhaps being that the principles of space-time perceived in manifested force are effectively non-existent, though potentially present, in un- or pre-manifested force.

    As to perception, I suggest the left brain works primarily with manifested force and the right brain with pre-manifested force, and as Lao Tsu suggests, there is a little of the yin in the yang and a little of the yang in the yin. Today we might say they meet in the Tao, accessed through the corpus callosum.

    As to function, perhaps the right brain works primarily with the undifferentiated aetheric memory, calling out the knowledge that is immediately available without being stored, while the left brain depends for its data on the "five senses" and tests intuitive knowledge with the probe of negation to clarify it for function in the manifested world. The corpus callosum is the balancing force between them.

    The above may seem too mechanical and impersonal, but the unmanifested reality may be viewed as the manifestor of energy-spirit-consciousness. Therefore, it is more pre-personal than non-personal, as the voice of the actor is pre-personal to the character represented by the mask, the prosopon of the actor who plays many parts, if not all.

    With that, I think I've given you plenty to think about until we next meet.

✳

Interlude

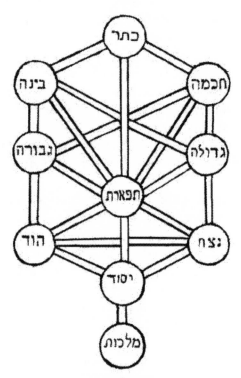

Etz Chayim
The Tree of Life
A tree with its roots in the sky

Canto XLIV

Innocence and Infallibility

*We have paid so much attention to Original Sin that we
have forgotten Original Innocence.*

~ Innocent III, Pope of Francis of Assisi
and the Albigensian Crusade

Time: 1963
Place: Rome, The Second Vatican Council
Personae: Pope John XXIII
             Fr. Jung, the Pope's liaison to the Council,
             (no relation to Carl Jung)

John: Well, young man, what reports on today's session?
Fr. Jung: Before I report on today's session, Your Holiness, may I
           make an urgent observation?
John: Of course!
Fr. Jung: Your Holiness, we cannot make the changes necessary to
           the survival of the Church as long as Papal Infallibility is
           in place.
John: (*Chuckling*) Oh, that's easy, I'll just go in there tomorrow
           and infallibly declare myself fallible!
Fr. Jung: As you have suggested before, Your Holiness, the next big
           obstacle is Original Sin.
John: As I recall, our Lord never had anything to say about that,
           one way or the other. It was Paul of Tarsus, wasn't it? You
           know, I am not very fond of that fellow. It seems to me he
           did what the Sanhedrin hired him to do—dispose of those
           early Followers of the Way in Damascus by claiming to
           see Jesus, joining up with Ananias, and then making
           changes in our Lord's teachings to suit himself, and to suit
           those who had hired him.
Fr. Jung: So, perhaps there wasn't any Original Sin after all?
John: I am inclined to think there wasn't, at least not in the way
           we've been presenting it.
Fr. Jung: Does that have anything to do with recent archaeological
           findings?

255

John: Yes. Especially a finding in which your fellow country-
           man, Carl Jung, the analyst, participated at Nag
           Hammadi.

Fr. Jung: You mean the *Gospel According to Thomas?*

John: It is clearly Gnostic. Ever since Nicea in 325 AD we have
           been contemptuous of Gnostics because they claim to
           know and we insist you have to *believe.* Frankly, I think
           they were right, and we ought to apologize for misrepre-
           senting them.

Fr. Jung: Is that what you mean when you say we need to pay
           more attention to Original Innocence?

John: Perhaps it is, as it is obvious that our Innocence has been
           interfered with by something.

Fr. Jung: Other than the devil, I presume?

John: Other than the devil as we know, or say we know, him.
           The answer may also be archaeological.

Fr. Jung: You mean the finding of Ur at the end of the first archae-
           ological trail in Mesopotamia?

John: Yes, exactly. It seems that Sumerian records in cuneiform
           on well-preserved clay tablets tell that we were colonized
           450,000 years ago by people from another planet and that
           they made some genetic alteration to disempower us in
           order to make us slaves.

Fr. Jung: And this is what we are teaching as Original Sin?

John: I think so. The crucial difference is that Adam and Eve
           didn't do it. It was *done to us.*

Jung: Truly? But that would mean the *entire* theology of the
           Church would have to be rethought from the beginning!
           May I ask, Your Holiness, is that why you called this
           council?

John: No. I called this council to undo the mischief done by that
           frightened little man whom you know as Pio Nono, Pius
           IX, who was so mad about losing the Papal States to
           Garibaldi that he wanted to compensate himself by taking
           on the mantle of infallibility. He refused to give the *Urbe
           et Orbe* blessing until he got himself declared infallible at
           Vatican I!

Fr. Jung: I understand that he manipulated the council shameless-
           ly to get his infallibility accepted and did some very un-
           Christian things in the Vatican Museum.

John: Yes. He couldn't get a majority of the bishops to agree so he sent them home on a break, meanwhile telling his co-conspirators to stay in Rome. When the others were gone he called his conspirators together in a *rump council* and got his infallibility through while the majority of the council was out of town. As to the un-Christian things, I am ashamed to mention what they were.

Fr. Jung: He could very well have doomed the Church by railroading infallibility past the bishops.

John: That is exactly my fear. We have a lot of problems in the Church, but as long as we claim to be infallible, we can't even approach solving any of them. Who is less entitled to be believed than a man who claims he cannot err? Or to put it more lightly, it is a mistake to claim that you can't make a mistake.

Fr. Jung: It seems to me that the next big problem is Paul of Tarsus. What do you think, Holiness?

John: Again, I think he did what he was hired to do, destroy the followers of James in Damascus, the true companions of Jesus. He also seems to have replaced Jesus' brother James with Peter who was surely not one of Jesus' favorite people, even according to the Gospels.

Fr. Jung: My idea exactly. As you said before, Paul was hired by the Sanhedrin "to root out the Followers of the Way in Damascus." He was a very clever man and he knew the best way to beat them was to join them. So he told the story of a vision of the Lord, pretended to be blind, asked the way to Ananias in Damascus and then tearfully proclaimed his conversion to "Christ Jesus." Immediately he promoted Jesus to be God, taught that he died on the cross for our sins, claimed that Jesus had established a church on Peter, and alleged that Jesus had given us his body to eat at the Last Supper. Few of these concepts are in the recorded teachings of Jesus.

            Paul thus accomplished two pivotal things: first, he made the Followers of the Way non-Jewish; second, he did the bidding of the Sanhedrin by setting up a Roman-oriented religion. Later on, Eusebius modeled Paul's work into a religion for Constantine's army.

John: Do you think we could get a program like that past Cardinal Ottaviani and his Roman Empire gang?

Fr. Jung: I doubt it, but at least we could put down a marker for someone to pick up who is genuinely interested in saving the Church after we've gone.

John: I am sure the Lord Jesus is a Master, and that he answers prayers. However, I am afraid Jesus is in chains in this Church and vastly underrepresented. Francis of Assisi basically had it right. We treated those who followed Francis very badly. And I fear we will be treated badly as well.

Fr. Jung: Oppenheimer quoted Shiva: "I am become death, the destroyer of worlds" in reference to the atom bomb. It appears we have such a bomb in those conservatives who, by protecting the Church of yesterday, will doom the Church of tomorrow.

John: The real question is, will there be a Church of tomorrow? More importantly, should there be a Church of tomorrow?

Fr. Jung: Going back to the start of this conversation about making changes, perhaps the diagnosis reveals that too many changes are going to be required, and though the operation may be a success, the patient may die.

John: A distinct possibility. The decline of the Church in Europe is already approaching catastrophic levels. And as I consider our conversation about Paul of Tarsus and its implication that the Church is supported by untrustworthy documents, I become aware that our attempts to save the Church may prove fatal to the very existence to the Church.

Fr. Jung: If the Church was not founded by Jesus, but by a Roman Emperor, then it has probably been serving the Empire it was founded to serve, and not Jesus.

John: I think these thoughts have occurred to Cardinal Ottaviani, and that is why he is so opposed to the Council. He has the feeling that our tinkering will be fatal to the institution that he has given his life to serve, although, in fact it has served *him* very well indeed.

Fr. Jung: Perhaps, Holiness, the truth is a dangerous thing for those who have based their lives on the teachings of the Masters of Deceit.

Interlude

Prosopon

The Masks of God

Every being is a mask of God. For the fullness of the Divinity, in which there is no emptiness, rests in each one of all that is—entire, from the smallest to the greatest.

There is no emptiness save that which illusion perceives—nothing but the truth is That is that which is That before that is Who.

There is nowhere or nowhen that is not All, for he who can be his own should not be another's.

For the only Master whose mastering we may trust is the one who seeks not to be a master of slaves.

~ In memory of Paracelsus the Wanderer

I, I wander. I with the Vasus, I with the Rudras, I with the Adityas. I, I wander.

~ First line of the *Rig Veda*

Canto XLV

Gift of a Name

Time: July 1985
Place: London, British Museum
               Camelot
Personae: Myself
               Robert Johnson
               Merlin

It was closing time at the British Museum, rush hour, five o'clock. We had come there from Greenwich and the Royal Naval Academy where you can stand with one foot on either side of the Prime Meridian. We had not had much time to visit the section of Mesopotamian and Egyptian Antiquities. I had come there in honor of its most illustrious curator, Wallace Budge, whose book *Amulets and Talismans* had shattered my scientific and religious orthodox prejudices. The guards were hurrying us toward the exit that faced a roar of London traffic and the declining summer sun.

As we exited to the roofed porch, Robert, who was hosting my tour of London, said, "Well, what now? Should we take in a play at Piccadilly?"

"No," I replied. "I want to visit Camelot."

"But," said Robert, "that's 150 miles!"

"Well, it's not a far piece in California, and you have motorways."

We departed, not on motorways, but traveled back roads instead. There was very little traffic. The coming storm was accompanied by fires burning along the way, mingling smoke with mist. Shadows of the Beltaine fires! It grew very dark as we approached the village of South Camel. There was no sign of life other than the trees, and an eerie stillness.

The village seemed deserted. There were no lights anywhere. It was about ten o'clock. Suddenly the bells in the squat little cupola of the stone church began to ring deafeningly, just as we entered the village. I would have clapped my hands over my ears if I hadn't been driving. Robert, however, did just that.

We pulled to a stop at a dead end street where a skinned pole had been placed horizontally to protect what looked like an old shed.

260

There in the headlights, pointing to the right was a hand-lettered sign, "Camelot." Suddenly the bells stopped, still no lights in the village, no sign of a person.

We walked in the direction the sign bid us, but soon lost the trail. We crossed what seemed a small cow pasture and came to a steep and tapered wall covered with trees. All attempts to climb it failed. I sensed an opening to my left, although it was pitch-black. My feet somehow found a trail. After about fifty yards I was impelled to look to my right. A long ramp became visible, with stars shining through the silhouettes of tree braches and a cow against the sky. I found my way back through the dark to where I first started.

I said, "Robert!" No answer. I repeated, "Robert!" No answer. More insistently I called, "Robert!!"

Finally his response, "Yes?"

"What were you doing?" I asked.

"Praying!"

"Robert, I think I have found the gate of Camelot!"

"How did you find it?"

"I don't know. I think Merlin…"

All at once a huge white owl swooped down from the walls of Camelot. I felt his feathers brush my hair as he descended. Speechless, we walked to the long earthen ramp, went up the ramp and out through the tree-guarded gate, and there, spread out in the starlight, was the great field where Camelot once stood.

Postscript

I have since learned that Merlin visits people in such ways with some frequency, and is not satisfied with "waiting for the call." I have also learned that ancestors like Merlin enter easily into conversation with those descendants who are willing to listen. Speaking of that still small voice, if it be the voice of God, it respects your fragility by pressing an ancestor to its service.

The great field of memory reaches far beyond one's prior experience, even to the knowledge of what only God could know—like the time of the emergence of the solar system. What is the Golden Age of which Plato and the "old ones" speak? How long ago was it? When did it begin? When did it end, and why? Should we ask Plato, or should we ask Merlin with his "charm of making?"

Interlude

Truth is not so much something that is taught
As it is something that is felt.

Truth is not so much something that is believed
As it is something that is known.

Truth is not so much something that is recalled
As it is some thing that is remembered.

Truth is not so much something that is thought
As it is something that is felt.

Does your truth come from outside you?
Or does your truth come from within you?

Is the Divine only some reality in the distant heavens?

Or is the Divine a reality within the memory of your heart?

Canto XLVI

Merkabah

Time: July 1985

Place: Camelot

Personae: Myself
            Merlin

Me: Master Merlin, was there a Golden Age?
Merlin: Yes, it was very long ago.
Me: When did it begin to end?
Merlin: 450,000 years ago with the coming of the gods, but really 350,000 years ago when the gods enslaved us. However, the Golden Age is still with us where the gods have not yet reached.
Me: How do you know this, Merlin?
Merlin: You know it too, Bear Cub. I just have a little better practice with remembering it. It involves the use of the power.
Me: What was a day like in the Golden Age?
Merlin: What kind of a day do you prefer, a day so long ago, or a day now?
Me: Let's start with now: Time, Place and Persons.
Merlin: It's best to go to Africa where what is human in us began, and where the most remarkable of our "powers of innocence" may still be found—Burkina Faso.
Me: Burkina Faso? Where's that?
Merlin: Place: West Africa, east of Timbuktu, below the Niger River and above Ghana and Le Cote d'Ivoire. Time: any day when one of the village women reaches her first trimester. Persons: the woman herself and the women of the village.
Me: You mean the "day of the quickening?"
Merlin: That's it! On that day the women of the village gather around the expecting mother who stands in the center of the circle. All are nude. The child in the womb does what we all do at the trimester.
Me: You mean kicks the mother for the first time?

263

Merlin: Yes, that. But before that, we tergiversate.

Me: What's that?

Merlin: It means turn your back. Before that day we are looking back toward the beginning of the illusion of time and living through the experience of becoming—time-traveling the cosmos. On that day, we turn our attention toward the space-time where we will be living for a while. We call that *here and now*.

Me: You mean we all tergiversate? And we all have access to what is remembered, although we usually don't recall that?

Merlin: So it seems. But the kick doesn't come first. The first thing is the name. While you are a time traveler you find your name, and the first thing you do is speak it telepathically. The women are all in a unanimous telepathic state of listening, and when they hear your name they sing it back to you as one voice, both in telepathy and sound. Then they send a question, "Why have you come?" You answer and tell them. They sing that back. They ask another question, "What gifts do you bring?" You answer and tell them. They sing that back.

Me: All the while you are still in the womb?

Merlin: Yes, and there's more. Now it's six months later and you are ready to be born. The women gather again, mother and midwife in the center. As your head appears in the vulva, the women sing your name, and you are born laughing, with no whack on the behind. Our Judaeo-Christian tradition perhaps remembers this in the name of Isaac, son of Abraham, for his name means *laughing child*. Then they sing what gifts you bring and why you have come.

Me: That would be a lot better start than we get today.

Merlin: Unless you were born in Burkina Faso. Wait, there is more. It's their Department of Corrections. Usually the offender is a man because of the testosterone overdrive. He is placed in the center with four attendants. All the people, both men and women, gather around the transgressor. From the surrounding circle they begin to sing his name. It is said that no man can take it for more than fifteen minutes without falling to the ground, doubling up in a fetal position and crying his eyes out. The name-song goes on for an hour, and then the attendants hold him up. All the people reach out their hands to him and sing the gifts he has brought and why he has come. The recidivism rate in Burkina Faso is close to zero.

Me: You wouldn't need a lot of prisons in Burkina Faso! And if you remembered that was going to happen, you wouldn't do it in the first place.

Merlin: The people just described were largely the kind of people who were made into slaves by the Arab slave traders and the white masters. This is what we have lost to the Empire.

Me: So, that is what it was like in the Golden Age 500,000 years ago, plus or minus? And this is the society the gods took from us?

Merlin: Yes, Bear Cub.

Interlude

The entheogenic, ethnobotanical, ithyphallic vortiginal spin of essence evokes the deva, the Earth spirit which, spiraling upward in Golden Section progression from the intersection of standing waves emanated by cylindrical subterranean flows, exemplifies the orthogonality of the inter-dimensional flow of the emergent Divine and evokes as well the *Manes*, the spiritual remains of ancestral beings who emerge from and return to the trans-spatial, trans-temporal aetheric dimension of essential existence.

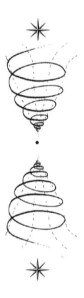

Canto XLVII

Sacrifice

Time: Easter, 1995

Place: Chichicastenango, Western Highlands,

               Guatemala

Personae: Roberto Cruz, a Mayan Shaman
               A Norteño

Setting: The Pascal Stone, on top of a mountain

Norteño: Thank you for bringing me here! This forest is cool delight—so deep in tropical America!

Shaman: We call this continent Turtle Island.

Norteño: This particular place seems an island in the sky. Is it much changed from the time my ancestors came to plunder your gold?

Shaman: Very little. Your ancestors did not offend us much by pillaging gold. It was the melting down of our spiritual truths, not our statues and jewelry, that impoverished us.

Norteño: Do remnants of that truth still remain among some of you?

Shaman: If you look upon this Pascal Stone and see what true memories it wakens, you will know not only that the truth still remains among us, but that truth dwells also in you.

Norteño: I see someone approaching on the trail from the city below. Who would it be?

Shaman: Another shaman similar to myself. He comes daily to the Pascal Stone to perform the sacrifice, today with compliant birds and chickens.

Norteño: What does the sacrifice consist of?

Shaman: Observe and you will see.

Norteño: Does it involve killing?

Shaman: In this case, yes. In the words of our local priest sacrifice means *Sacrum Facere*, or to make holy.

Norteño: What is it that you make holy?

Shaman: That which is unholy, in this case, the taking of a life.

Norteño: How can you possibly make the taking of a life holy?

Shaman: By awakening the *Ecstasy of Death* in the victim before the stroke.

Norteño: The ecstasy of death? What is that?

Shaman: The Great Spirit has shown us compassion. Compassion upon the woman in labor through the trials of childbirth. Compassion upon all creatures through the ecstasy of dying which comes by nature in the hour of their death and dispels the fear and suffering of the passing from this Earthly life.

It is the greatest purpose of the shaman to use the power of his spirit to awaken the joy of childbearing in the woman, and to awaken the ecstasy of dying in the one who passes. These are the times of making holy, the times of sacrifice.

Norteño: A consummation devoutly to be wished. Remarkable! Does the shaman over there at the Pascal Stone use his power to waken the ecstasy of death in that chicken?

Shaman: Yes, exactly. Thus he serves himself, the Great Spirit and the one who dies.

Norteño: But why with an animal or a bird?

Shaman: Because all creatures are our brothers and sisters, no matter how great or how small. We can each feel the fullness of the life of the Great One in all beings, no matter how small or how great, that flow forth from the One.

Norteño: Would not such thoughts make us fastidious as we walk? Stepping on the ant and breathing in the virus and the bacteria?

Shaman: Not if we try our best to walk in constant awareness, blessing all those we slay unknowingly and blessing all those who have given, as it were, their lives for us.

Norteño: What effect does this awakening of the ecstasy of dying have upon the creatures we slay? For instance, what effect does it have on their bodies that we consume?

Shaman: Ask any hunter, even those Norteños who know nothing of sacrifice, and they will tell you: "If you chase down an animal in flight and fear, the meat is tough, the blood reeks and the flies come. If you slip up on the animal before it is awakened to fright, and kill with a single stroke before it is aware, the meat is tender, the blood smells sweet, and the flies don't come."

Norteño: But you say that the ecstasy of death is "awakened" in the hour of death. You mean this happens without our conscious awareness?

Shaman: Yes, the ecstasy of death is different from the sense of the meaning of life, unless interfered with it occurs automatically in the hour of death.

Norteño: Very interesting. I was talking to a rabbi the other day and he told me that in the Talmud there is a saying: "Never a fly was seen in the Temple of Jerusalem, though the blood of the sacrifice poured into the funereal valley of Kedron in a constant stream twenty four hours a day."

Shaman: The priest in our church tells us that Beelzebub, a name of the Christian devil, means "idol of the flies" in Aramaic. So, I guess if you do the sacrifice properly the flies don't come, and neither does Beelzebub, but if you botch the sacrifice both the flies and the "Lord of the flies" come together.

Norteño: The rabbi told me if that happened, not only did the priest not get paid, but he lost his job as well.

Shaman: Our Catholic priest tells us that this was why the sons of Heli the Priest were unacceptable to Samuel's God.

Norteño: Amazing! What that means to me is that not only is life eternal, but by the fullness of joy in knowing the ecstasy of dying, even the fear of death will fade away.

Shaman: This is what our ancestors taught us, and what your Christian religion tried to make us forget.

Interlude

Sacerdos

The instrument of a priest is a knife.
The action of the priest is to kill.
The power of the priest is to get the consent
of the victim before the stroke,
by awakening the Ecstasy of Death.
The purpose of the priest is to give God
A good reputation in a predatory universe.

~ Shamanic Utterance

How?

By awakening the Ecstasy of Death in the victim.

How?

With the Wounding Sword of Blessing,
The sword that strikes to heal
Like the surgeon's scalpel.

Any day is a good day to be born.
Any day is a good day to die.

Canto XLVIII

May The Heart of Earth...

Place: Chichicastenango, Guatemala

Time: 1995 Winter Solstice

Personae: Shaman
                A woman in mourning

Woman: Good evening. Are you a guest here at the Hostel of the
        Flowers?
Shaman: No, my bed is in the forest where the spirits of my ances-
        tors can visit more easily in my dreams.
Wom: Then, you know the ways of the Maya?
Shaman: From my mother's womb. I sense that death has deprived
        you of the presence of one you love.
Woman: Yes. My son.
Shaman: Have you come here from the land of the Norteños to
        seek solace from us mountain dwellers, or do you come
        for reasons you do not understand?
Woman: Neither. I have come here to seek the spirit of my son.
Shaman: Why here?
Woman: Because my son often prayed and sang songs of Earth and
        the Mayan prophesies.
Shaman: Very much as I do. May I tell you of the great prayer we
        all sing?
Woman: Oh, please!
Shaman: First I must tell you that only a month ago it could have
        cost my life to sing it for you. Until the meeting last
        month in Chiapas there was a death penalty on any of us
        who sang in the ancestral way.
Woman: I'm not surprised. Until 1978 there was a law in our coun-
        try placing such a penalty on all native spiritual practices
        by shamans. Your country is only 25 years slower than
        the United States.
Shaman: Christians, it seems, fear any truth they have not been
        told by their authorities, either secular or ecclesiastic, and
        are ready to kill anyone who openly disagrees with them.

271

I find that sad because among our people we have a say-ing: "Only those who lie kill those who disagree with them."

Woman: I have long regretted that such practices have been com-mon in the Christian church.

Shaman: Yes, and it is strange that the most Christian of all prayers, the Our Father, is based upon this prayer that I would sing for you.

Woman: I am sure it will be a prayer well known to my son.

Oh! Look! Is that a quetzal bird? My son told me they are named for Quetzalcoyotl, the plumed serpent who was revered in these lands like a messiah who would come to save his people. Do my eyes deceive me?

Shaman: By no means. See that long tail and that bright plumage? We are truly honored, as this holy bird is seldom seen today. We understand that our ancestors come often to visit in the guise of birds, especially this resplendent bird. Perhaps our descendants could come as well if they die before us. Perhaps the thought of this prayer I am about to sing for you could call such a descendant!

Woman: Please.

Shaman: May the heart of Earth
Flow to the heart of the heavens
Through my heart
And through all our hearts together.

And may our hearts be
The heart of every being
In all the starry sky.

And may the heart of the heavens
Flow to the heart of Earth
Through my heart
And through all our hearts together.

And may our hearts be
The heart of every Earthly creature.

Woman: My tears are of joy and gratitude.
In your song I feel the presence of my son!

Interlude

Is not all transcendent experience the result of a boundless hope which, while fragile, is founded in eternal permanence, a permanence that, though flowing, is perceived never to cease?

And is not this hope the existential base of that perception that past all fragility and despair the ecstasy that is life will never cease, even in its most infinitesimal manifestations?

And does not the upwelling of this quiet but ecstatic hope in those who persist in seeking, at last quell the anger of rebellious youth so grimly attached to the bitterness of despair?

And if it does not upwell, or is diverted by scorn, does not that very dawning at last await on the portals of death, even for those who have most despaired of it?

What else shall we call it but the ecstasy of death—that most profound outflowing of what we call the love and mercy of God?

Perhaps, after all, this is the Gate of Heaven.

Canto XLIX

Confession

Time: Now

Place: Here

Personae: Oneself
             The Voice

Voice: You should forgive me.
Self: God, is that you?
Voice: Yes, it's me.
Self: Forgive you? But God, how could I ever admit that you have offended me? I thought it went the other way around.
Voice: Well, we'll get back to that, but for now you should forgive me.
Self: But God, how could I ever think that you have offended me?
Voice: Well, don't you?
Self: Don't I what?
Voice: Don't you think I have offended you?
Self: No, of course not.
Voice: Liar.
Self: Liar? But God, please help me with that.
Voice: Ooookay. I have made a predatory universe in which everything is eating everything else, including you and your friends. Doesn't that offend you? It should.
Self: Well, I have thought about that, but I still can't admit that you have offended me. Please help me.
Voice: Well, how about death? Here I am with all this eternity and I've given you these few turns around the sun. Don't you think I'm stingy? Don't you think that you would have been more generous if you were me?
Self: Well, I have thought about that.
Voice: So you should forgive me.
Self: Now just a minute, God! Now that you have shown me

274

what a perfect right I have to be offended by what you have done, how do you expect me honestly to forgive you?

Voice: Well, now we're having some honesty here. I like that. So, let me help you. You know what the love of God is, don't you?

Self: Well no, not exactly.

Voice: I'll tell you what it is—it's ecstasy. I've given the power to experience ecstasy to every sentient being in the universe, and all beings are sentient—the Unwinking Vigilance of Ecstasy.

Self: What? Every being is capable of ecstasy? But all those religious people are afraid to use that word. They think the word "ecstasy" is irreverent, even scurrilous.

Voice: Yes, I know, but that doesn't mean they don't want it. Ecstasy never blinks, and neither do I, and I do mean never.

Self: Are you saying even plastic can experience ecstasy?

Voice: At some level, yes.

Self: And that is the love of God?

Voice: Why yes, what else would it be? So, you should forgive me.

Self: Oh, I don't know, God, I'm still pretty offended.

Voice: Yes, I know; it's this death thing. Well, you know, we eternal beings have a problem: we don't know how to make anything that doesn't last forever.

Self: What? You mean everything lasts forever? Me too? I don't have to earn it?

Voice: No, my friend. You're stuck with it.

Self: Now, wait a minute! Everything is capable of ecstasy ... and everything lasts forever? God, I forgive you.

Voice: Well, good. Now that you have had the goodness to forgive me, do you know what I am going to do for you? I am going to waken in you your memory of your power to forgive yourself. What do you think of that?

Self: I forgave myself, and truly, I am better now.

Interlude

The Signs of Illumination

The first physical sign of illumination is Radiance of the face.

The first mental sign of illumination is Clarity of perception.

The first spiritual sign of illumination is Joy of the heart.

The first social sign of illumination is Compassion with all.

The first pragmatic sign of illumination is Humor against anger.

The first Divine sign of illumination is Freedom.

Canto L

Summation of The Course of Empire

Time: Near future

Place: A Court of the Law of Nature

Personae: Judge
                 Jury
                 District Attorney
                 Defense Attorneys
                 General public

Setting: Closing Argument by the District Attorney

The Protestant Revolution shattered the unity of the Roman Church.

The French Revolution denied the "Kingship of Christ" by denying the image of Christ as Emperor.

The Communist Revolution asserted atheism, a denial that the God of Israel was God.

But neither the Protestants, nor the French revolutionaries, nor the Communists suggested replacements.

What Might They Have Suggested as Replacements?

Protestants: That instead of communion with the body of Christ represented by the "Host," bread, or wafer, perhaps Jesus wished to proclaim the immanent unanimity of heart-mind of every being in the universe.

French Revolution: That though Jesus was entitled to be the Emperor, he wished to eliminate the Empire in favor of Democracy and Original Innocence.

Communists: That the God of Israel was only a demiurge and therefore too small to be the Manifestor of the Universe.

What is the Source of Authority?

In making this investigation we must be aware that the Church is the de facto origin of the very concept of authority in all of Christendom, or, as they say at Stanford, Western Civilization. In the Empire, authority comes from "God" to the Emperor via the Pope, thus the Divine Right of Kings. This authority started with the crowing of En-me-dur-an-ki, Enoch, and was reinforced by the Donation of Constantine and shared with Charlemagne.

What Must Change?

If Christianity is to survive, it must acknowledge that its "god" has not been the Manifesting Power, but the demiurge El, the god of Israel. Though Jesus was truly the heir to this Empire, he did not consider the Empire a thing to be clung to.

Through the Paedophilia Crisis of Trust, the bishops have lost their de facto corporate immunity. If the Church can be held responsible for the misdeeds of its priests, it can be held responsible for the misuse of its power; it can be investigated for the source of its authority, and can be cross-examined as to its veracity. Testimony can be admitted as to its reputation for veracity. Is this intransigence of the clergy and the Vatican due to failure of those persons to realize that the Church is the Roman Empire and that it never fell? Or do they realize that fact and deliberately refuse to acknowledge it publicly?

The difficulty for the Roman Catholic Church is infallibility, the belief that God protects the head of the Church from error when he speaks of faith or morality. The Church's errors, both deliberate and indeliberate, are so numerous that no human agency could possibly correct them. Correcting these errors would be beyond the demiurge as well. However, with the Manifesting Power all things are possible, even the correction of an infallible papal declaration!

Christianity needs to change its worship service from one which creates slavery to one patterned after the Buddhists which creates empowerment and unanimity. This would return the sacrament of communion to its original intention, creation of unanimity of heart-mind.

Christianity cannot revive unless reconciled with modern science. Modern science is not based on faith but on knowledge and is therefore Gnostic. Christianity must look to its own Alexandrian Gnostic roots. In other words, it must give up Empire and realize that the Jesus it purports to serve was a Gnostic Master who said: "You shall know the truth and the truth shall set you free!" That statement is the very essence of Gnosticism and does not include faith as a mode of "salvation."

Christianity, in particular the Roman Catholic Church, must apologize to the Buddhists, whom they have so long persecuted. They must acknowledge that Siddhartha is a true master as well as Jesus, remembering that it was Siddhartha's Buddhist priests and their successors at Alexandria who founded Qumran, the Essene monastery in Palestine where Jesus took the Nazarite vow of Leviticus to expedite the recovery of spirituality in a Judaism that had been sterilized by the maladministration of the Sadducees and Pharisees.

We have been denied the definition of a master by many of our religions. Why? Because these religions claim their master is the only one. They claim there aren't any other masters so we don't need a definition of a master. But in truth each is a master only to his or her Self. The true definition of a master makes it immediately clear that we're all born masters—every single one of us. Christianity must acknowledge that Jesus is a true master, one of many, and also that it has betrayed the true Jesus by identifying him with the demiurge.

Fear of death is a most corruptive force in society. Christianity teaches that death is inevitable, and it is, for the material body. The great failure of almost all religious systems, which may be deliberate, is to confuse eternal life with longevity. The Christian Creed says, "The resurrection of the body and the Life Everlasting." The resurrection of the body has nothing to do with life everlasting. It never did and it never will. Life everlasting is solely about the continuation of the spirit.

The biggest change Christianity and other organized religions must make is in its responses to those peoples whose theology or world view is different. First is censorship, in extreme cases, the burning of books. If they are truly satisfied with their knowledge of truth, why should Christians make war on other peoples' views? But the books are the smallest problem. Killing those who disagree is a much greater problem. Can we really trust people who kill other people who disagree with them? Hardly. It seems Christianity and Islam have been the guiltiest in this respect.

We are all, no matter what our religious faith or lack thereof, the victims of those Masters of Deceit who ruled the Church and much of Christianity and other religions. It may appear that all of this is only a religious phenomenon, but the Modern State that now rules almost every square inch of the Earth's surface is, in fact, an embodiment of the same lineage of dominance.

The Masters of Deceit have been responsible for the death and suffering of tens of millions of innocent people. Nonetheless, we must remember that though those Masters of Deceit and their lackeys may be abandoned by their jealous god, demiurge—the True God, the Manifesting Power, loves them too.

Interlude

There is Religion.
And there is Organized Religion.

Religion is as old as life for it is a function of the phenomenon of bonding.
Organized Religion is a new order of affairs arising from the imposition of authority.

Religion is founded on the motive of the Primal Ecstasy of Original Innocence.
Organized Religion is founded on the motive of Primal Fear that presumes Original Guilt.

Religion is the mode of Bonding.
Organized Religion is the mode of Bondage.

Religion places the Divinity and its fullness as the root and stem of every being.
Organized Religion places the Divinity and its fullness as separate and remote from every being.

The knowledge of Religion is the quest of true Masters.
The origin of Organized Religion is the machinations of Masters of Deceit.

Religion is the mainspring of true Democracy.
Organized Religion is the tool of Empire.

A nation is a dream, a dream that will perish for lack of dreamers
to dream the dream that the nation is.

So what is a true patriot?
Someone who dreams that dream—and not just sometimes.

E pluribus unum
Out of many one
Out of many dreams one dream.

Ex uno plures
Out of one many
Out of one dream many dreamers.

Out of many dreamers with one dream—a true nation.

Motto from the great seal of the
United States as shown on the dollar bill:

"For God has nodded with approval
upon the things we have begun,
a New Order of Affairs that out of many should be one
that in God alone we may trust."

(*Annuit coeptis novus ordo seclorum*
e pluribus unum
—in God we trust.)

Or, by contrast, the motto remembered:

"For the Divinity has breathed in approbation
upon the things we have begun,
a renewal of the Ancient Order of Affairs
that out of many should be one
in order that in the Divinity and each other
we may forever trust."

(*Annuit coeptis renovatio ordinis saeculorum*
e pluribus unum ut in
Deo et in nobis semper confitemur?)

Which is the voice of a Master of Truth,
and which is that of a Master of Deceit?

Canto LI

Remembering Original Innocence

Remembering True Democracy:
Freedom, Equality and Sister-Brotherhood

We can take refuge in the words of Jean Jacques Rousseau who, paraphrased, said, "The source of authority must arise from the Social Contract because true authority over the people must arise from the people."

One must be careful in a true democracy not to set up an Us *vs* Them scenario, recognizing that we all have the seeds within us. Resist not evil, yet most of Christianity has always fought sin, which is a phantom. In the struggle against evil one is dominated by what one fights against.

In democracy, authority comes from "the consent of the governed." Democracy is government of the people, by the people, for the people. A republic is a government of representatives of the people, by the representatives of the people, for representatives of the people and their cronies.

Democracy can only exist when all the people are enlightened and empowered. This is what Original Innocence means. The only way to have a democracy is to come together. Noam Chomsky said, "True democracy cannot exist in any nation unless there are many small groups in it that are practicing it."

So we must do it in groups. All humans have the inalienable right to make any important decisions alone, but no human being should *have* to do it alone. Every community should have a body of people available to provide the circle that provides the energy to support the decision-making.

The purpose of government is to make decisions. In government, the legislative branch makes strategic decisions, the administrative branch makes the tactical decisions, and the judicial branch reviews the above. Decision-making bodies, in a truly well-ordered world, work like the Quakers, in the unanimity of the heart-mind, not by rule of the majority.

The Iroquois Nation and its mode of government influenced Thomas Jefferson and the creation of the United States' constitution. The primary decision makers were a group of women elders. They were the legislative branch. The men's council was executive in nature, acting on decisions tactically to fulfill the administrative needs of the group. Four times each year the two councils came together at equinoxes and solstices to become the judicial branch, reviewing the group's decisions and actions.

True leaders do not demand obedience, and thus are offered, instead of obedience, allegiance by the people. All, then, are leaders in a group of people where each regards himself or herself as equal to all others in the group. By living in this way we can show the world what true democracy is. This is the essence of freedom, which is our birthright. Gnosticism, remembering the truth, is the real basis of democracy and freedom.

Freedom is the greatest mystery. Why was freedom made possible for us? Is it because the Divinity wants to be our equal, and not lord over us? Is not the primary mode of equality the perception of the fullness of the Divinity in every being, no matter how great or how small?

Is not a primary mode of that perception the capacity, activated or inactivated, of every individual to find the truth to be self-evident, and to find that self-evident truth in their own heart-mind? Is not the activation of one's capacity to find self-evident truth the basis of freedom put forth in the maxim: "You shall know the truth and the truth will set you free"?

Is it not true that democracy as a social form could only function in a society of beings all of whom have activated, or seek to activate, their power of perceiving self-evident truth, and who are committed to seeking that truth together in the experience of unanimity?

Consider the formula of the Golden Age: "For the Divinity has breathed in approbation upon the things we have begun, a renewal of the ancient order of affairs that out of many should be one in order that in the Divinity and each other we may forever trust."

Freedom depends upon the activation of one's ability to discover self-evident truth in one's own heart-mind. Equality depends upon respect for each person's innate ability to find such truth. Sister-brotherhood is the spiritual bond between those who meet in the quest for unanimity to find self-evident truth together.

285

We hold these truths to be self-evident that all human beings are created equal, endowed by their creator with an inalienable right to life, liberty, and the pursuit of the sense of the meaning of life.

Remembering Ecstasy, the Only Dependable Motive

A little boy is two years old and his brother is newborn, maybe four weeks or so. The mother can't get the little boy to come out of the newborn's room; he's always looking at his brother. He's just looking at him and they're looking at each other. Finally his mother comes in and says, "What are you doing John? Why are you here all day?"

"Mommy," he said, "I'm beginning to forget and he still remembers."

What can we do to remember? It is as simple and complex as developing our muscle of remembrance, to learn to listen for, and heed, our own inner voice. Some call it meditation.

How do we know which voice to listen to? Our heart-mind is like a crystal set radio and our will is like the wire whisker that must be moved upon the crystal's face until we find where the voice may be heard. The still, small voice never shouts. If you are quiet, you will hear the true voice within. When we get quiet enough that we can feel that flow, then the outside world begins to loosen its grip on us.

We were born in the ecstasy of hope. We were born in innocence, not guilt. We were born knowing that life is eternal. We must return to the innocence of the womb and be born again in the ecstasy of hope, which is our heritage. The only dependable motive is ecstasy.

In ecstasy and innocence we have a knowing of the bond that can never be broken with the living universe, the mysterious, Nameless essence of all that is. We know a choice is poor when it doesn't produce that ecstasy. This is more accurately what sin is; sin in Greek means to miss the mark. So if we miss while making a choice, we simply aim more accurately next time.

We are happy when ecstasy flows constantly; it is the motive *with* life, the manifestation of the love of God. One of the surest ways to feel the ecstasy is to feel deeply grateful. Then we find that gratitude *is* the flow of ecstasy.

When we are in ecstasy, we never ask about the meaning of life. We know that each person has been called into the world to be a catalyst of divine reaction, to activate the heart-mind, to remind others that they have the power. We catalyze each others' divine reactions to mutually catalyze the realization in our heart-minds.

The evolution of religion is one and the same with this evolution of the self. Both can bring people into remembering how to bind themselves back to the original covenant of heart-mind. Ecstasy rises as each heart-mind remembers—we become joyous, and those around us become joyous.

Gentleness is the key, within and without. Become, and listen to, the quality of voice that treasures joy. Become and hear a voice that never shouts, a voice that never gives commandments, that never tells us what we must believe or not believe, that never demands assent, but that speaks like the master of the Tao, the Way.

We need to listen with compassion to ourselves and to those awakening to the truth of their own heart-minds. The power to perceive self-evident truth that rests in the heart of every person is a surer foundation of human dignity and peace in the world than the idea that some people are intrinsically better than others.

For those who have chosen a life of seeking truth, is not their truest vow to serve the authentic teachings of the masters, Jesus among them? And, when we awaken and see clearly, does this not ignite in us the love for freedom and our zeal to be manifest expressions of the Divinity? Your true brothers and sisters are calling to you. Turn toward them. It is time to honor the bidding of Jesus, "Love one another as I have loved you."

> Love to you my Brothers and Sisters.
>
> May you be the cause of joy in the heart of everyone you love.
>
> For ecstasy is the only dependable motive of conduct of every being in the universe!
>
> And this is the natural result of the Love of the Divinity.

✳

Interlude

Gnostic: a seeker of knowledge in her/his own heart-mind.
Gignostic: one who decides to devote her/his life to that search.

Gignostic Doggerel

Doggerel is poetry
That lacks the muse
And some you find acceptable
And some you must refuse.

If you seek the knower
You will surely find the known
No matter how much time you spend there
It will surely take you home.

If you find it beautiful
You are surely on the way
But if reprehensible
You will not wish to stay.

The fullness of all knowledge
Lies in every breast
But 'till you find the access
You have not passed the test.

Canto LII

What Kind of Fool Am I

The fool says in his heart there is no God.

The Tarot deck brought from Egypt by the gypsies contains twenty-one "Major Trumps" that describe the journey of the initiate to illumination. The card numbered zero (0) is called the fool. This is the first card of the series. There is also a card at the end that might be numbered infinity (∞). This is the "second fool" that appears in some playing card decks as the "second joker." In ancient times the first fool is seen as "wise to the world and a fool to wisdom." The second fool was regarded as the destination of the first fool and seen as "wise to wisdom but appearing to the world to be a fool." So the full deck of the Tarot is 23, the number of the bundles of genes on a DNA particle.

I am that fool who does *not* say, "there is no God."
I am that fool who says, "there has to be something."
I have learned from my good atheist friends who say,
"I don't believe in your god, but there has to be something."

I am that fool who thinks that war is a *racket*
by means of which a few become fabulously rich
at the cost of the suffering and death of many.
To those who cause others to die and kill
in the name of their god, I say:
"Your god is too small for me."

I am that fool
who cannot choose a name for God
from the 72 names of God
Suggested by the Jewish rabbis.
I am foolish enough to believe
that God has no name

because no name is either great enough
nor small enough to limit the limitless.

I am that fool
who hears a soundless voice
that speaks wordlessly
in my heart-mind and sends me spinning
in the world of metaphor to find a comparison
that evokes the depth of a priceless but limitless understanding.

I am like the *jongleur de Dieu*, God's juggler,
trying to express the infinite,
that though beyond limitation of words,
is not beyond wordless understanding.

I am that fool
who seeks to know the unknowable
and sees the fullness of the Divinity in every creature
no matter how great or how small,
no matter how near or how distant in time or space or dimension.

I am that fool who believes
that Ecstasy is the only dependable motive of conduct
of every being in the Universe
and that the ubiquity of Ecstasy as a motive
is the primary evidence of the Love of God.

I am that fool who believes
that grace and gravity are the same thing—
the mysterious power of mutual attraction,
and who believes that true religion, true bonding, is the result of
that mutual attraction.

I am that fool who believes
that God never gives commandments
but only suggests advice,
advice that only a certain kind of fool can understand.

I am that fool who believes
that God never gives doctrine
but only urges me to remember the teaching of my heart-mind.

Canto LII

I am that fool who remembers
that there are olden gods
who stole our innocence
disempowered us
and reduced us to slavery.
But I am also that fool who believes
That God loves them too.

I am that fool who believes
that sin does not exist
because who is powerful enough to make God angry?

I am that fool who believes in *amartia*
"To miss the Mark" and who believes
that Ecstasy is always the mark,
and that he who misses
needs only to shoot straighter next time.

I am that fool who believes
that suffering is the question
and compassion is the answer.

I am that fool who believes
that we can all know everything
without ever knowing why.

I am that fool who believes
that everyone I meet is a master,
whether they have remembered yet or not.

I am that fool who believes
that every master needs a fool
to remind him or her not to take themselves too seriously,
especially when they are contradicted.

I am that fool who believes
that there are holy places
where devas spin upward from the Earth,
like a ladder to heaven from deep to deep.

I am that fool who believes
that mathematics is a spiritual discipline
that gives focus to the flow of the Divine Mind.

I am that fool who believes
that seekers seek masters who can awaken them,
and devotees seek charlatans to adore,
an adoration no true master will allow.

I am that fool whom wise kings seek
to tell them truth that sycophants do not dare speak.
I know the need of the powerful to wrestle to control their power
lest their power control them.
I know that Emperors are the
lackeys of the olden gods and that
true kings regard themselves as only first among equals.

I am that fool who loves to sing
and walk the mountain paths beneath the starry heavens
to gaze upon the nude body of the Goddess,
the Shekina who is the first manifestation of the unmanifest.

I am that fool who believes
that a saint is not so much an unusual person
as someone who is very good at being a usual person.

I am that fool who believes
that joy and life are natural companions
and though sorrow has its value
it is best when it is but the guest of a night.

I am that fool who is fascinated
with the astonishing intelligence of wood lice
and the amazing social decorum of chickens.

I am that fool who looks for God
down in instead of up out,
because the Divine Presence is more comfortable
in infinite smallness.

I am that fool who believes
that civilization is for cities
and culture is for the wilderness
where the wild things are.
And that deserts are only uninhabited by humans.
I am that fool who believes
that I should never ask anyone to believe me—
after all, who believes a fool?
And is a wise man ever wise who thinks he is?

I am that fool who remembers
that death is an illusion as an end
and a reality as the Gate of Eternity.

I am that fool who believes
that Eternal Life is inevitable
and that there is no need to earn it.

I am that fool who believes
that the best way to get Ecstasy
is to give it away.

Chronology

<table>
<tr><td rowspan="3">Golden Age</td><td colspan="2">Year BCE   Event</td></tr>
</table>

	Year BCE	**Event**
Golden Age	4 billion	Sumerian Creation Story of Earth by collision of Nibaru with Tiamat
	66 million	Dinosaur and human footprints together
	65 million	Asteroid hits the Earth, resulting in extinction of the dinosaur
Empire of the Gods	450,000	Arrival of the Anunnaki Beginning of the calendar of the gods
	350,000	The genetic breeding of humans by the gods

	Year	**Event**
Course of Empire	3760 BCE	Creation of first human Emperor by the gods
	1600	Agamemnon
	1500-1300*	Moses
	1100	Hebrews still worshiping the Goddess
	562	Nabuchodonosor II
	475	Pythagoras
	483	Siddhartha the Buddha
	399	Socrates
	331 BCE	Alexander dies in Babylon
	0	Beginning of Common Era
	66 CE	Paul on road to Damascus
	245	Origen, Plotinus, Ammonius Saccus
	325	Council of Nicea; Constantine & Eusebius
	500	Bodhidharma in the Himalayas
	527	Merlin on Isle of Avalon
	632	Muhammad
	751	Donation of Constantine
	800	Church-state partnership, the Pope and Charlemagne

Chronology

Year	Event
1226	Francis of Assisi
1274	Thomas Aquinas
1324	Marco Polo
1453	Guttenberg Press
1546	Martin Luther
1558	Charles V
1564	John Calvin
1500s	Michelangelo & Leonardo da Vinci
1775	Benjamin Franklin and Thomas Jefferson
1800s	Beginnings of Archeology
1850s	Rise of fundamental Christianity
1870	Declaration of corporate immunity in the United States
1927	Carl Jung & Sigmund Freud
1929	Lateran Pact between Italy & the Vatican
1930	Justice Cardozo & Oliver Wendell Holmes
1938	Carl Jung and Albert Einstein
1945	Discovery of Gospel According to Thomas and other Gnostic writings

(Course of Empire)

For an individual, the year is the year of death, exact or approximate.
*Depending upon interpretation, Moses could have lived at any time over the course of these two centuries.

The Capitals of the Course of Empire

The Empire commences in 3760 BCE (Before Common Era) with the crowning of Enmeduranki aka Enoch at Erech in Mesopoamia.

Eridu, Sumer
Akkad, Mesopotamia
Babylon I, Egypt
Nineveh, Assyria
Babylon II, Mesopotamia
Persepolis, Iran
Alexandria, Egypt
Rome
Paris
London
Washington, DC

295

Periods of the Catholic Church
As taught in seminaries in the United States in mid-1900's

313-565	Caesaro-Papist Imperialism	Original form of Christianity founded by Constantine Should technically be named Caesaro-Episcopal Imperialism as the Bishop of Rome was not the Pope until 751 when Zachary forged a document by Constantine to establish the Bishop of Rome as the Pope, Vicar of Christ. (See Donation of Constantine in the Glossary.)
565-843	Feudal Diarchy	Rule of the Empire by Bishop of Rome and the Emperor
843-1059	Feudal Anarchy	Dark Ages, authority largely ineffective
1059-1274	Clerical Theocracy	Government run by the Church
1274-1453	Secularizing Theocracy	Rule by the secular instead of the clergy
1453-1776	Secular Humanism	Putting man before God in the study of religion; introduction of the principle of democracy and the idea of the consent of the governed versus the divine right of kings.
1658-1789	Rationalist Humanism	Emergence of modern science with Descartes
1789-1870	Liberal Agnosticism	Emergence of the question: is there a God or not?
1870-present	Materialistic Agnosticism	Emergence of Atheism; Emergence of American Empire over American Democracy, with the declaration of Corporate immunity

Ancient Mesopotamia

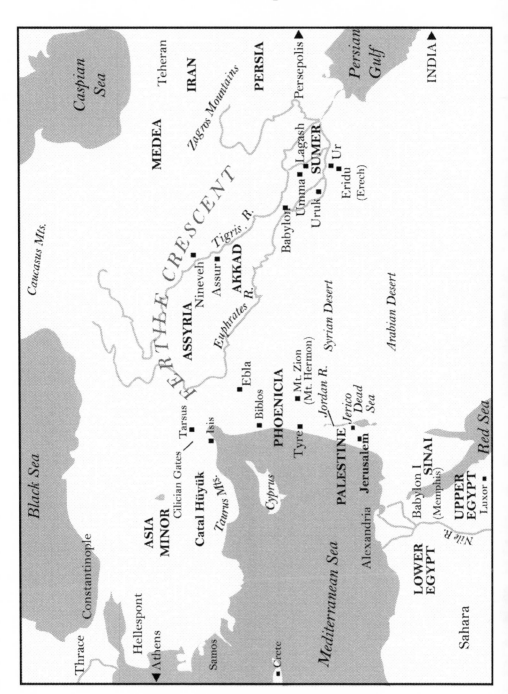

Anunnaki Genealogy

The "Begots"

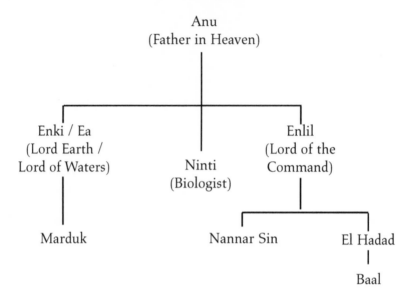

Anu
(Father in Heaven)

Enki / Ea
(Lord Earth /
Lord of Waters)

Ninti
(Biologist)

Enlil
(Lord of the
Command)

Marduk

Nannar Sin

El Hadad

Baal

Glossary

Abiru, Ha-abiru   Sumerian: *ha*, people, *-beru*, an astronomical distance. Thus, "People of the Crossing."

Abraham   Hebrew *Avraham*, Latin *Abrahamus*, Arabic *IbrÇh¥m* is the patriarch of Judaism, recognized by Christianity, and a very important prophet in Islam. The story of his life is told in the Book of Genesis and in the *Quan.* Abram, means "the Brahmin."

Acarusia   An ancient Druid kingdom on the Bosphorus in what is now European Turkey. The Acarusian tree alphabet was devised by the Druids to record their poetry. The Phoenician trade route to Scandinavia ran through the Bosphorus. The Phoenicians found the alphabet useful for commercial transactions. They adapted it to their own use and are given credit for inventing the alphabet.

Adapa or Adapu   Sumerian for Adam.

Albion   The most ancient name of Great Britain, though often used to refer specifically to England. Occasionally it refers to only Scotland, whose name in both Gaelic and Irish is Alba. Pliny the Elder, in his *Natural History*, applies it unequivocally to Great Britain: "It was itself named Albion, while all the islands about which we shall soon briefly speak were called the Britanniae." The name is perhaps of Celtic origin or older, from the Proto-Indo-European root that denotes both "white" and "mountain." The Romans took it as connected with *albus*, white, in reference to the chalky White Cliffs of Dover.

Al Chem   One of the three names of Egypt: Egypt, Mesamim, and Al Chem.

Amartia   Greek for "sin;" literally, to miss the mark, an archery term.

Ammonius Saccus   3rd Cent. CE. Ammonius Saccus was a Greek philosopher and Buddhist master of Alexandria, often called the founder of the Neoplatonic school. Origen and Plotinus were among his principal pupils at Alexandria. He was considered the greatest teacher in Alexandria in his time. He wore a robe, probably of saffron color. It was for this robe, a "sack," that he was named. Saca was the name of Siddhartha's tribe. (See *Saca.*)

Anaxagoras   Circa 500–428 BCE. A Greek philosopher. Pericles learned to love and admire him and the poet Euripides derived from him an enthusiasm for science and humanity. Some authorities assert that even Socrates was among his disciples. His influence was due partly to his astronomical and mathematical eminence, but still more to the ascetic dignity of his nature and his superiority to ordinary weaknesses, traits which legend has embalmed. His observations of the celestial bodies led him to form new theories of the universal order, and brought him into collision with the popular faith. Anaxagoras' thinking marks a turning point in the history of philosophy.

Ancient Order of Affairs   is remembering Original Innocence. The American Declaration of Independence is based on a society of Original Innocence. Democracy is only possible in a nation that believes in the equality of all people, which means that people have the potential to access all truth in their own heart-mind. In contrast, the New Order of Affairs is based on Original Guilt.

Animism   The religion that presumes that a spiritual force is behind the emergence of matter.

Anunnaki   Sumerian for "those-who-from-heaven-to-Earth-came." A group of Sumerian and Akkadian deities. Some theorists such as Zecharia Sitchin, Sherry Shriner, Laurence Gardner and David Icke state that the Anunnaki came to Earth in antiquity and created or tampered with the genetic makeup of primitive humans. According to Sitchin in his book *The 12th Planet*, these beings were the Biblical *Elohim* or *Nephilim* and lived on a planet called Nibiru, an alleged 12th planet of the solar system. Sitchin claims the Anunnaki came on a colonial expedition to Earth to mine gold. The worker Anunnaki revolted in protest to the working conditions. Because of this the Anunnaki set up a project to blend the DNA of *Homo erectus* with that of their own, thus giving rise to *Homo sapiens*. He proposes that fallout from their nuclear weapons was the "evil wind" that destroyed Ur and all of Sumer circa 2000 BCE, as recorded in the "Lament for Ur." (See Abiru, Bel-Marduk, *El*, *Elohim*, Enmeduranki, Erd, Ereck, Eridu, Enakim, *Enuma Elish*, *Epic of Gilgamesh*, *gods*, *Il*, *Iluahim*, and *Nephilim*.)

Apohelion, perihelion   These terms derive from the Latin *apo-* away from, and *helion* the sun: *apohelion* – away from the sun; and *per-* close to, and *hellion: perihelion* – close to the sun. Aphelion is the spelling from the Greek, meaning the same as apohelion. Many ancients thought the sun moved around Earth, as it appears to do, and therefore thought we were close to the sun at summer solstice and far from the sun at winter solstice, thus perihelion and aphelion.

Aquinas, Thomas   1225–1274 CE. An Italian Catholic philosopher and theologian in the scholastic tradition. Aquinas had a mystical experience while celebrating mass on December 6, 1273 after which he stopped writing, leaving his great work, the *Summa Theologica*, unfinished. He is considered by the Catholic Church to be its greatest theologian and one of the thirty-three Doctors of the Church. On the other hand, the Catholic Church adamantly rejects the possibility that Thomas Aquinas could have written the *Aurora Consurgens* which presents a more alchemical view reflecting the Gnostic tradition.

Armageddon   Greek transliteration of the Hebrew *Har Megiddo* meaning literally "the mount of Megiddo." Megiddo occupied a strategic location on the eastern ridge of Mt. Carmel between Esdralon and the plain of Sharon, southeast of Haifa and northwest of Jenin in Israel. It sits at the northern end of an important pass through the Carmel mountain range near the fertile Jezreel Valley. From 2350 BCE up until the 1973 war, at least 34 bloody conflicts have been fought at the ancient site of Megiddo and adjacent areas by Egyptians, Canaanites, Israelites, Midianites, Amalekites, Philistines, Hasmonaeans, Greeks, Romans, Muslims, Crusaders, Mamlukes, Mongols, French, Ottomans, British, Australians, Germans, Arabs and Israelis. Control of Megiddo provided control over one of the major trade routes of antiquity, the Via Maris (the "Way of the Sea") that wound through Israel past Megiddo. This strategically placed road ran between Egypt in the south, and Mesopotamia (modern Iran/Iraq) and Anatolia (modern Turkey) in the north. So much fighting occurred at Megiddo that the author of the Book of Revelation was convinced Megiddo would also be the site of the apocalyptic battle between good and evil to be fought at some time in the future.

Augustine of Hippo   354–430 CE. A saint and the pre-eminent Doctor of the Church according to Roman Catholicism. Influenced by Plotinus, Augustine was important to the "baptism" of Greek thought and its entrance into the Christian and the European intellectual tradition. Many Protestants also consider him to be a spiritual ancestor of Protestantism. Protestantism's founder Martin Luther was trained as an Augustinian monk. Protestantism followed in Augustine's footsteps, making original sin its main focus and leading to a more pessimistic assessment of human reason and action apart from Divine grace. (See Plotinus and Original Sin.)

Aumakua   (See Uhane, and Unihipili.)

Babylon   The Greek variant of Akkadian *Babilu*, means Gateway of the Gods. In the Hebrew Bible, the name appears as *Babel,* interpreted by popular etymology to mean "confusion." (See *Ilu.*)

Babylon I   Ancient Memphis, Egypt. Called Babylon I as Memphis also means Gateway of the Gods. One of the centers in the Course of Empire.

Babylon II   The capital of the Babylonian Empire from circa 600 BCE, Modern Al Hillah, Iraq. (See *Enuma Elish.*)

Bahrain   A 25 km-long island, once part of the coast of Arabia, said to be the landing place of the old Sumerian gods, the Anunnaki. Bahrain's earliest recorded reference dates to the third millennium BCE, when it was known as Dilmun. With its lush vegetation, abundant fresh water springs and its ideal location between Mesopotamia and the Indus Valley (India and Pakistan), Dilmun became a popular haven on the sea trade route. Dilmun grew in prosperity until the fall of the Indus Valley civilization around 1700 BCE. The era was chronicled in the *Epic of Gilgamesh,* who called Dilmun the land of immortality.

Bartolomeo de las Casas   (See Charles V.)

Bel-Marduk   Marduk is the god of Babylon II and may be the origin of the name of the Roman god of war, Mars. Marduk, son of Enki, counterattacks against the descendants of Enlil. Enlil means Lord of the Command and as such is an Emperor giving orders whereas Enki is Lord Earth, more kindly inclined to Earth's natives. In a sense Marduk represents a god who is at war with his fellow gods as to how to treat the natives (humans). As such, he is the archetype of the Messiah who comes to set the captives free.

Benben   The mound in Egyptian mythology that arose from the primordial waters, Nu, that Atum sat upon, the rising or setting sun. It was said to have turned into a small pyramid, located in Annu, or Heliopolis, one of the most ancient Egyptian cities which was the principal seat of sun-worship, the place Atum was said to dwell within. The sacred Benben stone, named after the pyramid, was located in the solar temple of Heliopolis. It is thought to have been the prototype for later obelisks. The capstones of the great pyramids were based on its design.

Bishop   In Greek, *Episcope;* "overseer, as in slavery." Episcopalian is derived from *Episcope.*

Blessing   From the Norman French *blessure,* which means "wound." Hence, the wounding sword of blessing is like a surgeon's scalpel: it wounds in order to heal. (See Charm of Making.)

Bodhidharma   Born 482 BCE, is credited with bringing Chan teachings to China and is the first patriarch of Chinese Chan (Zen) lineage. He was born in Southern India, the third son of an Indian King in a royal family of the Brahmin caste. Bodhidharma's Buddhist Master, Prajnatara, the 27th patriarch of Indian Buddhism, taught Bodhidharma for many years, gave him mind transmission, made him the 28th Patriarch, and gave him his name. Following the instruction of his master to transmit Dharma to China, Bodhidharma traveled east to Southern China in 526 CE where he was ceremoniously welcomed and greatly honored by the local military official named Shao Yang.

Caesarea Philippi   Caesarea Philippi was a new town built around a spring at the foot of Mt. Hermon in present day Lebanon. It was named after Tiberius Caesar and his local tetrarch (regent) Philip, a son of Herod the Great. Matthew puts Jesus at this town with his disciples while on a break from his duties in Galilee and reports the famous conversation in which Jesus is said to tell Peter that he intends to found his gathering on *petros*, a little stone. (See Petra, Petros.)

Çatal Hüyük   Turkish for fork-mound, a very large Neolithic and Chalcolithic settlement in southern Anatolia (Turkey) whose deepest layers date from around 7500 BCE. It is perhaps the largest and most sophisticated Neolithic site yet uncovered. Although no identifiable temples have been found, the graves, murals and figurines suggest that the people of Çatal Hüyük had a religion that was rich in symbol. Rooms with concentrations of these items may have been shrines or public meeting areas. The people appear to have lived relatively egalitarian lives without social classes, as no houses with distinctive features (belonging to kings or priests, for example) have been found so far. The most recent investigations also reveal little social distinction based on gender, with both men and women receiving equivalent nutrition and apparently having relatively equal social status.

   This mound contains the remnants of matrilineal goddess worship which proclaimed the living power of the unmanifested dark, and the glory of the manifested womb dark of the night sky, known to Egypt as Nut and to Israel as the Shekinah. It also had altars with a great set of bullhorns at each end proclaiming the Great Bull of the Heavens, the sun, the Son of God, purveyor of the light and the visible world, incarnate. (See Mithraist and Gnostic Trinity in the Interlude at end of Canto XIV.)

Chaldeans   A semitic people of Arabian origin who settled in southern Mesopotamia in the early part of the 1st millennium BCE. During the period of Assyrian domination of Babylonia, the Chaldeans formed some of the strongest resistance to Assyrian rule, and several kings of the period were of Chaldean origin. When Babylonia finally reestablished its independence, it was under the Chaldean dynasty of Nabopolassar. After the conquest of Babylonia by the Persians, the Chaldeans disappeared as a separate people.

Charles V   1500-1558 CE. The Holy Roman Emperor from 1519-1556 CE whose capital was at Valladolid, northwest of Madrid, Spain. In 1550, Charles convened a conference at Valladolid to consider the morality of the force used against the indigenous populations of Spanish America. Bartolomeo de las Casas was a planter in Santo Domingo, (Haiti and Dominican Republic.) Bartolomeo treated his Indian slaves as equals to the extent of his ability, enraging his fellow planters who insisted that the Indians were only animals and without a human soul and therefore could be treated like cattle. The planters succeeded in killing off a million of the Arawak people and began the slave trade with Africa to replace them. In the process they ran Bartolomeo off the island. He went to Chiapas, became a Bishop and defended the rights of the Mayas. The planters never relented in their hostility against him and the trial parodied here was on a single question: "Do American Indians have a soul?" Nearly every "august theologian" in Europe said they did not, and Sepulveda, philosopher and theologian, took the planters' side as advocate. The trial is remembered as the greatest judicial event of the 16th Century. Both Sepulveda and Bartolomeo have streets in California named after them. Charles V sided with Bartolomeo. The English sided with Sepulveda. The planters ignored Charles' decision and went on with the massacre of the Indians, as did the English.

Charm of Making   The mysterious chant of Merlin the Chief Druid: *Annal Nathrach Bethod Utwas Dochiel Dielve*. The last word *Dielve* means "delve" which is an invocation of sending out the wounding sword of blessing. (See Blessing.)

Chthonic   From Greek *khthonios*, of the Earth. Chthonic or telluric energies are energies emitted by the Earth.

Coven   From the Latin root word *convenire* meaning "to come together or to gather," as in the English word "convene." A gathering of beings who seek the unanimity of bonding and the empowerment of union with the Manifesting Power.

Covenant   A solemn contract or similar undertaking. In this text, a bonding between heart-minds.

Creation Date of Earth   Current science: 4 billion BCE. Fundamentalist Christian: 4004 BCE, a date derived from the Jewish calendar. Jewish: 3760, derived from the Sumerian calendar, the coronation date of Enoch (Enmeduranki), the first human emperor.

Culture   Latin, *cultura*, "to till, to prepare the ground for growing". Improvement by mental or physical training, education, refinement. For this text, culture is the way of life of a people, including how inherently telepathic heart-minds have the ability, passed on from generation to generation, to come into unanimity with Manifesting Power. Empire-supported organized religion provides the medium for producing Masters of Deceit by negating the heart-mind.

Cyrus I   Circa 600 to 580 BCE; or possibly circa 652 to 600 BCE. Cyrus the Persian, who sent the Jews home from the Babylonian captivity. Cyrus is not a Persian word but a Greek one: *kurio* means lord. The Bible often refers to Cyrus as a sort of latter-day Pharaoh.

Danites   One of the Twelve Tribes of Israel.

Darius III   380-330 BCE. Great Emperor of Media and Persia and King of Egypt, Darius was the man Alexander beat at the battle of Isis and later at the battle of Arbela. They had taunted each other through letters for years and their letters may still be seen. When Darius was wounded by one of his own generals and about to die, he wrote his last letter to Alexander giving him his Empire, *the* Empire. He asked only one favor: that Alexander, still in his twenties, should marry Darius' daughter, Statira, so their children would carry Darius' blood as well as Alexander's. It is reported that Statira gave Alexander a son and heir, Alexander IV of Macedon, in 323 BCE, six months after his death.

Demiurge   From Greek *demiourgos*, "artisan." Refers in some belief systems to a deity responsible for the creation of the physical universe and the physical aspect of humanity. The term occurs in a number of religious and philosophical systems, most notably Platonism and Gnosticism. The precise nature and character of the demiurge varies considerably from system to system, being the benign architect of matter in some, the personification of evil in others. Plato used the term in the dialogue Timaeus to describe the force that produces all the physical things of the world out of chaos. In some philosophies, the demiurge is a subordinate deity. The demiurge is the God of the "Religions of the Book," Judaism, Christianity, and Islam, an angry and vengeful deity involved in "creating" the material universe, who demands obedience and punishes sin.

Deva   Sanskrit and southern Iranian word for "god, deity." An entity of spiraling chthonic or telluric energies that rise from the Earth perpendicular to underground water streams that cross at different depths and create a "standing wave" of energy. The created vortex has the ability to affect humans gathered in unanimous telepathy. Coming into resonance with a deva assists people in entering into unanimity with the Manifesting Power. Ahura or asura is a northern Iranian word for deva.

Diocletian   Roman Emperor 284-305 CE. In Latin, *Dios Kaleos*, means "the man who calls himself God." He destroyed all the old nations of the Roman Empire by decree issued in the Imperial palace at Split on the Adriatic coast of Croatia. He re-divided the Empire into new districts, called dioceses, after his name. This was done to destroy all local allegiances and replace them with allegiance to himself, "the True God," as in "Hail Caesar, we who are about to die salute you." Diocletian is said to have been the last persecutor of the Christians. When he died, Constantine moved to become emperor.

Donation of Constantine   A Roman imperial edict forged in 731 CE by Bishop Zachary, making the Bishop of Rome the Vicar of Christ on Earth, as Christ is Vicar of God in heaven. Hence, the power to appoint all kings and queens. This was the origin of the Divine Right of Kings that was the supreme authority in Europe until the social contract that arose out of the French Revolution. It purports to reproduce a legal document in which the Emperor Constantine the Great, reciting his baptism and the cure of his leprosy at the hands of Sylvester, Bishop of Rome 314-336, confirmed the privilege of that pontiff as head of all the clergy and supreme over the other four patriarchates; conferred upon him extensive imperial property in various parts of the world.

Doubt   The faithful consider doubt sinful, whereas for the Gnostic, methodical doubt, like that of science, is used to make truth more specific.

Druids   Those who followed the pre-Christian nature religion among the Celts of ancient Britain, Gaul and Ireland, including many wise men and women who worked as teachers, healers and advisors to kings and common people. Druidism emphasized connection with nature and living things. Druids often appeared in Irish and Welsh sagas and Christian legends as magicians, wizards and bards.

Ebionites   Hebrew for "poor ones." The earliest followers of Jesus were known as Nazarenes, and perhaps later as Ebionites, and form an important part of the picture of Palestinian Jewish groups in late Second Temple times. The Ebionite/Nazarene movement was made up of mostly Jewish/Israelite followers of John the Baptist, and later Jesus, who were concentrated in Palestine and surrounding regions, were led by James the Just, the oldest brother of Jesus, and flourished between the years 30-80 CE.

Ecstasy   From the Greek *ekstasis*, "to stand outside of." The concept of Zen meditation, "to watch oneself watching," parallels the original meaning of ecstasy. The Sufis refer to ecstasy as the cosmic emotion wherein pain and joy are conjoined. Ecstasy is the power that leads to the sense of the meaning of life

Ecstasy can be an awesomely powerful experience. We need to find the balance between too much and too little. It is interesting to note that the planet Earth is between Mars, named for the god of war, and Venus, named for the goddess of love. If Earth's orbit were to get too close to the Sun in the direction of Venus, we would burn up; too close to Mars, we would freeze. Too much ecstasy can blow you up, too little leaves you frozen solid. Our course needs to be like a sine wave, weaving around a midline.

El, Eloahim, Elohim   Hebrew for "god" or "gods," from the Akkadian *Ilu, Iluahim*. *El* is a masculine singular; *-ah* or *-ach* is the feminine plural; *-im* is masculine plural. *Eloahim* is the feminine plural followed by masculine plural. *Elohim*, is an aberration of the masculine plural. Depending on which is used, the deity becomes either hermaphrodite gods or a single male god, and therefore shapes a world view.

El is the Sumerian god renamed Jehovah in Chanaan. He is brother of Nannar Sin, the god of Sinai and Sind (India). These gods are not to be confused with the Manifesting Power. (See Anunnaki, *Enuma Elish, Ilu, Iluahim,* and Manifesting Power.)

El Hadad   (See El.)

Emrys   Welsh for Child of Light, or eagle.

Emperor   The Empire with a human as Emperor began on the fall equinox 3670 BCE with the crowning of the first human Emperor whose name was Enoch. The crowning occurred at Erech, the high holy city of ancient Sumer, and was performed by Anu, the "Father in the Heavens." Enoch's name in Sumerian is Enmeduranki meaning "Lord of the Encoded Information for the Maintenance of the Bondage between the Gods and Man."

Enakim   Hebrew word for Anunnaki, "those who-came-from-the-night-sky-to-Earth;" the gods of Sumer.

Enmeduranki   Summerian for Enoch. Lord of the Encoded Information for the Maintenance of the Bondage between the gods and humans. Enmeduranki was the vicar of Enlil the Emperor on Earth. Enlil was the only Begotten son of Anu and was Anu's vicar on Earth (See Anunnaki, Enoch, Annunaki Genology page 298 and Canto X, page 59.)

Enoch   Father of the Hebrew nation who God took to heaven after living 65 years. (See Donation of Constantine.)

Enuma Elish   Sumerian for "when in the heights." The *Enuma Elish* is the *Tree of Knowledge*. The words *Enuma Elish* appear at the beginning of the Sumerian creation story, which is the basis of the creation story in Genesis. The opening words of Genesis are *B'rashid bara Eloahim w ha shamayim w et ha eretz*, meaning, "In the beginning God created the heavens and the earth." The Sumerian story opens with a spatial reference, Genesis with a time reference, and the Genesis story assumes there is a beginning to the universe while the Sumerian story leaves that open. (See Anunnaki and *Ilu*.)

Epic of Gilgamesh   The *Epic of Gilgamesh* is the *Tree of Life* and the original story of the quest of the Holy Grail (*San Graal*, actually *Sang Real*, Holy Blood. It nourishes the awakening of awareness of the Inevitability of Eternal life). Gilgamesh is king of Erech, the Holy City Of Anu, the Father in Heaven. The keeper of the sanctuary is Inanna, Granddaughter of Anu and lover of Tammuz. (In Greek, this is the story of Venus and Adonis, Adonai of the Bible.) Gilgamesh sets out on his quest for the Holy Bread and the Holy Blood, taking with him Enkidu whom he finds dancing round the watering place enjoying his Original Innocence with all the wild creatures. They embark in quest of a substance that is said to be in far off Chanaan where the pure waters flow from Mt. Zuen (Zion or Hermon), into the Waters of Merom north of the sea of Kennethereth (Galilee). Enkidu dies along the way in a struggle with nameless powers, but Gilgamesh comes within earshot of the landing place of the eagles (Baalbeck) and retrieves the Grail-Bearing Plant from the Waters of Merom. But a serpent comes and steals it while he sleeps, and so he must return to Erech and the temple of Anu empty-handed. This substance appears in Exodus as a form of Manna that is used to prepare the "show bread" that only the priest may eat. The preparer is Eleazar, the goldsmith. The substance is probably monatomic gold in the high spin state, described as the White Powder of Gold. (See Anunnaki.)

Episcopal   (See Bishop.)

Erech (Uruk)   Sumerian, *Unug,* Biblical, *Erich,* and Arabic, *Warka.* An ancient city of Sumer and later Babylonia, situated east of the present bed of the Euphrates in a region of marshes about 140 miles from Baghdad. The modern name of Iraq is derived from the name Uruk. It was one of the oldest and most important cities of Babylonia. Its walls were said to have been built by order of Gilgamesh who also constructed the famous temple called Eanna, dedicated to the worship of Inanna or Ishtar. (See *Epic of Gilgamesh.*)

Eretz   (See Eridu.)

Eridu   The Sumerian name for the first city ever established, perhaps circa fifth millennium BCE. It was located near the Euphrates River in Iraq, and its founder was Enki, Lord Earth, known in Egypt as *Ptah,* the god of creation. Its Arabic form is *ard,* its Hebrew form is *eretz,* and its German form is *erd.* (See Anunnaki.)

Esselen   The Esselen Indian tribe of the Big Sur Coast of California still survives. Their language was discovered recently in Spain, and surviving Esselens are seeking certification from the Bureau of Indian Affairs. Their language has been restored by a remarkable linguist at the University of Arizona.

Essenes   (See Qumran, *Saca.*)

Eusebius   Circa 275–339 CE. Eusebius of Caesarea was an archbishop and is often referred to as the father of church history because of his work in recording the history of the early Christian church. He is said to have known 40 languages. He was Constantine's associate in building Christianity at the Council of Nicea 325 CE.

Ezra, Book of   A single scroll of the Egyptian Book of the Dead translated by Ezra (originally Osiris-Ra) from Egyptian hieroglyphics into Hebrew. This scroll replaces the Egyptian Torah with the Babylonian Torah. (The plural of the word Torah is Tarot.)

First Among Equals   A phrase which indicates a person is the most senior of a group of people sharing the same rank or office. The concept is also known by its Latin equivalent, *primus inter pares,* from which it originates. In the tenth century, Constantinople split from Rome. Photius, the Patriarch of Constantinople, said the Pope was not an emperor entitled to give orders to bishops, but only a First

Among Equals who called meetings, etcetera. The Pope, relying on the Donation of Constantine, said that he was the vicar of Christ on Earth as Christ was God's vicar in heaven, and, "you must obey the Pope or go to hell." The patriarch replied: "That 'donation' is a forgery done by Pope Zachary in 751 and you have no such powers." The Pope responded by sending a German Cardinal to Constantinople who stomped up the aisle of Sancta Sofia (Holy Wisdom), the greatest church in Constantinople, and slapped a papal decree of excommunication against the Patriarch on the altar just as the Patriarch was raising the chalice in consecration on Sunday morning. The schism has never healed to this day, and the Patriarch was right: The Donation of Constantine is a forgery and the Holy Roman Empire is a fraud. (See Donation of Constantine.)

Fortnight Current usage has this as 14 days and nights. Originally it was 45 days, each one making up one of the Eight Seasons of the Sun.

Gilgal A stone circle. The first encampment after crossing the Jordan River mentioned in connection with the entering of the promised land. Joshua set up the twelve stones, taken from the middle of the riverbed (Joshua chapters 4 and 5). Stonehenge is a Gilgal.

gods As used in most of this book, the "gods" refer to the individuals described in the Sumerian and Akkadian cuneiform tablets, the Anunnaki, Elohim and Nephilim. According to the scholar Zecharia Sitchen, they came to Earth from the planet Nibiru beginning circa 450,000 BCE. These gods or tall people violated human culture by bio-engineering humanity to produce slaves. (Note the similarity to defying the "Prime Directive" in the Star Trek fictional universe. Starfleet's General Order #1 dictates that there be no interference with the natural development of any primitive society, chiefly meaning that no primitive culture can be given or exposed to any information regarding advanced technology or alien races. It also forbids any effort to improve or change in any way the natural course of such a society, even if that change is well-intentioned and kept secret.) (See Anunnaki, Erech and Ilu.)

Goyim god *Goy* is Hebrew for "gentile" or non-Jewish. A *goyim* god is a "gentile god." Of course the Manifesting Power really does not play favorites and whether the god is Jewish, *goy*, Muslim, Hindu or pagan makes little difference. God loves them all, even when they are naughty.

Grand Vizier The Moslem authority in Jerusalem in St. Francis' time. Vizier is the Anglicized form of the Arabic word *wazir*, a minister, usually chief minister, to a caliph or Muslim ruler or sultan. On occasion a vizier was in effect the governor.

Gyre Any manner of circular, swirling, or spiral form or motion; a vortex; often used to describe wind or ocean currents.

Hapsburgs Austrian-based dynasty that ruled much of central and parts of western Europe from the thirteenth to the twentieth centuries and produced many Holy Roman emperors.

Hasmonean Kings 140–37 BCE. The Hasmonean, meaning "heart-mind," kingdom in ancient Judea. Its ruling dynasty was established under the leadership of Simon Maccabaeus two decades after Judah the Maccabee defeated the Seleucid army in 165 BCE and ended the Babylonian captivity. Hanukkah was instituted to celebrate this event. The Hasmonean bureaucracy was filled with men with Greek names. The last known scion of this priestly line of kings was Mary Magdalene. The line was descended from Aaron, not Moses. (See Maccabeans.)

Heart-Mind A "way of knowing" that filters the intellectual capacities through the intuitive, emotional center of the heart, as in "The heart has a mind of its own." Recent studies in neuro-cardiology suggest that the heart acts as a physical informer and interpreter of the total human organism, assisting in balancing the whole. Also conceptualized in modern Buddhist literature.

Hellas-pont Now spelled Hellespont, also referred to as the Dardanelles, named after the ancient Greek hero Dardanus. The Hellespont together with the Sea of Marmora and the Bosphorus forms the most famous part of the boundary between Europe and Asia. *Hellas* means "Greece;" *pont* means "bridge." The Persians who ruled the Empire before Alexander saw this saltwater stream as the "Bridge to Greece," and Alexander's crossing of the Hellespont was the beginning of his conquest of the Empire.

Hellenistic and Hellenic periods The Hellenic period, circa 500 BCE, occurred during and following the invasion of Greece by waves of Hellenes, a hyperborean blonde-haired, blue-eyed people who pushed out the previous Mycenaean inhabitants. The Hellenes were a tribal democratic people. The Hellenistic period, refers to the post-Alexandrian time when Empire replaced the ancient democratic society. (See Hyperborean.)

Heresiarch From the word heretic. A high leader of heretics.

Hyperborean In Greek, *boreal*, as in *Aurora Borealis*, means "north." *Hyper* means "above or beyond." Most of the Greek or Hellenic invaders of Greece were fair people from the north, so northerners were called Hyperboreans.

Ilu, Iluahim   In Akkadian, *ilu* means "tall people" This has been translated as "gods," resulting in the interpretation that the Sumerians and Akkadians had deities, when the tablets were actually speaking of "tall people." This is shown in images of the *ilu* and ordinary people, where the *ilu* are much taller. It is also corroborated by the four-foot human femur bone recently unearthed in Ereck, making these people 13 feet tall. Perhaps the current day prejudice for tall men originates back to *ilu*. (See Anunnaki, El and gods.)

Infallibility   Papal Infallibility did not become an issue until 751 CE when Bishop Zachary forged the Donation of Constantine granting to the Bishop of Rome extraordinary powers that other bishops did not have. Since that time many bishops of Rome have sought to broaden those powers even further. One of those powers is infallibility when, speaking from the "Chair of the Peter," the Pope makes declarations concerning faith and morals (what you should believe and how you should act). Garibaldi united the city states of Italy into one nation in the 1870s, and he also took the Papal States away from the Pope. Pius IX, Pope at that time, was so angry that he refused to act as Pope until he got the Papal States back. When he failed, as compensation for losing the Papal States, he had himself declared infallible at the First Vatican Council of 1870. (See Donation of Constantine.)

Innocence   From the Latin *in*, not, and *nocere*, to hurt or injure. Innocence is commonly understood to mean not guilty; it more correctly means uninjured, retaining the capacity to know the truth and the law in one's own heart-mind. Original Innocence is the source of individual sovereignty.

Irenaeus   Circa 130–202 CE. A Father of the Catholic Church, Bishop of Lyon, France. He was author of the five-volume *On the Detection and Overthrow of the So-Called Gnosis*, normally referred to as *Adversus Haereses (Against Heresies)* whose prime purpose was to refute the teachings of various Gnostic groups. His careful listing of heresies gives a good sense of the original teachings of Christianity that were subverted, changed or eliminated by the Church authorities to consolidate their control. Eusibus and Constantine used Irenaeus' writings as a basis for their work at the Council of Nicea. Lyon was the original capital of Gaul, the crossroads of main Roman roads and the site of the major camp of the Roman army.

Isis   In Egyptian mythology Isis is the spouse and sister of Osiris, the Sun god, and the mother of Horus, the solar hero. Her name appears also in various other places such as Paris, originally Parisis. Her shrine there lies concealed under the Church of San Sulpice as referred to in *The Da Vinci Code*. Most all old Christian churches in Europe are built on top of pagan shrines, many of them dedicated to Saint Michael, the hyperborean warrior angel who deals with the evil spirits that Christians presume inhabit old holy places. Another place name is Atlantis, originally *A-tklan-isis*, meaning in Old British the gathering at the most holy low place, *isis* meaning in Welsh, lowest place. The *Isis* here is at Iskandar, formerly Alexandretta, where the coast of Turkey does a ninety-degree turn to become the coast of the Levant. It is at this *Isis* that Alexander beat Darius and sent him packing, only to be killed by one of his generals after the Battle of Arabela.

Ixtklan   *Tklan* in Welsh means "a group of people." When asked the name of their group, most native peoples replied "The people." Since the Spaniards most likely heard this response as *Ix tklan*, this may explain the origin of the word *Esselen*.

Jurisprudence   Jurisprudence studies the origin and meaning of the concept of law or, to view it practically, a study of the moral and ethical principles from which the law derives.

Kaaba   A stone shrine that is the holiest place in Islam. According to the *Qur'an*, the Kaaba was initiated by the prophet Ibrahim (Abraham) and his son Ismail (Ishmael). The Kaaba is located inside the mosque known as Masjid al Haram in Mecca (Makkah) which was built around it.

Kaaba Stone   A holy relic set into a cornerstone of the Kaaba, Muslims say the Stone was found by Ibrahim and his son Ismail when they were searching for stones with which to build the Kaaba, reputed by some to have been given to Ibrahim by the angel Gabriel. They recognized its worth and made it one of the building's cornerstones. Early chroniclers say the Kaaba was rebuilt during Muhammad's youth. Secular historians point to veneration of the stone in pre-Islamic times and say that it is likely that the Stone is a meteorite. Muhammed "cleansed" the stone of images of "pagan" gods. These images may be seen today at a museum in Riyadh. All are gods of India.

Kabode   A Hebrew invocational word for awesomeness or holiness.

Lacedaemonians   People from Laconia, also known as Lacedaemonia, on Greece's Peloponnesian peninsula. Its most important city was Sparta. *La cedamon* is derived from Cedmon, mythical founder of the Greek nation.

Lateran Pact   Also called the Lateran Treaty of 1929, effective until 1985, between Italy and the Vatican. It was signed by Benito Mussolini for the Italian government and by cardinal secretary of state Pietro Gasparri for the papacy and confirmed by the Italian constitution of 1948. Upon ratification of the Lateran Treaty, the papacy recognized the state of Italy, with Rome as its capital. Italy in return recognized papal sovereignty over the Vatican City, a minute territory of 44 hectares (109 acres), and secured full independence for the Pope. A number of additional measures were agreed upon. Article 1, for example, gave the city of Rome a special character as the "centre of the Catholic world and place of pilgrimage." Article 20 stated that all bishops were to take an oath of loyalty to the state and had to be Italian subjects speaking the Italian language.

Maccabeans   Judas Maccabeus and his father Mathathias, rebelled against the Seleucid overlords of Judea. They founded the Hasmonean royal line and established Jewish independence in Israel from 165 BCE to 63 BCE. Antiochus Epiphanes, a Seleucid, had made an exercise yard out of Ezra's Second Temple in Jerusalem for young, naked and uncircumcised Greek men. Young Jewish men yearned so much to join them that they made foreskins from the flesh of pigs so as not to be identified as Jews. "Enough!" said the Maccabees and drove the defilers out, and restored the temple. (See Hasmonean and Sicarri.)

Manifesting Power   The All That Is, the Creator of the Universe, the Divinity, called The Nameless by Buddha. Not to be confused with the demiurge, which the Bible erroneously refers to as God. Since the Manifesting Power is fully present in you and speaks the truth to your heart-mind, there is no need for Organized Religion, for every person can "sit under their own vine or their own fig tree." (See Demiurge.)

Marduk   (See Bel-Marduk.)

Masters of Deceit   Those who use the Power for the control of others, and the furtherance of Empire. The deceit is that the Power is only available to elites. The Masters of Deceit use the Principle of Continuous Assent, in which a series of self-evident truths are recited to support statement of faith. Faith is, of course, not a self-evident truth. However the Masters of Deceit modify this principle to support an ultimate lie.

Meh   In Sumerian mythology, the *Tablets of Destiny* stolen by Enzu from Enlil. Supposedly whoever possessed the tablets ruled the universe.

Mithraist   One who follows the Mithraic religion. *Mithra* is the Persian name for the constellation Perseus which is seen as a Bull Rider astride the constellation of Taurus. Mithra is seen stabbing the bull in the heart while looking away from the stroke. Mithra was a Solar Hero, like Horus of Egypt and Mabon of Wales. Constantine and his army followed this religion that had been acquired earlier from a king of Pontus called *Mithradates* (Mithra gives). The religion developed by Constantine and Eusebius at Nicea cobbled together the teachings of Jesus and those of Mithraism. (See Çatal Hüyük and Solar Myth.)

Mountains of the Bull   The Taurus Mountains above Tarsus in Cilicia. They are so called because of a species of giant bulls, aurocs, eight feet high at the shoulder that inhabited those mountains in ancient times. To the north of the Taurus Mountains lies Çatal Huyuk. (See Çatal Huyuk.)

Natural Law vs. Law of Nature   The Law of Nature is how things work. Natural Law is how the church says that Christ says that God says they work. The confusion between Natural Law and the Law of Nature lies at the base of the conflict between science and religion. The Law of Nature is that authority comes from the consent of the governed. Natural Law says that authority comes from God through the Pope, hence, the divine right of kings. (See Positive Law.)

Nazarite   From the Latin verb *nazir* meaning "to separate." A vow which may be taken by either sex that sets the aspirant apart from others for the service of God (Numbers 6:1-21). The vow may be for life or for a particular period of time. Nazarite vows do not appear to have been understood by the Gentiles, as Paul demonstrated, nor are they even mentioned in patristic writings. "Nazarite" or "Nazarene" is the more likely source of the Hebrew and Aramaic epithets for Jesus, rather than "of Nazareth," as the first century necropolis where Nazareth now stands is an unlikely site for Jesus' childhood home, because it didn't exist in Jesus' time!

Nephlim   Sumerian for "those-who-came-down." The Catholic Encyclopedia says "the Hebrew word *nephilim* rendered gigantes, may mean "fallen ones." (See Anunnaki.)

Nineveh   The present Iraqi city of Mosul where the second great archaeological dig was done in the middle of the nineteenth century after Troy was discovered. Its most famous reference is in the story of Jonah and the Whale. It was a seat of Empire in the following series: Sumer, Akkad, Babylon I, Nineveh, Babylon II, Persepolis, Alexandria, Rome, ...Paris, London, Washington D.C.

Omphalos   A rounded stone in Apollo's temple at Delphi regarded as the center of the world by the ancients. (Canto I, page 13.)

Oracle   A person or agency considered to be a source of wise or prophetic counsel; an authority, usually spiritual in nature. In the ancient world many sites gained a reputation for the dispensing of oracular wisdom; they too became known as "oracles," as did the oracular utterances themselves, whose name is derived from the Latin verb *orare*, "to speak." The Delphic Sibyl was among the most renowned; she lived on Mount Parnassus and was believed by many to be a prophet. The Sibyl of Cumae was consulted by Roman Emperors and was said to have been the first writer of the book of the Bible.

Oracle of Anun   Located at Siwa in Egypt, this oracle was a man gifted with "the sight"; the second oracle in Alexander's life. Also, spelled Amon or Amen, and in Greek as Ammon, and Hammon.

Oracle of Delphi   In classical Greece, the pre-eminent oracle, the Sibyl (or Pythia), operated at the temple of Apollo at Delphi on Mount Parnassus. Apollo had snatched the Pythia away from Gaia, the Earth goddess, and her guardian dragon Python long ago in a primal struggle between intuition and reason in which Apollo the sun god of reason had triumphed. Still the oracle at Delphi remained, a young girl gifted with the intuitive sight in a temple of the god of reason, sought after by kings anxious to know through her precognition what fate held in store. This oracle exerted considerable influence throughout Hellenic culture; the Greeks consulted her prior to all major undertakings, such as wars and the founding of colonies. The semi-Hellenic countries around the Greek world, such as Macedonia, Lydia, Caria, and even Egypt also respected her. Croesus of Lydia consulted Delphi before attacking Persia, and according to Herodotus was told, "If you do, you will destroy a great empire." Believing the response favorable, Croesus attacked, but it was his own empire that was ultimately destroyed by the Persians. The Oracle of Delphi was the first oracle consulted by Alexander the Great.

Origen   Circa 182–251 CE was a Christian scholar and theologian and one of the most distinguished of the Fathers of the early Christian church. His writings are important as one of the first serious intellectual attempts to describe Christianity. (See Ammonius

Saccus.)

Original Sin This religious doctrine, shared in one form or another by most Christian denominations, holds that human nature is morally and ethically distorted due to the disobedience of humankind's earliest parents to the revealed will of God. In the Bible, the first human transgression of God's command (i.e., the *original* sin) is described as the sin of Adam and Eve in the Garden of Eden called "the fall." The doctrine holds that every person born into the world is tainted by the wrong-doing of the first ancestors and that all of humanity is ethically debilitated and powerless to rehabilitate themselves, unless rescued by God. There are wide-ranging disagreements among Christian groups as to the exact understanding of this doctrine, with some denying it altogether. Eastern Orthodoxy, Judaism, and Islam acknowledge that the introduction of sin into the human race affected the subsequent environment for humankind, but tend to deny any inherited guilt or necessary corruption of human nature.

Pascal Stone The Pascal Stone is a stone on top of a mountain in Chichicastenango, a city in Guatemala. This Stone is used by Mayan shamans to perform sacrifices. Pascal refers to the Jewish Passover.

Pelagius 354–420 CE. A monk and reformer who denied the doctrine of Original Sin and was declared a heretic. He was well educated, fluent in both Greek and Latin, and learned much theology. Until his more radical ideas saw daylight, even such pillars of the Church as Augustine of Hippo referred to him as "saintly" with great austerity. However, he was later accused of lying about his own teachings in order to avoid public condemnation. Most of his life was spent defending himself against the Roman Catholic Church, the agents of which eventually hounded him to death. (See Augustine of Hippo and Original Sin.)

Perihelion (See Apohelion.)

Petra, Petros *Petra* Greek for rock or large stone; *petros*, Greek for small stone. Peter's name comes from *petros*. Peter is translated into Greek as *Petros*. Christianity uses a conversation at Caesarea Philippi as the sole basis of its doctrine: "Jesus founded his church on Peter." In Rome to this day the Church is not called the Roman Catholic Church but the "Church of Peter and Paul."

Phalanx The Phalanx was Alexander's secret weapon with which he "conquered the world." It was a sort of tank with feet. The soldiers in the phalanx carried shields that fitted together on all four sides and across the top, and wore strong greaves, ankle and shin shields. They would run forward into the midst of the enemy, drop down and attack through well-designed ports with sword and pike.

Philosopher's Stone   The quest of alchemy is to find "The Philosopher's Stone" believed by alchemists to confer the ability to convert base metal, usually lead, into gold and/or to create an elixir that would make humans immortal. Nicholas Flamel, reputed to have been the most celebrated of alchemists, put these words on the title page of his great work: "The Philosopher's Stone is the White Powder of Gold."

Pleiades   The "Seven Sisters" of stars in the constellation Taurus, often used for celestial navigation. Six are visible by the naked eye. For northern hemisphere viewers, the cluster is above and to the right of Orion the Hunter as one faces south. A story from Borneo tells of a whirlpool island with a tree that allows a man to climb up into the heavens and bring back useful seeds from the land of the Pleiades.

Plotinus   Circa 205-270 CE. Plotinus viewed man as a prismatic trinity veiling and alternatively looked through by the spirit in the "unwinking vigilance of ecstasy." He is the founder of neo-Platonism, the philosophy of the Church until Thomas Aquinas. Plotinus never became a Christian. His fellow student Origen did become a Christian and is among the most influential of the Fathers of the Church. He was never proclaimed a saint because he castrated himself in order to avoid the torture of abstinence. The Church opines that the agony makes you holy, and a saint prefers to suffer; a suspiciously sadomasochistic opinion.

Positive Law   Law codified into written form. The term is often used in contrast with common law or law of nature. The normative theory of law gave pre-eminence to positive law because of its rational nature. Libertarian philosophers usually favor the superiority of the law of nature over positive law. (See Natural Law.)

Primus inter pares   (See First Among Equals.)

Prosopon   Greek for "mask." These masks worn by actors in the Greek theatre enabled them to play many parts. Shakespeare's famous line comes from this: "All the world is a stage and each man in his time plays many parts." At the Council of Nicea, *prosopon* is the origin of the word "person" in order to support the phrase "One God in three persons" as it appears in the Nicene Creed.

Pythagoras   Circa 569–475 BCE. He invented the word philosophy to describe the pursuit of the Greeks. His influence upon philosophy, mathematics and music has been extensive. The Hippocratic Oath, with its central commitment to "First do no harm," has its roots in the oath of the Pythagorean Brotherhood. Iamblichus in his book *On the Pythagorean Life* circa 300 CE points to what may be the origin of the concept of Original Sin. He reports that Pythagoras said: "The gods are good and human beings are wicked." (See Original Sin.)

Python   The oracular serpent of Delphi in Greek mythology. In one myth, it was the offspring of Gaia and the mud that was left over after the flood of Deucalion. In the Homeric Hymn to Apollo, Python was the offspring of Hera, the Olympian lady who bore him out of her own being, parthegenetically, in the manner of Gaia, to spite Zeus. Apollo killed it and remade its former home as his own oracle, the most famous in Greece. Python refers to the vortex.

Qumran   Located on the northwestern shore of the Dead Sea, several kilometers south of Jericho. A religious sect of Essenes who took vows of dedication to God inhabited the site around second century BCE. The Dead Sea Scrolls were unearthed here in 1947. The founding of the monastery at Qumran and the order of the Essenes is a great mystery. It now appears most probable that it was founded by Jewish/Buddhists from Alexandria in order to bring true spirituality back to the Holy Land. Jesus himself was a Nazarite who studied at the monastery of the Essenes at Qumran, the center of spirituality in Judaism at the time. So, did Jesus become a Buddhist and graft a Buddhist shoot on a Jewish root? (See Nazarite, *Saca*.)

Romani-ta   To be Roman, that is, Roman-ness; usually described as the influence or "fine hand" of the Roman Church. Its secular equivalent is diplomacy.

Rump Council   A council deliberately called to make decisions when it is known that most of its members are absent.

Sacerdos   From Latin *sacerdos*, "priest," literally "one who presents sacred offerings," *sacer*, "sacred," and *dare*, "to give." Sacerdotalism is a term applied (usually in a hostile sense) to the system, method, and spirit of a priestly order or class, under which the functions, dignity, and influence of the members of the priesthood are exalted in the ministry of religion, and in the Church, at the expense of the laity. This exalting of the priesthood in the Christian church is based on the claim that the priest exercises sacrificial and supernatural powers in the celebration of the Eucharist.

Saca (Saka)   In Nepal on the Gangetic Plain lived the people called the Saka. Their king was the father of Siddhartha who would find the Buddha in himself and discover that the Buddha lived in every creature. Buddha was also known as the "Lion of the Tribe of Saca" and as Sakyamuni. There were active trade routes from Egypt to India since before the fall of Sumer.

When Alexander I left India he took six Buddhist monks with him. After he died, his general Ptolemy took those monks with him to Egypt where he founded the city of Alexandria, which replaced Tarsus as the philosophical center of the western world.

In the first centuries CE there were more Jews in Alexandria than there were in Palestine. One of their teachers was Ammonius Saccus who wore a saffron robe called a sak. He was the teacher of Plotinus and Origen, two powerful influences among the followers of Jesus. Christians are in a rigorous state of denial that Buddha could have influenced Jesus and his story. In view of the evidence we now possess, it is nearly impossible to believe that influence was lacking, especially given what we know of Ammonius Saccus. (See Ammonius Saccus, Essenes, Nazarite, Origen and Plotinus.)

Sakyamuni   (See Saka, Siddhartha.)

Science   From the Latin, *scientia*, "knowledge." A Greek word for knowledge is *gnosis*.

Seleucus   Circa 358–281 BCE. One of Alexander's Macedonian generals, Ptolemy aquired Egypt. Seleucus inherited the remainder of the Alexander's empire except for Macedonia and Greece proper. Seleucus took up residence in Babylon after Alexander's death but soon moved his capital north to a new city he built for himself called Seleucia. With that move Babylon began its decline into ruin until Saddam Hussein rebuilt it in our time. Later the capital of the Seleucid Empire was moved to another new city in Syria, Antioch, where the Maccabeans rebelled against Antiochus Epiphanes. (See Hasmonean Kings and Maccabeans.)

Septentrionalis   Latin for "of the North." It has an interesting derivation. In looking for north at night one seeks the pole star, but it is near the zenith and difficult to find being quite small. Most people have learned to look for the big dipper, follow the first two stars of the ladle "straight up" until they find Polaris, the North Star. The ancients had a different procedure. They started with the Pleiades that are much lower on the horizon and very easy to spot. The Pleiades has six visible stars and one "invisible" one, seven altogether, hence *Septentrionalis*. Interestingly, the original Latin name of North America is: America *Septentrionalis*. (See Pleiades.)

Sicarii   A sect named after a kind of dagger, a terrorist weapon of assassination frequently wielded in crowds to avoid detection. Several of Jesus's disciples were Sicarii. They followed the tradition of the Maccabees, but this time against the Romans. (See Maccabeans.)

Siddhartha   Siddhartha found the Buddha in himself and discovered that the Buddha lived in every creature. He was moved to realize the first noble truth: suffering. He made his way (*veda*) into the forest (*thera*) and at last found the answer to suffering: compassion. He went back to Raj Gir from which he wandered the Gangetic Plain, helping others to find the Buddha in themselves as he had found the Buddha in himself. Buddha was also known as the "Lion of the Tribe of Saca" and as Sakyamuni or Saka-yamuna.

Siddi   Sanskrit for "hit the mark."

Silk Road   Around 300 BCE the Silk Road was an interconnected series of trade routes through southern Asia traversed by horse and camel caravans connecting the silk trade of Chang'an (today's Xi'an), China with traders from Antioch, Syria and points further west. Its influence carried over into Korea and Japan. The route was critical to the development and flowering of the civilizations of ancient Egypt, China, India and Rome that influenced the cultural foundations of the modern world. The continental Silk Road diverged into northern and southern routes through formidable mountain ranges and around extensive desert regions as it extended from the commercial centers of North China. The northern route passed through Eastern Europe and the Crimean peninsula, and from there across the Black Sea, Marmara Sea and the Balkans to Venice. The southern route passed through Turkestan-Khorasan into Mesopotamia and Anatolia, through Antioch in Southern Anatolia into the Mediterranean Sea, or through the Levant into Egypt and North Africa.

Siwa   (See Oracle of Ammon.)

Solar Cross   One of the oldest religious symbols in the world, appearing in Asian, American, European, and Indian religious art from the dawn of history. Composed of an equal armed cross within a circle, it represents the solar calendar, the movements of the sun, marked by the solstices. Sometimes the equinoxes are marked as well with another cross, giving an eight-armed wheel.

The swastika is also a form of solar cross.

Solar Myth   The story of a Solar Hero who models his life after the yearly course of the sun: born on December 25th, espoused in May, triumphs at middle age, declines in autumn, dies on a solar cross between two thieves, lies in the tomb for the four days of the sun-stand (solstice), and resurrects on December 25. Typical solar heroes: Horus, Krishna, Mithra, Buddha, Mabon, and Jesus. They were the bearers of the cults of the sun as the living symbol of the Unmanifest Divinity. The solar myth adds that the sun is crucified on a cross between two thieves, the illusions of space and time. (See Eight Seasons of the Sun, Jeseus.)

Spin   The phenomenon of spin and its effects on us are largely uncommented upon. Three spins are part of our life: the spin of the Earth on its axis; the spin of the Earth around the sun, and the spin of our solar system around the center of the Milky Way. To lift our spirits and become in greater harmony with the Earth, in the northern hemisphere, spin clockwise; in the southern hemisphere, spin counterclockwise. This hemispherical difference of spin on the human aura is why sailors were thrown in the water as ships crossed the equator.

Stoics   Stoics are named for the Greek word *stoa*, "a white garment." The Latin word is toga. The Sumerian word is tug. Stoicism is a school of philosophy founded 308 BCE in Athens by Zeno of Citium (Cyprus). It teaches self-control and an indifference to pain or pleasure while advocating a staunch detachment from emotions. This allows one to be clear thinking, level-headed and unbiased. It is designed to empower an individual with virtue, wisdom and strength while allowing one the ability to readily refuse corruption, temptation, and degradation. Students of Stoicism are also encouraged to help those who are in need, knowing that those who can, should. Stoicism also teaches independence and self-sufficiency. Independence from society, regarded as a chaotic and unruly entity, is also considered of utmost priority. Virtue, reason, natural law and common sense are prime directives. By mastering passions and emotions, it is possible to overcome the discord of the outside world and find peace within oneself. This philosophy is usually contrasted with Epicureanism, which preferred enjoyment over restraint. The stoic center of the Roman Empire was Tarsus. (See Tarsus.)

Synthesis   From Hegel's philosophy that all logic is dialectical in character, as in thesis-antithesis-synthesis. Hypothesis or thesis comes as a function of the right brain. Antithesis comes as a function of the left brain, as in scientific doubt. Synthesis is the combining of the two. The corpus callosum of the brain plays a major role in compiling this synthesis. Much of Catholic (and therefore Christian) philosophy is based on the *Summa Theologica*, the synthesis written by Thomas Aquinas.

Tao   Refers to a Chinese character that was of pivotal meaning in ancient Chinese philosophy and religion. As used in modern spoken and written Chinese, Tao has a wide scope of usage and meaning, and its semantics vary widely depending on the context. Tao may be rendered as religion, morality, duty, knowledge, rationality, ultimate truth, path or taste. Tao is generally translated into English as "Way."

Tarsus   A city of Asia Minor near the Taurus Mountains in Cilicia, where Paul of Tarsus was born. Tarsus was also the home of the Cilician pirates who controlled the commerce of the Roman Empire (which always had inferior sailors). The Cilicians learned navigation from the Phoenicians. Also the seat of the Stoics.

Telepathy   The transference of thought-feelings between heart-minds without the involvement of the five senses.

Theodosius   Greek for "friend of God." Theodosius is a common name to three emperors of ancient Rome and Byzantium. Theodosius I was Roman Emperor from 379-395 CE. He cleaved closely to the Nicene Creed, the Creed that predominated in the west and was held by the important Alexandrian church. He and Gratian published an edict that all their subjects should profess the faith of the bishops of Rome and Alexandria (i.e., the Nicene faith).

Theurgy   From the Greek *Theos*, god and *ergos*, working, means the Divine Works, or that which the Divine does. Theology is what God says. Theurgy is what God does, i.e. the Manifesting Power. Theology is to Theurgy as dogma as is to "pragma" as words are to action.

Tri-skel   Three-Rays-In-One: Energy, Life Force, Consciousness. The Triskel has been used in many early cultures and most often is a three interlocked spiral, or any similar symbol, including three bent human legs—as in the Heraldry of the Isle of Man.

Tyre   A well-walled and fortified island near Sidon on the coast of Lebanon. The Siege of Tyre was Alexander's only major siege on his march from Isis to Babylon. Alexander's siege engines couldn't get to the walls, so though it took his army over a year out of his ten-year forced march, they filled in the estuary between the city and the shore. Then the city was totally destroyed. When the Egyptians heard about the fall of Tyre, they sent Alexander a messenger and surrendered. Tyre remains today, not as an island, but as a peninsula.

Unihipili, Uhane, and Aumakua   These terms correlate with Freud's notions of id, ego and superego, and with Jung's individual unconscious, conscious and collective unconscious. *The Secret Science Behind Miracles*, by Max Freedom Long, inspired the dialogues between Jung and Freud in Cantos XXXVIII and XXXIX. Mr. Long spent much time with the Kahunas, the shamans of the secret Huna traditions of Polynesia and Hawaii.

Urbe et Orbe   The city and the world, the city being Rome. One of the Pope's most public and most popular duties is to come out on his balcony overlooking St. Peter's Square to give the Urbe et Orbe blessing to the city and the world and the assembled multitude.

Ureck   (See Erech.)

Valladolid   (See Charles V.)

Further Reference

Allegro, John Marco, *The Sacred Mushroom and the Cross, A Study of the Nature and Origins of Christianity within the Fertility Cults of the Ancient Near East,* Doubleday & Company, Garden City, NY, 1970.

Aquinas, Thomas, *Summa Theologica,* Five Volume Set, Translated by Fathers of the English Dominican Province, Ave Maria Press, Notre Dame, IN, 1948.

Atwill, Joseph, *Caesar's Messiah, The Roman Conspiracy to Invent Jesus,* Ulysses Press, Berkeley, CA, 2005.

Aurora Consurgens: A Document Attributed to Thomas Aquinas on the Problem of Opposites in Alchemy, A Companion Work to C.G. Jung's Mysterium Conjunctionis, Edited by Marie-Louise Von Franz, Translated by R. F. C. Hull and A. S. B. Glover, Inner City Books, Toronto, 2000.

Bacon, Sir Francis, *The Letters and the Life of Francis Bacon,* Including all his occasional Works, namely letters, speeches, tracts, state papers, memorials, devices and all authentic writing not already printed among his philosophical, literary, or professional Works, *Collected Works of Sir Francis Bacon,* 7 Volumes, Classic Books, 2000.

Baigent, Michael, Leigh, Richard and Lincoln, Henry, *Holy Blood, Holy Grail,* Dell Publishing, New York, 1982.

Bryant, Dorothy, *The Kin of Ata Are Waiting for You,* Random House, New York, 1997.

Budge, E. A. Wallis, *Amulets and Talismans, The Original Texts with Translations and Descriptions of a Long Series of Egyptian, Sumerian, Assyrian, Hebrew, Christian Texts.* Dover Publications, New York, 1978.

Bushby, Tony, *The Bible Fraud,* The Pacific Blue Group, Inc., Hong Kong, 2001.

Carroll, James, *Constantine's Sword, The Church and the Jews,* Houghton & Mifflin Company, San Francisco, 2002.

Clay, Albert Tobias, *Neo-Babylonian Letters from Erech, Enuma Elish & Epic of Gilgamish,* Yale University Press, New Haven, CT, 1919, (out of print).

De Santillana, Girogio and Von Dechend, Hertha, *Hamlet's Mill, An Essay Investigating the Origins of Human Knowledge and It's Transmission Through Myth*, David R. Godine Publisher, Jaffery, NH, 1977.

The Declaration of Independence and the Constitution of the United States, Edited by Roger Pilon, Cato Institute, Washington, DC, 2000.

Dourley, John P., *The Illness That We Are, A Jungian Critique of Christianity*, Inner City Books, Toronto, 1984.

Eberhardt, Father Newman, *A Summary of Catholic History*, B. Herder Book Company, St Louis, MO, 1962.

Einstein, Albert, *Why War?, The Correspondence between Albert Einstein and Sigmund Freud*, Chicago Institute for Psychoanalysis, Chicago, IL, 1978.

Eisler, Riane, *The Chalice and the Blade, Our History, Our Future*, Harper & Row, San Francisco, 1987.

Enuma Elish, The Seven Tablets of Creation, The Babylonian and Assyrian Legends Concerning the Creation of the World and of Mankind, Volume One & Two, Editor Leonard W. Kin, Book Tree, San Diego, 1998.

Feinberg, Barbara, *The Articles Of Confederation*, 21st Century, 2002.

Fortune, Dion, *Mystical Qabalah*, Weiser Books, York Beach, ME, 2000.

Gardner, Laurence, *Lost Secrets of the Sacred Ark: Amazing Revelations of the Incredible Power of Gold*, Element, London, 2003.

Hall, Manley P., *The Secret Teachings of All Ages, An Encyclopedic Outline of Masonic, Hermetic, Qabbalistic, and Rosicrucian Symbolical Philosophy*, Jeremy P. Tarcher, New York, 1928, 2003.

Hamilton, Alexander, Madison, James and Jay, John, *The Federalist Papers*, Penguin, New York, 1987.

Hancock, Graham and Bauval, Robert, *The Message of the Sphynx, A Quest for the Hidden Legacy of Mankind*, Three Rivers Press, New York, 1996.

Henry, William, *Cloak of the Illuminati, Secrets, Transformations, Crossing the Stargate*, Adventures Unlimited Press, Kempton, IL, 2002.

Iamblichus, *Iamblichus' Life of Pythagoras*, Translated by Thomas Taylor, Inner Traditions, Rochester, VT, 1818, 1986.

Jung, Carl G., *The Basic Writings of C. G. Jung*, Edited by Violet S. De Laszlo, Modern Library, New York, 1959, 1991.

Keyes, Jr., Ken, *The Hundredth Monkey*, DeVorss Publications, Marina del Rey, CA, 1981.

Kharitidi, Olga, *Entering the Circle, Ancient Secrets of Siberian Wisdom Discovered by a Russian Psychiatrist*, HarperCollins, New York, 1996.

Lao Tzu, *The Complete Works of Lao Tzu, Tao de Ching & Hua Hu Ching*, Translation and elucidation by Master Hua-Ching Ni, Seven Star Communications, Los Angeles, 1979.

Long, Max Freedom, *The Secret Science Behind Miracles, Unveiling the Huna Tradition of the Ancient Polynesians*, DeVorss Publications, Marina del Rey, CA, 1948, 1976.

Long, Max Freedom, *The Huna Code in Religions, The Influence of the Huna Tradition on Modern Faith*, DeVorss Publications, Marina del Rey, CA, 1965, 1990.

Loy, David, *A Buddhist History of the West, Studies in Lack*, State University of New York Press, Albany, NY, 2002.

Martin, Malachi, *Windswept House*, Main Street Books, New York, 1998.

Merton, Thomas, *The Seven Storey Mountain, An Autobiography of Faith*, Harcourt, San Diego, 1948, 1999.

Michell, John, *The New View over Atlantis*, Thames & Hudson, London, 2001.

Monroe, Douglas, *The Lost Books of Merlyn, Druid Magic from the Age of Arthur*, Llewellyn Publication, St. Paul, MN, 2002.

Newton, Sir Isaac, *The Principia, Mathematical Principles of Natural Philosophy*, University of California Press, Berkeley & Los Angeles, CA, 1999.

Pagels, Elaine, *The Gnostic Gospels*, Vintage Books, a division of Random House, New York, 1979.

Plato, *The Republic of Plato*, Translated by Allan Bloom, Basic Books, Philadelphia, PA, 1968, 1991.

Ruck, Carl A.B., Staples, Blaise Daniel and Heinrich, Clark, *The Apples of Apollo, Pagan and Christian Mysteries of the Eucharist*, Carolina Academic Press, Durham, NC, 2001.

S, Acharya, *The Christ Conspiracy, The Greatest Story Ever Sold*, Adventures Unlimited Press, Kempton, IL, 1999.

Shakespeare, William, *William Shakespeare: The Complete Works*, Gramercy, New York, 1990.

Shlain, Leonard, *The Alphabet Versus the Goddess, The Conflict Between Word and Image*, Penguin, New York, 1998.

Sitchin, Zecharia, *Genesis Revisited, Is Modern Science Catching Up with Ancient Knowledge?*, Avon, New York, 1990.

Starbird, Margaret, *The Woman with the Alabaster Jar, Mary Magdalene and the Holy Grail*, Bear & Company, Sante Fe, NM, 1993.

Talbot, Michael, *The Holographic Universe, A Remarkable New Theory of Reality that Explains: the Paranormal Abilities of the Mind, the Latest Frontiers of Physics and the Unsolved Riddles of Brain and Body*, HarperCollins, New York, 1991.

The Epic of Gilgamesh, Translated, with notes and introduction by Maureen Gallery Kovacs, Stanford University Press, Palo Alto, CA, 1985.

The Gospel According to Thomas, Coptic text established and translated by Leiden, A. Guillaumont, H.-Ch. Puech, G. Quispel, W. Till and Yassah 'Abd Al Masih E. J. Brill, Harper & Row, San Francisco, 1959.

Van Der Zee, John, *Agony in the Garden, Sex, Lies and Redemption from the Troubled Heart of the American Catholic Church*, Thunder's Mouth Press/Nation Books, New York, NY, 2002.

Wasson, Eleanor, *28,000 Martinis and Counting, A Century of Living, Learning and Loving*, Santa Cruz, CA, 2004.

Yogananda, Paramahansa, *Autobiography of a Yogi*, Self Realization Fellowship, Los Angeles, 1946.

Index of Cantos

Invocation

Oh Great Manifesting Power
You
Who are fully present
In every being in the Universe
No matter how great or how small
No matter how near or how distant
in time or space or dimension
Thank You
For the gift of life
That you have given me today
And Thank You
For the gift of gratitude
That You have given me as well.
Oh Great Manifesting Power
I only ask You one more favor
That You would help me to listen and to hear
The still small voice
In which You constantly utter
all Truths
In my heart-mind
Forever
As you do in the heart-mind
of every sentient being.

Oh Beauty
So old and so new
Late have I loved You
I had sought You outside myself
Because I was outside myself
But behold You were within
And it is there I found You.

—Confessions of St. Augustine

CPSIA information can be obtained
at www.ICGtesting.com
Printed in the USA
BVHW03*2320060918
526209BV00007B/7/P